who is even contemplating public office, as well as for every patriot in the land."

—**PAMELA GELLER**, president of the American Freedom Defense Initiative

"Robert Spencer has written a courageous and enormously important book, analyzing Islam's global effort to destroy free speech. This is the most important book of the year. Read it and act! The choice is simple: Speak out against Islam or lose freedom forever."

—**GEERT WILDERS**, member of parliament in the Netherlands and leader of the Dutch Party for Freedom (PVV)

The COMPLETE INFIDEL'S GUIDE to FREE SPEECH (and Its Enemies)

The
COMPLETE
INFIDEL'S GUIDE

to

FREE SPEECH

(and Its Enemies)

ROBERT SPENCER
NEW YORK TIMES BESTSELLING AUTHOR

REGNERY
PUBLISHING
A Division of Salem Media Group

Regnery® is a registered trademark of Salem Communications Holding Corporation

Cataloging-in-Publication data on file with the Library of Congress

ISBN 978-1-62157-627-3

Published in the United States by
Regnery Publishing
A Division of Salem Media Group
300 New Jersey Ave NW
Washington, DC 20001
www.Regnery.com

Manufactured in the United States of America

10 9 8 7 6 5 4 3 2 1

Books are available in quantity for promotional or premium use. For information on discounts and terms, please visit our website: www.Regnery.com.

Distributed to the trade by
Perseus Distribution
www.perseusdistribution.com

Dedicated to all of those who, despite everything,
are still unafraid to speak the truth

CONTENTS

Chapter One

"JUST STAY QUIET AND YOU'LL BE OKAY"

The man who summed up the entire ethos of the war against the freedom of speech was none other than Mohamed Atta, the most prominent of the 9/11 hijackers.

On September 11, 2001, Atta boarded American Airlines flight 11 in Boston, bound for Los Angeles. Once he and his fellow jihadis had hijacked the plane, Atta told passengers: "Just stay quiet and you'll be okay.… Nobody move. Everything will be okay. If you try to make any moves, you'll endanger yourself and the airplane. Just stay quiet."[1]

The passengers heeded his warning and stayed quiet—but they weren't okay. Atta flew American Airlines Flight 11 to New York City and crashed it into the North Tower of the World Trade Center.

Atta had unwittingly uttered an epigram: the contrast between his words of reassurance and the passengers' horrifying fate is emblematic of the global effort to destroy the freedom of speech.

As the global jihad advances, we are told in innumerable ways that if we just stay quiet, we will be okay.

Spearheading these efforts is a little-known organization that comprises most of the Muslim governments around the world today. The foremost foe of the First Amendment right to free speech, and of the freedom of speech in general, in the world today is the Organization of Islamic Cooperation (OIC).

The Organization of Islamic Cooperation (formerly the Organization of the Islamic Conference), which is made up of fifty-six member nations plus the Palestinian Authority and constitutes the largest voting bloc at the United Nations, has been working for years to try to compel the West to restrict the freedom of speech, and particularly the freedom to criticize Islam.

Essentially, they want to impose a key principle of Islamic Sharia law—which forbids blasphemy against Allah, Muhammad, and Islam—on the entire non-Muslim world. That prohibition explains why the Islam world has no tradition of free speech. The West does, and our tradition of freedom must be extinguished in order to advance the Islamic agenda worldwide.

"Muslims will never accept this kind of humiliation. The article has insulted every Muslim in the world. We demand an apology!"

The OIC's initiative against free speech began in earnest in the wake of the publication of twelve cartoons of the Islamic prophet Muhammad in the Danish newspaper *Jyllands-Posten* on September 30, 2005. The paper wasn't trying to be gratuitously provocative; in the wake of the jihad murder of Theo van Gogh, Danish author Kåre Bluitgen had found it difficult to find an illustrator for his book about Muhammad: Danish artists were all too afraid of jihadis.[2] Frants Iver Gundelach, president of the Danish Writers Union, decried this submission to violent intimidation as a threat to free speech, and the largest newspaper in Denmark, *Jyllands-Posten*, took up the challenge. Flemming Rose, *Jyllands-Posten*'s culture editor, approached forty artists asking for depictions of Muhammad.

In response, Rose received the twelve drawings he published, nine of which were eminently forgettable—and immediately forgotten. The other three pointed out the link between Islam and violence; one of the three, a drawing of Muhammad with a bomb in his turban by Danish illustrator Kurt Westergaard, became notorious.

Editor-in-chief Carsten Juste explained his paper's decision to publish the cartoons: "We live in a democracy. That's why we can use all the journalistic methods we want to. Satire is accepted in this country, and you can make caricatures. Religion shouldn't set any barriers on that sort of expression. This doesn't mean that we wish to insult any Muslims."[3]

Danish imam Raed Hlayhel was not mollified: "This type of democracy is worthless for Muslims," he fumed. "Muslims will never accept this kind of humiliation. The article has insulted every Muslim in the world. We demand an apology!"[4]

Jyllands-Posten defended its publication of the cartoons by appealing to the core principles of the West: "We must quietly point out here that the drawings illustrated an article on the self-censorship which rules large parts of the Western world. Our right to say, write, photograph and draw what we want to within the framework of the law exists and must endure—unconditionally!"[5] Editor-in-chief Juste added, "If we apologize, we go against the freedom of speech that generations before us have struggled to win."[6]

Christians had already become accustomed to the mockery that Muslims were demanding protection from: in the United Kingdom, the secretary of an organization called Christians Against Ridicule complained in 2003 that "over the last seven days alone we have witnessed the ridicule of the Nativity in a new advert for Mr Kipling cakes, the ridicule of the Lord's Prayer on Harry Hill's TV Burp, the ridicule of a proud Christian family on ITV's Holiday Nightmare and the opening of a blasphemous play at London's Old Vic Theatre—Stephen Berkoff's Messiah.... Rarely a day goes by today without underhand and insidious mockery of the Christian faith."[8] Christians Against Ridicule, however, issued no death threats.

Muslims in Denmark were not so sanguine. After the cartoons were published, *Jyllands-Posten* had to hire security guards to protect its staff, as threats came in by phone and email.[9]

"I will never accept that respect for a religious stance leads to the curtailment of criticism, humour and satire in the press"

The anger was not limited to threat-issuing thugs. In late October, ambassadors to Denmark from eleven Muslim countries asked Danish Prime Minister Anders Fogh Rasmussen for a meeting about what they called the "smear campaign" against Muslims in the Danish press.[10] Rasmussen declined: "This is a matter of principle. I won't meet with them because it is so crystal clear what principles Danish democracy is built upon that there is no reason to do so."[11] He later added, "I will never accept that respect for a religious stance leads to the curtailment of criticism, humour and satire in the press."[12] The matter, he said, was beyond his authority. "As prime minister I have no tool whatsoever to take actions against the media and I don't want that kind of tool."[13]

As far as one of the ambassadors was concerned, that was the wrong answer. Egyptian officials withdrew from a dialogue they had been conducting

STICKS AND STONES MAY BREAK MY BONES, BUT WORDS WILL NEVER HURT ME

"Religious feelings cannot demand special treatment in a secular society. In a democracy one must from time to time accept criticism or becom[e] a laughingstock."

—*Jyllands-Posten* culture editor Flemming Rose[7]

with their Danish counterparts about human rights and discrimination. In addition, Egyptian Embassy councilor Mohab Nasr Mostafa Mahdy said, "The Egyptian ambassador in Denmark has said that the case no longer rests with the embassy. It is now being treated at an international level. As far as I have been informed by my government, the cartoon case has already been placed on the agenda for the Islamic Conference Organization's extraordinary summit in the beginning of December."[14]

The crisis escalated rapidly. By early November, thousands of Muslims in Denmark were marching in demonstrations against the cartoons.[15] Two of the cartoonists went into hiding, fearing for their lives. The Pakistani Jamaat-e-Islami party offered fifty thousand Danish kroner (around $7,500) to anyone who killed one of the cartoonists.[16] The Organization of the Islamic Conference (OIC) lodged a protest with the Danish government.[17] To take a stand against the cartoons, business establishments closed—in Kashmir.[18] Ghulam Nabi Azad, the chief minister of Jammu and Kashmir, was reportedly "anguished" by the cartoons, and asked India's Prime Minister to complain to the Danish government.[19] And the most respected authority in the Sunni Muslim world, Mohammad Sayed Tantawi, Grand Sheikh of Al-Azhar University in Cairo, declared that the cartoons had "trespassed all limits of objective criticism into insults and contempt of the religious beliefs of more than one billion Muslims around the world, including thousands in Denmark. Al-Azhar intends to protest these anti-Prophet cartoons with the UN's concerned committees and human rights groups around the world."[20]

"I find alarming any behaviors that disregard the beliefs of others. This kind of thing is unacceptable"

The UN, apparently uninterested in the principle of freedom of speech, was happy to take up the case. Louise Arbour, the UN High Commissioner for Human Rights, wrote to the OIC, "I understand your attitude to the images that appeared in the newspaper. I find alarming any behaviors that disregard the beliefs of others. This kind of thing is unacceptable."[21] She announced that investigations for racism and "Islamophobia" would commence forthwith.

Despite Arbour's solicitude for Muslims' sensibilities, the crisis continued to escalate. A Denmark-based imam, Ahmad Abu Laban, toured Middle Eastern countries in December 2005 with a dossier of cartoons that contained three additional images, each more inflammatory than anything that had been published in *Jyllands-Posten*, in an attempt to stir up outrage. These images included a photograph of a man wearing a toy pig nose; it was not a depiction of Muhammad at all.[22] At a meeting of the leaders of the Muslim world in Mecca that same month, the OIC decided to make the cartoons an abject lesson in the perils of Western secularism, and a weapon to force the West to discard the freedom of expression. Soon after that, in late January 2006, Muslim gunmen seized an EU office in Gaza, demanding apologies from Denmark and Norway (where another publication had reprinted the cartoons).[23] The following day, demonstrators chanted, "War on Denmark, death to Denmark," as they burned Danish flags. Said Islamic Jihad leader Nafez Azzam, "We feel great rage at the continued attacks on Islam and the Prophet of Islam and we demand that the Danish government make a clear and public apology for the wrongful crime."[24]

Arab interior ministers, meeting in Tunis, declared, "We ask the Danish authorities to take the necessary measures to punish those responsible for this harm and to take action to avoid a repeat."[25] Libya and Saudi Arabia recalled their ambassadors from Copenhagen. In Saudi Arabia, an angry mob beat two employees of the Danish corporation Arla Foods. Throughout the Islamic world, Arla Foods was subjected to a crippling boycott—endorsed by Muslim officials worldwide.[26] Iraqi Foreign Minister Hoshiyar Zebari complained to the Danish ambassador to Baghdad when Danish troops were put on alert there after a Muslim cleric issued a fatwa against

Danish troops because of the cartoons.[27] These incidents followed diplomatic protests from the Muslim World League, protests in Kashmir, death threats emanating from Pakistan, and more.[28]

"These totally outrageous cartoons against Islam"

As all this was unfolding, even Bill Clinton got into the act. But not, as one might expect, in the role of a former president of the United States standing up for the freedom of speech and denouncing the mad killing of innocent people because someone else had drawn a cartoon. Instead, Clinton came out firmly for self-censorship to protect Muslims' delicate sensibilities. He decried "these totally outrageous cartoons against Islam," huffing self-righteously, "So now what are we going to do?... Replace the anti-Semitic prejudice with anti-Islamic prejudice?"[30]

Of course not. The cartoons were not a manifestation of anti-Islamic prejudice: criticism of Muhammad or even of Islam is not equivalent to anti-Semitism. Islam is not a race; the problems with it are not the product of fear-mongering and fiction, but of ideology and facts—facts that have been stressed repeatedly by Muslims themselves, when they have committed violence around the world in the name of Islam and justified that violence by the teachings of their religion. To note, as some of the Danish cartoons do, that there is a connection between the teachings of Muhammad and Islamic violence is simply to exhibit an awareness of something that has been repeatedly asserted by Osama bin Laden, Ayman al-Zawahiri, Abu Musab al-Zarqawi, Abu Bakr al-Baghdadi, and so many other jihadists.

Do all these men and so many, many others misunderstand and misrepresent the teachings of Muhammad and Islam? So the leaders of the free nations of the West

NOT THE FUNNY PAPERS

Around the world, riots over the Danish Muhammad cartoons killed at least 139 people and injured 823, and the cartoonists now live under death threats.[29]

STICKS AND STONES MAY BREAK MY BONES, BUT WORDS WILL NEVER HURT ME

. . . .

"What is freedom of expression? Without the freedom to offend, it ceases to exist."

—Salman Rushdie[31]

insist. But that question, as crucial as it is to our relationship with the Muslim world—and even to our very survival—is irrelevant to an ethical assessment of the cartoons. The simple if unwelcome fact is that those and other jihad terrorists claim Muhammad's example and words as their inspiration. Some of the cartoons called attention to that fact. To do so was not illegitimate.

The freedom of speech encompasses precisely the freedom to annoy, to ridicule, and to offend. If it doesn't, the doctrine of free speech is a dead letter. After all, inoffensive speech doesn't need the protection of a constitutional amendment. The instant that any person or ideology is considered off-limits for critical examination and even ridicule, an ideological straitjacket replaces the freedom of speech. Westerners seem to grasp this principle easily when it comes to affronts to Christianity, even when they are as determinedly offensive as Andres Serrano's *Piss Christ* or Chris Ofili's dung- and pornography-encrusted *Holy Virgin Mary*. But the same clarity of thought doesn't seem to carry over to an Islamic context.

"The Islamic world took the satirical drawings as a different version of the September 11 attacks against them"

The OIC doesn't seem to be able to see the difference between publishing annoying cartoons and murdering thousands of innocent people. As Ekmeleddin Ihsanoglu, the OIC's secretary general, insisted to Javier Solana, the

High Representative of the Common Foreign and Security Policy of the European Union: "The Islamic world took the satirical drawings as a different version of the September 11 attacks against them."[32]

After the riots, the OIC, playing good cop to the rioters' bad cop, offered the free world a solution to end the riots: making criticism of Islam a crime. Ihsanoglu told Solana that he wanted action to ensure that such catastrophes wouldn't happen again. "I hope the EU will adopt a new ruling to fight against Islamophobia."[33]

Solana was apologetic and reassuring: rather than defend the freedom of speech to Ihsanoglu and try to explain its importance, he told him, "We never had the intention of harming. Please feel assured that we will do our best to preclude the cartoon crisis from re-occurring, because we need each other."[34]

Solana was not the only official in the West who was anxious to shield Islam from criticism. In 2007, Doudou Diène, the United Nations Special Rapporteur on contemporary forms of "racism, racial discrimination, xenophobia and related intolerance," suggested that it was "Islamophobic" even to quote the Qur'an in order to show how jihadis use Islamic texts and teachings to justify violence and supremacism: "the manipulation and selective quoting of sacred texts, in particular the Qur'an, as a means to deceptively argue that these texts show the violent nature of Islam has become current practice."[35]

So could even quoting the Qur'an—if the quotation showed Islam in a negative light—be outlawed?

That appeared to be what the OIC wanted. Ihsanoglu told the OIC's Council of Foreign Ministers in March 2008 that "Islamophobia cannot be dealt with only through cultural activities but [through] a robust political engagement."[36] What kind of robust political engagement? Agitating for restrictions on the freedom of speech, apparently. Abdoulaye Wade, president of Senegal and the chairman of the OIC, explained, "I don't think freedom of expression should mean freedom from [sic] blasphemy. There can be no freedom without limits."[37]

Ihsanoglu was confident that Western leaders could be persuaded to get onboard: "In face of the adverse and mounting phenomenon of Islamophobia in the West, we placed this issue at the top of our priorities and preoccupations, while conducting a large-scale world-wide effort to confront it at four levels." The first of these was "the official level of countries and governments of the West, where this phenomenon is rampant and widespread." This involved actively lobbying Western leaders to restrict the freedom of speech in order to stamp out perceived "Islamophobia": "We have exhorted the officials in these countries to assume their inherent legal responsibilities in order to stem this illegal trend in conformity with international and domestic laws which prohibit discrimination based on incitement to hatred towards individuals or groups because of their religion, race, or other grounds."

"Hatred towards individuals or groups because of their religion" is an extremely elastic concept. Is counter-terror analysis of the motivating ideology behind Islamic jihad terror "hatred" toward Muslims? That was the consistent contention of the Council on American-Islamic Relations (CAIR) and other Islamic advocacy groups in the United States. If Ihsanoglu got his way, this "hatred" would be outlawed: it would be legally forbidden to examine the ways in which the religious beliefs of terrorists incite them to commit acts of terror.

Ihsanoglu said that this initiative was advancing on "the level of major international organizations, such as the United Nations General Assembly in New York or the UN Human Rights Council in Geneva, as well as organisations concerned with Dialogue among Civilizations, or inter-religious and interfaith dialogue."

He happily reported that the anti-free speech initiative had "proven its merit and we have been able to achieve convincing progress at all these levels mainly the UN Human Rights Council in Geneva, and the UN General Assembly," for "the United Nations General Assembly adopted similar resolutions against the defamation of Islam."

"In confronting the Danish cartoons and the Dutch film 'Fitna', we sent a clear message to the West regarding the red lines that should not be crossed"

In Ihsanoghlu's eyes, the Islamic world was showing the West who was boss, making it obey Islamic restrictions on criticism of Islam: "In confronting the Danish cartoons and the Dutch film 'Fitna', we sent a clear message to the West regarding the red lines that should not be crossed. As we speak, the official West and its public opinion are all now well-aware of the sensitivities of these issues. They have also started to look seriously into the question of freedom of expression from the perspective of its inherent responsibility, which should not be overlooked."[38] *Fitna* was a short film by Dutch politician Geert Wilders with a very simple structure: it showed verses from the Qur'an exhorting Muslims to violence, followed by scenes of modern-day jihad violence inspired by those Qur'anic passages.

The OIC continued to win victories. In 2010, the UN General Assembly condemned the "vilification of religion"—without, of course, explaining in any useful detail what did or did not constitute such vilification, or who would be given the enormous power to define it.[39] In an impressive display of unanimity in opposition to the freedom of speech, every majority-Muslim nation in the entire world voted in favor of this condemnation. Their intent was clear: to make criticizing Islam an international crime. The UN resolution condemned "Judeophobia and Christianophobia" as well as "Islamophobia," but its true intent was obvious.

In March 2011, Ihsanoglu called upon the UN Council on Human Rights to set up "an Observatory at the Office of the High Commissioner to monitor

A MARTYR FOR FREE SPEECH

. . . .

Stéphane Charbonnier had told an interviewer in 2012, "I'd rather die standing up than live on my knees."[44] He was killed in the January 2015 massacre at the offices of *Charlie Hebdo*, where he was the editor.

acts of defamation of all religions.... as a first step toward concerted action at the international level."[40] Then on April 12, 2011, the UN Council on Human Rights passed Resolution 16/18, which called upon the nations of the world to ban speech involving "defamation of religion."[41] Two months later, Ihsanoglu reiterated that such laws were "a matter of extreme priority" for the OIC.[42]

"I'm not killing you because you are a woman and we don't kill women but you have to convert to Islam, read the Qu'ran and wear a veil"

The bad cop counterpart to the OIC's good cop showed itself again in January 2015, when Islamic jihadists murdered twelve people and injured eleven others in the Paris offices of the satirical magazine *Charlie Hebdo*, which had featured cartoons of Muhammad in several issues.

Laurent Leger, a *Charlie Hebdo* journalist who survived the attack by hiding, recalled, "We thought it was a joke, that it was fire crackers. Then we heard footsteps. The door opened. A guy shouted 'Allahu Akbar.' They called out the name of Charb [*Charlie Hebdo* editor Stéphane Charbonnier]. But after that they fired into the group."[43]

An incident during the *Charlie Hebdo* attack made the Islamic motives behind it undeniable. The jihad killers pointed a gun at the head of magazine staffer Sigolène Vinson, but then instead of shooting her, one of them said: "I'm not killing you because you are a woman and we don't kill women but you have to convert to Islam, read the Qu'ran and wear a veil." The attackers shouted "Allahu akbar" and left.[45]

The Islamic character of the entire initiative—both violent and non-violent—against the freedom of speech could not be clearer.

After the massacre there was an outpouring of public defense of free speech, with people all over the world proclaiming, "Je suis Charlie." But this enthusiasm didn't last long. Western resolve faltered, while the jihad against the freedom of speech continued unabated.

"Who will deal with this rascal for me?"

But why do Islamic groups see restricting the freedom of speech as such an "extreme priority"?

The answer is rooted in Islamic law and the example of the man whom the Qur'an designates (33:21) as the supreme model for conduct: Muhammad, the prophet of Islam. Islamic law presents a model for society that is a radical contrast with the one that currently prevails in the West. The differences are rooted in actions of Muhammad that are considered exemplary for Muslims for all time. And one of the chief differences is the freedom of speech.

Islamic tradition recounts that during Muhammad's prophetic career, a man named Ka'b bin Al-Ashraf, who was not a Muslim, heard of a Muslim victory in battle against some other Arabs. Ka'b asked, "Is this true? Did Muhammad actually kill these whom these two men mention? These are the nobles of the Arabs and kingly men; by God, if Muhammad has slain these people 'twere better to be dead than alive."[46] He began to compose verses criticizing Muhammad and bewailing the fate of the men the Muslim prophet had killed. When some Muslims answered him with verses of their own, the war of words escalated, until finally Ka'b was writing lewd verses about Muslim women.

Muhammad had had enough. He asked his followers, "Who will rid me of Ibn u'l-Ashraf?"[47]

One of his disciples, Muhammad bin Maslama, was eager for the job: "I will deal with him for you, O apostle of God, I will kill him."[48]

Muhammad replied, "Do so if you can," and granted Maslama and a comrade permission to deceive Ka'b in order to get close enough to him to kill him.[49] Maslama's fellow assassin was wounded in the struggle, but Ka'b was duly killed, and the killers reported the success of their mission to Muhammad.

A precedent was set. Those who insulted Muhammad's followers could be killed.

Later, an elderly poet, Abu Afak, mocked Muhammad in verse for having divided people by saying "'Permitted', 'Forbidden' of all sorts of things."[50] The poet declared to the Arabs, "Had you believed in glory or kingship, you would have followed Tubba," a rival of Muhammad. [51]

The messenger of Allah was not disposed to receive such criticism with equanimity. He asked his followers, "Who will deal with this rascal for me?"[52] One of them duly murdered Abu Afak, and another Muslim mocked the slain poet in verse of his own:

You gave the lie to God's religion and the man Ahmad [Muhammad]!
By him who was your father, evil is the son he produced!
A hanif [monotheist] gave you a thrust in the night saying,
"Take that, Abu Afak, in spite of your age!"
Though I knew whether it was man or jinn
Who slew you in the dead of night (I would say naught).[53]

Another precedent was set: those who criticized, mocked, or challenged Muhammad deserved death.

And that precedent was quickly reinforced. Asma bint Marwan, a poetess, appalled by the murder of Abu Afak, called for Muhammad to be killed in verses of her own, asking Muhammad's followers:

Do you expect good from him after the killing of your chiefs
Like a hungry man waiting for a cook's broth?

Is there no man of pride who would attack him by surprise

And cut off the hopes of those who expect aught from him?[54]

A Muslim poet answered her with this warning:

When she called for folly woe to her in her weeping,

For death is coming.

She stirred up a man of glorious origin,

Noble in his going out and his coming in.

Before midnight he dyed her in her blood

And incurred no guilt thereby.[55]

Muhammad was anxious that this prophecy be fulfilled, asking his followers, "Who will rid me of Marwan's daughter?" Once the deed had been done, Muhammad praised the killer, Umayr bin Adiy al-Khatmi: "You have helped God and His apostle, O Umayr!"[56]

When Umayr asked Muhammad if he would face punishment for having murdered Asma; Muhammad reassured the killer: "Two goats won't butt their heads about her."[57]

In another incident, Muhammad decreed that the murderer of a woman who had disparaged the Muslim prophet should not be punished. As one hadith (hadiths are collected Islamic traditions reporting the words and deeds of Muhammad) recounts,

A blind man had a slave-mother [a slave who bore children for him] who used to abuse the Prophet and disparage him. [The blind man] forbade her but she did not stop. He rebuked her but she did not give up her habit. One night she began to slander the Prophet and abuse him. So [the blind man] took a dagger, placed it on her belly, pressed it, and killed her. A child who came between her legs was smeared with the blood that was there. When the morning came, the Prophet was informed about it.

[Muhammad] assembled the people and said: I adjure by Allah the man who has done this action and I adjure him by my right to him that he should stand up. Jumping over the necks of the people and trembling the man stood up.

[The blind man] sat before the Prophet and said: Apostle of Allah! I am her master; she used to abuse you and disparage you. I forbade her, but she did not stop, and I rebuked her, but she did not abandon her habit. I have two sons like pearls from her, and she was my companion. Last night she began to abuse and disparage you. So I took a dagger, put it on her belly and pressed it till I killed her.

Thereupon the Prophet said: Oh be witness, no retaliation is payable for her blood.[59]

IF I STRIKE YOU DOWN, I WILL BECOME MORE POWERFUL THAN YOU CAN POSSIBLY IMAGINE

. . . .

The murder of Asma bint Marwan occasioned the conversion to Islam of the Arab Khatma tribe, who saw in the incident "the power of Islam," according to Ibn Ishaq, Muhammad's first biographer.[58] That same power would be manifested again and again throughout history, as Muslims killed those who spoke out against Islam or were perceived to have insulted the religion, its followers, the Prophet Muhammad, or Allah. Western leaders and opinion-makers only shore up that power when they make accommodations to calls for restrictions on the speech of those who are critical of Islam.

There are many such incidents. Another hadith reports, "A Jewess used to abuse the Prophet and disparage him. A man strangled her till she died. The Apostle of Allah declared that no recompense was payable for her blood.[60]

That is, no one was to be penalized for killing her; her death was just.

Capital punishment for criticizing Muhammad or Islam became codified in Islamic law, which stipulates that non-Muslims are forbidden to say "something impermissible about Allah, the Prophet.... or Islam."[61]

The popular Islamic website IslamQA (Islam Question and Answer) declares that if non-Muslims "insult Allaah and His Messenger," then Muslims "must respond and punish them so as deter them from their kufr [unbelief] and enmity. If we leave the kuffaar [unbelievers] and atheists to say whatever they want without denouncing it or punishing them, great mischief will result, which is something that these kuffaar love.... The Muslim has to have a sense of protective jealousy and get angry for the sake of Allaah [sic] and His Messenger.... Whoever hears the Prophet...being insulted and does not feel any protective jealousy or get angry is not a true believer."[62]

But jealousy and anger are not the end of it. The Qur'an exhorts believers, "Fight them; Allah will punish them by your hands and will disgrace them and give you victory over them and satisfy the breasts of a believing people, and remove the fury in the believers' hearts" (9:14–15). Believing Muslims are the executors of the wrath of Allah, bringing divine punishment on those who dared to insult the prophet of Islam.

This belief has had lethal consequences for untold numbers of people throughout Islamic history.

"I can't remember anyone ever suggesting that conservative views were illegitimate and unworthy of debate"

The OIC has an extraordinarily powerful ally in its effort to extend the principle that Islam must not be criticized: the international Left, which has its own reasons for refusing to tolerate dissent.

The Left in the United States has come a long way from the Free Speech Movement of the Sixties. Today the American Left is frankly authoritarian, intolerant of dissent, and increasingly intent on demonizing and destroying its opponents rather than engaging them in rational debate. Journalist Kirsten Powers, a long-time liberal who was active in the New York Democratic Party politics for years, recalls that when she was growing up, "I can't remember anyone ever suggesting that conservative views were illegitimate and unworthy of debate."[63]

Now, however, the disparagement of conservative views as beneath serious consideration, and worse, as manifestations of bigotry and racism is virtually universal on the Left. The answer to the positions enunciated by conservatives is not rational discussion of why the conservative views are wrong and would be bad for society, but moral outrage coupled with ridicule.

The transformation of the American Left from champions of free speech to its relentless enemies has been swift: Powers was born in 1969. The reason for the dramatic change is unclear, but the international Left has never been a friend of the freedom of speech. Whenever radical leftists have taken power, from eighteenth-century France to twentieth-century Russia, China, Cambodia and so many other places, they have begun their rule with a reign of terror that has targeted the critics of the new regime. Dissent is outlawed; dissenters are silenced. Conservative activist David Horowitz, a former leftist, has argued that the Left is inherently authoritarian, and that any leftist regime will move to crush dissent.

Because leftists envision establishing a truly just society on earth, those who oppose them are inevitably stigmatized as morally evil. Consequently, critics of the Left's program are accorded as little tolerance as the medieval Roman Catholic Church extended to those it considered heretics. No less a luminary than St. Thomas Aquinas argued that because the Catholic state had to be concerned with the moral and spiritual well-being of its people, heretics were enemies of the state, deserving of execution. The modern Left, in a similar vein, so closely identifies its agenda with all that is good that it considers those who oppose its imperatives to be beyond the pale of reasonable discourse. The foes of the Left cannot be decent human beings; they must be simply evil people who have to be shouted down, discredited, and destroyed altogether.

In endeavoring to weaken and destroy the freedom of speech, leftists in the United States have found ready allies in the Muslim community. Many observers have remarked that the Left and Islamic supremacists make strange bedfellows: the former advocate a moral libertinism; the latter are attempting to impose a repressive moral code. What binds these unlikely allies is a shared taste for authoritarianism. Both parties want to stifle dissent, and in doing so both find themselves fighting the same foes. Why not join forces?

> ## WHY WE NEED THE FREEDOM OF SPEECH
>
> . . .
>
> "If freedom of speech is taken away, then dumb and silent we may be led, like sheep to the slaughter."
>
> —George Washington[64]

The idea that certain ideas, groups, and individuals should be sheltered from criticism is inimical to the principle of the freedom of speech, which is the foundation of a free society and an indispensable shelter against tyranny. Most Americans are unconcerned about threats to free speech, which, after all, is enshrined in the Bill of Rights. The provisions of Islamic law forbidding criticism of Allah, Muhammad, and Islam are foreign elements of a foreign law. The First Amendment will protect us. Won't it?

Yes, it will—for now. But even Constitutional rights can have enemies. And the First Amendment's free speech protection has many powerful ones.

Chapter Two

"TAILORED IN AN APPROPRIATE WAY": CAN FREE SPEECH REALLY BE RESTRICTED IN THE UNITED STATES?

Could the U.S. government actually curtail the freedom of speech to restrict criticism of Islam? Would the U.S. government ever do such a thing?

There are precedents, of a sort.

Americans have enjoyed constitutionally protected freedom of speech since December 15, 1791, the day the Bill of Rights was adopted. The First Amendment states:

> Congress shall make no law respecting an establishment of religion, or prohibiting the free exercise thereof; or abridging the freedom of speech, or of the press; or the right of the people peaceably to assemble, and to petition the Government for a redress of grievances.

It is likely that this was the first of the ten amendments comprising the Bill of Rights because the five rights enumerated in it—freedom of religion, speech, press, assembly, and the right to petition the government regarding grievances—are the foundation of any free society. No free state hinders the practice of religion, muzzles critical or dissenting individuals or media voices, or forbids people to meet in groups or complain to the government.

If a government can forbid the enunciation of certain points of view, if it sets the acceptable spectrum of the public discourse, it is a tyranny.

"The liberty of the press is indeed essential to the nature of a free state"

Blackstone's *Commentaries on the Laws of England*, a key text for the founding of the United States, explains that "the liberty of the press is indeed essential to the nature of a free state.... To subject the press to the restrictive power of a licenser, as was formerly done...is to subject all freedom of sentiment to the prejudices of one man, and make him the arbitrary and infallible judge of all controverted points in learning, religion and government."[1]

Those who have the power to determine what is acceptable speech, and what is unacceptable, wield enormous power. The Founding Fathers did not envision anyone in the United States holding such power.

But the constitutional guarantee of free speech was threatened almost immediately. In 1798, the U.S. Congress, dominated by Federalists during the administration of President John Adams, passed the Sedition Act, criminalizing the "writing, printing, uttering or publishing" of "any false, scandalous and malicious writing or writings against the government of the United States, or either house of the Congress of the United States, or the President of the United States, with intent to defame the said government, or either house of the said Congress, or the said President, or to bring them, or either of them, into contempt or disrepute; or to excite against them, or either or any of them, the hatred of the good people of the United States, or to stir up sedition within the United States."[2]

Critics complained that the Sedition Act was an unconstitutional violation of the First Amendment. The principle of judicial review—the idea that the Supreme Court could declare laws unconstitutional—had not yet been established at that time, but the Kentucky and Virginia legislatures passed bills (written anonymously by Adams's political opponents Thomas Jefferson and James Madison) declaring the Sedition Act unconstitutional; the New Hampshire legislature responded by asserting "that the state legislatures are not the proper tribunals to determine the constitutionality of the laws of the general government; that the duty of such decision is properly and exclusively confided to the judicial department."[3] The controversy over whether the states could reject laws passed by the federal government was not resolved until the Civil War.

> ### FREE SPEECH: PRICELESS
>
> • • •
>
> The penalty for violating the Sedition Act was a fine of up to two thousand dollars and up to two years in prison.

"The grand object of his administration, has been to exasperate the rage of contending parties, to calumniate and destroy every man who differs from his opinions"

Controversy raged as the Adams administration began enforcing the Sedition Act. Congressman Matthew Lyon of Vermont got four months in an unheated Vermont prison cell and a $1,000 fine for saying that the Adams administration was demonstrating "an unbounded thirst for ridiculous pomp, foolish adulation, and selfish avarice."[4] Benjamin Franklin Bache, editor of the opposition newspaper *Aurora*, was arrested for criticizing "the blind, bald, crippled, toothless, querulous Adams," but died before his case went to trial.[5]

NOT THE VINDICATION HE WAS LOOKING FOR

· ·

Virginia resident James Callender wrote in his book *The Prospect Before Us* that John Adams was a "repulsive pedant, a gross hypocrite and an unprincipled oppressor" and "in private life, one of the most egregious fools on the continent."[6] Callender also declared Adams's administration "one continual tempest of malignant passions," and wrote that "the grand object of his administration, has been to exasperate the rage of contending parties, to calumniate and destroy every man who differs from his opinions."[7] Callender's claim was vindicated, but not in a manner he likely welcomed: he was sentenced to nine months in prison and fined $200.[8]

Printer Anthony Haswell, who reprinted material from *Aurora* charging that the Adams administration had deemed Tories, "men who fought against our independence, who shared in the destruction of our homes, and the abuse of our wives and daughters…worthy of the confidence of the government," was fined $200 and given a two-month sentence.[9]

In November 1798, a Massachusetts resident named David Brown led a group in setting up a liberty pole reading, "No Stamp Act, No Sedition Act, No Alien Bills, No Land Tax, downfall to the Tyrants of America; peace and retirement to the President; Long Live the Vice President." The vice president was Thomas Jefferson, Adams's chief political rival and a vociferous critic of the Sedition Act. Brown was fined $450 and sentenced to eighteen months in prison.[10]

The Sedition Act was the law of the land until March 3, 1801, the date specified in the bill itself for its expiration.[11] Its foremost foe, Thomas Jefferson, who became president the next day, pardoned those who were still in prison on Sedition Act charges. Their fines were repaid. Long afterward, in its 1964 ruling on *New York Times Co. vs. Sullivan*, the Supreme Court stated, "Although the Sedition Act was never tested in this Court, the attack upon its validity has carried the day in the court of history."[12]

"The most stringent protection of free speech would not protect a man in falsely shouting fire in a theatre and causing a panic"

Challenges to the freedom of speech, however, recurred. The Espionage Act of 1917 criminalized attempting to induce "insubordination, disloyalty, mutiny, or refusal of duty in the military or naval forces of the United States."[13] Charles Schenck, general secretary of the Socialist Party of America, was accordingly imprisoned for anti-draft leaflets. Schenck appealed on First Amendment grounds, but the Supreme Court upheld his conviction in a unanimous vote. Justice Oliver Wendell Holmes Jr. explained the Court's position: "The question in every case is whether the words used are used in such circumstances and are of such a nature as to create a clear and present danger that they will bring about the substantive evils that Congress has a right to prevent."[14]

"Clear and present danger" became a fundamental criterion for judging speech to be outside the protection of the First Amendment. And Holmes's decision in *Schenck vs. the United States* also contained another phrase that became a cornerstone of modern-day evaluations of whether speech was permissible or crossed an unacceptable line: "The most stringent protection of free speech would not protect a man in falsely shouting fire in a theatre and causing a panic."[15]

The Court shortly affirmed the *Schenck* decision in another Espionage Act case, *Frohwerk vs. the United States*, noting that "a person may be convicted of a conspiracy to obstruct recruiting by words of persuasion."[16] Those who objected on First Amendment grounds were reminded that the First Amendment, "while prohibiting legislation against free speech as such cannot have been, and obviously was not, intended to give immunity for every possible use of language.... We venture to believe that neither Hamilton nor Madison, nor any other competent person then or later, ever supposed that to make criminal the counselling of a murder within the jurisdiction of Congress would be an unconstitutional interference with free speech."[17]

The following year, Socialist Party leader Eugene V. Debs gave a speech in which he praised three "comrades" who had been "convicted of aiding and abetting another in failing to register for the draft."[18] Debs himself was then imprisoned under the Espionage Act, as the Supreme Court deemed his speech to have a "natural tendency and reasonably probable effect to obstruct the recruiting service."[19]

"The best test of truth is the power of the thought to get itself accepted in the competition of the market"

Also convicted under the Espionage Act, in *Abrams vs. the United States*, were four Marxists who had distributed leaflets favoring the October Revolution in Russia and criticizing President Woodrow Wilson for sending American troops to Russia to oppose it. One of these leaflets, entitled "The Hypocrisy of the United States and her Allies," denounced Wilson's "shameful, cowardly silence about the intervention in Russia," charging that his silence revealed "the hypocrisy of the plutocratic gang in Washington and vicinity."[20] Wilson, it said, was "too much of a coward to come out openly and say: 'We capitalistic nations cannot afford to have a proletarian republic in Russia.'" The leaflet included open calls for revolution: "The Russian Revolution cries: Workers of the World! Awake! Rise! Put down your enemy and mine! Yes! friends, there is only one enemy of the workers of the world and that is CAPITALISM.... Awake! Awake! you Workers of the World!"[21]

Another leaflet referred to "his Majesty, Mr. Wilson, and the rest of the gang; dogs of all colors" and declared that "America and her Allies have betrayed (the Workers). Their robberish aims are clear to all men. The destruction of the Russian Revolution, that is the politics of the march to Russia. *Workers, our reply to the barbaric intervention has to be a general strike! An open challenge* only will let the Government know that not only the Russian Worker fights for freedom, but also here in America lives the spirit of Revolution."[22]

Supreme Court Justice John Hessin Clarke, in upholding the conviction of the leafleters, pointed out that "this is not an attempt to bring about a change of administration by candid discussion, for, no matter what may have incited the outbreak on the part of the defendant anarchists, the manifest purpose of such a publication was to create an attempt to defeat the war plans of the Government of the United States by bringing upon the country the paralysis of a general strike, thereby arresting the production of all munitions and other things essential to the conduct of the war."[23]

Dissenting, Oliver Wendell Holmes delivered a ringing defense of the freedom of speech and the power of truth to defeat falsehood in an open arena. He conceded that "persecution for the expression of opinions seems to me perfectly logical," for "if you have no doubt of your premises or your power, and want a certain result with all your heart, you naturally express your wishes in law, and sweep away all opposition." However, "the best test of truth is the power of the thought to get itself accepted in the competition of the market." Holmes affirmed, "That, at any rate, is the theory of our Constitution."[24]

The idea that the government has a legitimate right to limit speech that is libelous or that calls for violence or the overthrow of the government has seldom if ever been controversial. But the dividing line between treasonous and seditious speech and speech that is simply unwelcome to the government has been a subject of controversy throughout American history.

The Sedition Act and the Espionage Act demonstrate that the U.S. government has placed severe restrictions on the First Amendment's protection of the freedom of speech in the past, and indicate that it could do so again in the future. This history also shows that First Amendment protections of free speech are most likely to be curtailed in a time of serious and imminent threats to the nation.

That time may be upon us now.

"Know the laws! Ignorance of the law will not help you if you get into trouble!"

From 9/11 and the Boston Bombing to numerous mass shootings across the nation (Ft. Hood, San Bernadino, the Pulse nightclub in Orlando, the Ft. Lauderdale airport, to name just a few), Americans have been at deadly risk of jihad attacks for more than a decade and a half now. Our government and media have responded to that threat by taking extraordinary steps to obscure the connection between the violence and the religion of Islam. The motivations behind this campaign of political correctness on the subject of jihad are complex and to some extent unclear. But it would seem that the authorities fear that identifying the danger with Muslims and their beliefs—admitting the expressed motivations of such killers as "Soldier of Allah" Major Nidal Hasan, for example, or even revealing the Muslim-sounding names of mass shooters—would only encourage the billion mostly peaceful Muslims (a quarter of the world's population) to identify with the violent

"DID ANY OF THEM HAVE EATING DISORDERS? THOSE CAN MAKE YOU CRAZY"

The political correctness hampering the free discussion of jihad attacks and the motives behind them is so egregious that it inspired a ½ Hour News Hour skit in which baffled TV reporters and an "international terrorism expert" wrack their brains about the 2005 London bombing plot, completely unable to think of anything that suspects with names like Muktar Said Ibrahim, Ramzi Mohammed, Yassin Omar, and Hussain Osman might have in common.[27]

jihadis against the West, and could also inspire Americans to take out their anger and fear on innocent Muslims. Thus the U.S. government first characterized the Ft. Hood attack as "workplace violence,"[25] and the Department of Justice originally redacted references to ISIS from the transcript of Pulse shooter Omar Mateen's 911 call.[26]

But most Americans, if they have thought about these issues at all, are confident that, however influential the politically correct conformism with regard to the jihad threat may be, it will ultimately recede, as restrictions on speech can never be codified in law in the United States. The First Amendment will always protect the freedom of speech.

Yet no law, not even a constitutional amendment, has any force unless duly constituted authorities have the will to enforce it. And when those authorities are determined to restrict the law rather than enforce it, they can always find ways to do just that.

The history of the Second Amendment provides an instructive analogy.

The Second Amendment to the U.S. Constitution reads, "A well regulated Militia, being necessary to the security of a free State, the right of the people to keep and bear Arms, shall not be infringed."

The precise meaning of this language is hotly contested, not only by constitutional lawyers, but also by politicians and concerned citizens. Some contend that the right to bear arms is an absolute right, like the freedom of speech, not to be infringed. Others claim that the Second Amendment refers only to the right of each state to have a militia, and doesn't grant the individual citizen any right to bear arms at all. Still others grant that it does recognize a right to bear arms, but with the caveat that the exercise of that right must be "well regulated."

For the Founding Fathers, the element of the Second Amendment that is most contested today was perfectly clear. The Massachusetts State Convention declared in February 1788 that the Constitution should "be never construed to authorize Congress...to prevent the people of the United

States, who are peaceable citizens, from keeping their own arms."[28] New Hampshire weighed in four months later: "Congress shall never disarm any Citizen unless such as are or have been in Actual Rebellion."[29]

That was over two centuries ago. In numerous localities today, the right to bear arms has been severely circumscribed, usually by choking it with so many regulations that it has become essentially a dead letter. The New York City Guns website notes that "the process for obtaining a handgun license in New York City is long (between 3–6 months, and waits up to 8 months are not uncommon), and compared to many other jurisdictions, rather expensive. It's not particularly difficult, but it is tedious and incredibly time consuming. It tests your patience, and there is a lot of bureaucracy to deal with."[30]

That's an understatement. New York City requires that the application to get a permit to carry a gun be typed or filled out electronically and then printed out; handwritten applications are summarily rejected. One must produce a driver's license, a passport, two U.S. postal money orders, two recent photographs, a birth certificate, proof of residence, a letter explaining why the gun is needed, and more. Documents must be originals, not copies. The application must be notarized and accompanied by an affidavit certifying that the applicant has read and understood the New York City laws regarding the responsibilities of gun owners, the use of deadly force, criminal possession of firearms, trigger locks, public safety zones, people who are forbidden to possess firearms, and a New York Police Department pamphlet about terrorism. If the applicant lives with someone, he or she must file an affidavit as well.

Once one has cut through all this red tape, the wait can be from between one and three months before an interview is scheduled between the applicant and a police officer. The applicant must also supply three character references. And then more forms are demanded. One applicant recalled, "I also had to supply my Social Security Card, current bank statements and

1040 Income Tax return along with photos of my home (because I am self employed), my marriage license, and my DMV abstract. I guess I'm just lucky."[31]

After the interview, there is another one- to three-month wait, followed by a letter approving or denying the application. If approved, one must go in person between nine a.m. and noon Monday through Thursday to pick up one's license, be photographed, and receive a Purchase Authorization, which allows the applicant to buy a handgun within ninety days from an approved firearms merchant.

Then the buyer must take the new gun back to the Police Department to be inspected and its serial number recorded on one's gun license. (If the serial number is written down wrong on the license and ends up not matching the one on the gun, the gun owner could be arrested.) Once that is done, the gun owner may buy ammunition. And if the gun owner wants to leave New York City with the gun, that triggers a new round of bureaucracy. The laws are extremely complicated, and the stakes high, as one New York City gun owner reminded potential buyers: "Read the booklet that NYPD gives you at the time of your Pistol Permit issuance. Know the laws! Ignorance of the law will not help you if you get into trouble!"[32]

The process of buying a handgun is somewhat easier in Chicago, but still lengthy and complicated. One must apply for a Firearm Owners Identification Card, complete a firearms safety course, and apply for a Chicago Firearms Permit before buying a gun. Once the

EMILY GETS HER GUN

Washington, D.C., reporter Emily Miller wrote a full-length book about the ridiculous hoops she had to jump through to acquire a gun legally in the nation's capital—even after the 2008 *District of Columbia vs. Heller* decision affirming that the Second Amendment protects an individual's right to own a firearm.

gun is obtained, something that must be done outside the city, it has to be registered with city officials within five days of purchase.[33]

Laws as complicated and regulations as time-consuming as these obviously deter many people from obtaining a gun at all. And that is clearly the idea. It is likely that these regulations were put in place by politicians who opposed the Second Amendment altogether, thinking it outmoded in the modern age. And so they hedged the right to bear arms around with a maze of rules so difficult to follow that the Second Amendment became essentially a dead letter.

"Every constitutional right and amendment can be tailored in an appropriate way"

The assault continues. Two hundred years after the Massachusetts State Convention warned that the Constitution should "be never construed to authorize Congress...to prevent the people of the United States, who are peaceable citizens, from keeping their own arms," Democratic presidential candidate Hillary Clinton declared that she rejected what she referred to as the National Rifle Association's "single-minded, absolutist theology about the Second Amendment being sacrosanct."[34] Her opponent Donald Trump charged, not without justification, that "Hillary Clinton wants to abolish the Second Amendment. Hillary Clinton wants to take your guns away and she wants to abolish the Second Amendment."[35]

The Clinton camp, however, scoffed at this accusation. Clinton spokesman Jesse Lehrich said of Trump, "It must be liberating to just have no regard for facts whatsoever."[36] And it was true that Clinton had not declared any intention to set in motion the Constitutional process that would have been necessary to repeal the Second Amendment. She had other plans to curtail it, declaring ominously that "every constitutional right and amendment can be tailored in an appropriate way without breaching the Constitution."[37]

That would include the First.

"The inalienable right of every citizen to live without fear and intimidation"

The enemies of the First Amendment right to free speech were at work in the House of Representatives on December 17, 2015. House Resolution 569 (HR569), sponsored by Muslim Congressmen Keith Ellison and Andre Carson, as well as other notable Democrats including Eleanor Holmes Norton, Loretta Sanchez, Charles Rangel, Debbie Wasserman Schultz, Joe Kennedy, Al Green, Judy Chu, Debbie Dingell, Niki Tsongas, John Conyers, José Serrano, Hank Johnson, and many others condemned "violence, bigotry, and hateful rhetoric towards Muslims in the United States."[38] HR569 was referred to the House Committee on the Judiciary on the same day it was introduced, and then in January 2016 to the Subcommittee on the Constitution and Civil Justice.

The implications of a condemnation of "violence, bigotry and hateful rhetoric" are ominous. That was what was so clever, and so ominous, about this Resolution. It conflated violence—attacks on innocent civilians, which have no justification under any circumstances—with "hateful rhetoric," which—while no decent person can be *for* it—is speech protected by the First Amendment.

It's worth pointing out that whether speech is "bigotry" and "hateful rhetoric" depends on subjective judgments. Condemning these things seems both obvious and high-minded—who would embrace or even defend bigotry or hate?—but this is the very language that Ellison, Carson, and their allies (including groups such as the Hamas-linked Council on American-Islamic Relations, CAIR) have used for years to condemn any and all honest examination of how Islamic jihadists use the texts and teachings of Islam to incite hatred and violence.

And in condemning "bigotry" and "hateful rhetoric" in the same breath as "violence," the Resolution equates legitimate debate of the motives and goals of those who have vowed to destroy us—absolutely necessary, if we don't want the jihad to advance unimpeded—with violence against innocent Muslims.

While what constitutes "violence" is more or less easy to establish, "bigotry" and "hateful rhetoric" are highly subjective terms. The person charged with the responsibility of determining what constitutes "bigotry" and "hateful rhetoric" and what does not would wield enormous and unprecedented power over the public discourse, a power that amounts to censorship of all public discource.

This would be the end of free speech. Public debate could proceed only within the parameters of what the guardians against "bigotry" and "hateful rhetoric" deem acceptable. With the end of free discourse would come the end of free society. A would-be dictator could deem any opposition to his policies "bigotry" and "hateful rhetoric," and rule it out of bounds.

Of course House Resolution 569 did not go that far. It did not mandate criminal penalties for "bigotry" and "hateful rhetoric." But if it had passed, it would have put the House of Representatives on record as conflating speech with violent crime, laying the groundwork for the eventual criminalization of speech.

The Resolution denounced "in the strongest terms the increase of hate speech, intimidation, violence, vandalism, arson, and other hate crimes targeted against mosques, Muslims, or those perceived to be Muslim"; paid tribute to the "countless positive contributions to United States society" that it said Muslims in the United States had made; and declared "that the civil rights and civil liberties of all United States citizens, including Muslims in the United States, should be protected and preserved," urging "local and Federal law enforcement authorities to work to prevent hate crimes; and to prosecute to the fullest extent of the law those perpetrators of hate crimes." It reaffirmed "the inalienable right of every citizen to live without fear and intimidation, and to practice their freedom of faith."

No one in his right mind could possibly object to any of that. But the Resolution made no attempt to distinguish the legitimate criticism of Islam, and even simply honest reporting of the facts about jihad doctrine and ideology—both of which have often been characterized as hatred and bigotry—from the irrational hatred of Muslims.

"As long as you continue to offend Islam and Muslims, you will be potential targets, and not just cops and Jews but everyone"

The importance of this frequently ignored distinction was underscored in December 2015, just days after House Resolution 569 was introduced, by Kahina Amimour, the wife of Samy Amimour, one of the jihad gunmen who killed 130 people in Paris in November 2015. Kahina was overjoyed by her husband's participation in the massacre: "I encouraged my husband to leave in order to terrorize the people of France who have so much blood on their hands.... I'm so proud of my husband and to boast about his virtue, ah la la, I am so happy." She added a threat to non-Muslims in France: "As long as you continue to offend Islam and Muslims, you will be potential targets, and not just cops and Jews but everyone."[39]

Kahina Amimour sounded as if she would have been quite happy with House Resolution 569's condemnation of "bigotry" and "hateful rhetoric" directed against Muslims. She represents the bad cop in the Islamic war on free speech, warning that non-Muslims are going to be "potential targets" of jihadists as long as they "continue to offend Islam and Muslims." The sponsors of HR569 represent the good cop, making the high-minded case that we really should stop doing anything that might offend Muslims.

NO JEWS OR DOGS ALLOWED

• • •

Where, if anywhere, would authorities eager to spare Muslims from all offense draw the line? Malaysia Airlines has become the world's first Sharia-compliant airline, banning alcohol and pork, which are, of course, forbidden in Islam.[42] If airlines that fly to Muslim countries, or airlines that sell tickets to Muslims in the United States, for that matter, continue to offer alcohol and pork, would that be a manifestation of "bigotry"? Already, Muslim cab drivers at the Minneapolis-St. Paul airport have refused to transport passengers with alcohol or dogs.[43]

But what offends Muslims? What is the price of the future, free of offense to Islam, that our leftist politicians, media elites, and much of the Western intelligentsia are actively working to make a reality?

For starters, to avoid "bigotry" and "hateful rhetoric," non-Muslims would have to refrain from drawing Muhammad. And would that be so bad? Many Americans would agree that we shouldn't go out of our way to insult anyone's religion, and the vast majority of U.S. citizens have no interest in creating Muhammad cartoons.

Unfortunately, however, there is a great deal more that offends Muslims than cartoons of their Prophet. In December 2015, three Muslim countries—Somalia, Tajikistan, and Brunei—officially banned Christmas celebrations.[40] Imams in Brunei explained, "Using religious symbols like crosses, lighting candles, putting up Christmas trees, singing religious songs, sending Christmas greetings…are against Islamic faith."[41]

Would these imams consider Christmas carols, and Christmas celebrations in general, a manifestation of "hateful rhetoric" against Muslims? The Brunei government banned all such public displays. Certainly this was very different from what Congressmen Ellison and Carson and their colleagues had in mind when they condemned "hateful rhetoric" against Muslims. But the distance between their idea of what was offensive to Muslims and that of the imams and government of Brunei is not as large as you may assume. Once the principle that nothing offensive to Muslims should be allowed is established, then Muslims can always claim that they are offended by something new, until the entire society is governed by Sharia law—because any deviation from it offends Muslims. Notice that Kahina Amimour's idea of what offends Islam and Muslims begins—though it does not end—with simply being a cop, or a Jew.

The average American may not consider it "bigotry" or "hateful rhetoric" to do and say things forbidden by Islam. But the fact is, many Muslims do find it offensive when non-Muslims simply go about their business, continuing to behave as non-Muslims in the presence of Muslims. Some Islamic authorities have suggested, for example, that Western women who have the nerve to go out in public uncovered deserve to be sexually assaulted.[44] That's a principle that thousands of Muslim men notoriously tried to enforce on New Year's Eve 2016 in Cologne, Germany.[45]

And uncovered women, alcohol, dogs, and Christmas are no more offensive to Islamic sensibilities than is a great deal of speech that Americans take it for granted we have the right to engage in. That applies to any criticism of Islam, of course. But even speech that simply disagrees with Muslim beliefs— as when a Christian asserts that Jesus is the Son of God, for example—is so offensive to Muslims that non-Muslims who attest to their own religious beliefs risk charges of "blasphemy," which is a capital offense in many Muslim countries. For saying, "I believe in Jesus Christ who died on the cross for the sins of mankind. What did your Prophet Mohammed ever do to save mankind?" a Christian woman named Asia Bibi is on death row in Pakistan,[46] where "wounding [Muslim's] religious feelings" is a crime and blaspheming against Muhammad is punishable by death.[47]

WHY WE NEED THE FREEDOM OF SPEECH

• • •

"The framers of the constitution knew human nature as well as we do. They too had lived in dangerous days; they too knew the suffocating influence of orthodoxy and standardized thought. They weighed the compulsions for restrained speech and thought against the abuses of liberty. They chose liberty."

—William O. Douglas[48]

Pakistan doesn't have the First Amendment. Americans in the United States are in no danger of execution for testifying to their religious beliefs. But the Asia Bibi case illustrates the utter futility of attempting keep Muslims from ever being offended—unless we are willing to give up our right to freedom of speech entirely.

Chapter Three

"NOW OBVIOUSLY THIS IS A COUNTRY THAT IS BASED ON FREE SPEECH, BUT. . . . ": THE U.S. GOVERNMENT VS. FREE SPEECH

The U.S. government vs. the First Amendment? Is that even possible? During the presidency of Barack Obama, it was reality.

Given the First Amendment, the Obama administration couldn't move directly to implement the OIC agenda and restrict speech critical of Islam. But it found creative ways to try to ensure that the First Amendment right to free speech would be "tailored in an appropriate way," particularly when it came to speech about Islam.

One way the Obama administration attempted to curtail the First Amendment was at the United Nations. In October 2009, the U.S. government lent its support to a UN Human Rights Council resolution declaring that "negative racial and religious stereotyping" should be outlawed.[1] The resolution

Did you know?

- Obama representatives at the UN actually agreed to limit the freedom of speech
- The Obama administration falsely blamed the Benghazi massacre on a video of Muhammad to build a case against free speech
- Obama administration officials routinely warned the public against certain kinds of speech

stated that UN member states should condemn and criminalize "any advocacy of national, racial or religious hatred that constitutes incitement to discrimination, hostility or violence."[2]

But who would decide that an unacceptable level of "national, racial or religious hatred" had been reached? Incitement to violence is relatively easy to spot, but "incitement to hostility" is very much in the eye of the beholder. Just as they would do with House Resolution 569, members of the U.S. government were working to advance the Muslim campaign against free speech by deliberately conflating speech (and even feelings) with actual violent crimes.

UCLA law professor Eugene Volokh pointed out that the resolution was a commitment to curtailing the First Amendment protection of free speech, and that administration officials would follow up with court briefings, judicial appointments, and even proposed constitutional amendments if they wanted to be consistent: "If the U.S. backs a resolution that urges the suppression of some speech," he explained, "presumably we are taking the view that all countries—including the U.S.—should adhere to this resolution. If we are constitutionally barred from adhering to it by our domestic constitution, then we're implicitly criticizing that constitution, and committing ourselves to do what we can to change it."[3]

To make its support for this resolution more than just symbolic, Volokh said, "the Administration would presumably have to take what steps it can to ensure that supposed 'hate speech' that incites hostility will indeed be punished. It would presumably be committed to filing amicus briefs supporting changes in First Amendment law to allow such punishment, and in principle perhaps the appointment of Justices who would endorse such changes (or even the proposal of express constitutional amendments that would work such changes)."[4]

"Will you tell us here today that this administration's Department of Justice will never entertain or advance a proposal that criminalizes speech against any religion?"

One Obama administration official refused to say that the administration was not contemplating such changes.

In July 2012, Thomas Perez, the Obama administration's Assistant Attorney General for the Civil Rights Division, who became chair of the Democratic National Committee after Donald Trump was elected president, was being questioned by Republican Representative Trent Franks of Arizona about the administration's commitment to free speech. "Will you tell us here today," Franks asked, "that this administration's Department of Justice will never entertain or advance a proposal that criminalizes speech against any religion?"[5]

Perez could have simply answered yes, and maybe even cited the First Amendment. Instead, he refused to answer the question directly. Franks persisted, ultimately asking it four times.

At one point the assistant attorney general claimed that it was a "hard question."[6] He simply refused to affirm that the Obama Justice Department would not attempt to criminalize criticism of Islam. While the Obama administration never did go that far, its nibbling around the edges of the First Amendment to appease Muslim sensibilities set a disturbing precedent, laying a foundation upon which criminalization of certain kinds of speech may be justified in the future.

It was a preview of how the First Amendment could be "tailored in an appropriate way"—ultimately, rendered essentially meaningless, just as the Second Amendment has been gutted in localities where gun laws are so restrictive as to make it nearly impossible for law-abiding citizens to own guns.

"The United States deplores any intentional effort to denigrate the religious beliefs of others"

The initiative to cater to Muslims' easily offended feelings got a massive boost from the massacre of four Americans by Islamic jihadis in Benghazi, Libya, on September 11, 2012. Secretary of State Hillary Clinton's initial statement on the violent attack suggested that it was a spontaneous reaction to a YouTube video, *The Innocence of Muslims*, which was critical of Muhammad—and other administration officials would make that claim outright. Clinton took the opportunity to deplore not only the violence, but also the criticism of Islam that was supposed to have motivated it: "Some have sought to justify this vicious behavior as a response to inflammatory material posted on the Internet. The United States deplores any intentional effort to denigrate the religious beliefs of others. Our commitment to religious tolerance goes back to the very beginning of our nation. But let me be clear: There is never any justification for violent acts of this kind."[7]

THE OLD GOOD COP–BAD COP ROUTINE

The attack on the freedom of speech after the Benghazi attacks followed the classic good cop–bad cop routine by which Islamic restrictions on free speech continue to gain ground in the free world. First, violent jihadis go on the attack. Then, diplomatic voices are heard making the case that it would really be wiser not to upset those hot-tempered thugs.

That was for public consumption. Behind closed doors, however, Clinton told Egypt's Muslim Brotherhood Prime Minister Hesham Kandil the very next day, "We know that the attack in Libya had nothing to do with the film. It was a planned attack—not a protest.... Based on the information we saw today we believe the group that claimed responsibility for this was affiliated with al Qaeda."[8]

The day after that, September 13, 2012, Clinton spoke at the Opening Plenary of the U.S.-Morocco Strategic Dialogue in Washington and referred to the video again. After the movie had been linked to the Benghazi massacre by Obama administration officials, there actually had been protests in other Muslim countries against it. In speaking about those protests, Clinton took the opportunity, once again, to deplore speech critical of Islam:

> I also want to take a moment to address the video circulating on the Internet that has led to these protests in a number of countries. Let me state very clearly—and I hope it is obvious—that the United States Government had absolutely nothing to do with this video. We absolutely reject its content and message. America's commitment to religious tolerance goes back to the very beginning of our nation. And as you know, we are home to people of all religions, many of whom came to this country seeking the right to exercise their own religion, including, of course, millions of Muslims. And we have the greatest respect for people of faith.[9]

The next day, at the transfer-of-remains ceremony for the Benghazi victims, Clinton said, "This has been a difficult week for the State Department and for our country. We've seen the heavy assault on our post in Benghazi that took the lives of those brave men. We've seen rage and violence directed at American embassies over an awful internet video that we had nothing to do with."[10] Whatever happened to, "I disapprove of what you say, but I will defend to the death your right to say it"?[11]

That same day, White House press secretary Jay Carney said, "We have no information to suggest that it was a pre-planned attack," despite the fact that administration officials knew it was exactly that, a pre-planned jihad attack, not a spontaneous eruption over the video. Carney added, "The unrest we've seen around the region has been in reaction to a video that Muslims, many Muslims find offensive."[12]

On September 16, 2012, Susan Rice, the U.S. Ambassador to the United Nations, perpetuated this falsehood on the morning news feature shows, saying on one, "What sparked the recent violence was the airing on the Internet of a very hateful, very offensive video that has offended many people around the world."[13] On another, she asserted, "But based on the best information we have to date, what our assessment is as of the present is in fact what began spontaneously in Benghazi as a reaction to what had transpired some hours earlier in Cairo where, of course, as you know, there was a violent protest outside of our embassy—sparked by this hateful video."[14]

Two days later, President Barack Obama himself added, "As offensive as this video was, and obviously, we've denounced it and the United States government had nothing to do with it, that's never an excuse for violence."[15]

It emerged later that White House Deputy Strategic Communications Adviser Ben Rhodes and other Obama administration officials had advised Rice and others to protect the administration by claiming that the Benghazi massacre had been "rooted in [an] Internet video, and not a broader failure [of] policy." In an email, Rhodes had laid out the administration's line: "[W]e've made our views on this video crystal clear. The United States government had nothing to do with it. We reject its message and its contents. We find it disgusting and reprehensible. But there is absolutely no justification at all for responding to this movie with violence. And we are working to make sure that people around the globe hear that message."[16]

Tom Fitton, the President of Judicial Watch, which obtained the Rhodes email and other Benghazi material through a Freedom of Information Act request, commented, "Now we know the Obama White House's chief concern about the Benghazi attack was making sure that President Obama looked good. And these documents undermine the Obama administration's narrative that it thought the Benghazi attack had something to do with protests or an Internet video. Given the explosive material in these documents, it is no surprise that we had to go to federal court to pry them loose from the Obama State Department."[17]

The controversy over the Obama administration's statements in the wake of the Benghazi massacre has centered on officials' dishonesty in claiming that the Benghazi attack was a reaction to a video about Muhammad when they knew that it was not. But even more ominous was the threat to freedom of speech from the highest levels of the U.S. government. By scapegoating a video criticizing Muhammad, the administration was placing the onus upon the freedom of speech. The unmistakable implication was that if only Americans would not criticize Muhammad, attacks of this kind wouldn't happen.

And soon, the administration found a human scapegoat: the filmmaker who had produced this infamous video about Muhammad.

"We will make sure the person who made that film is arrested and prosecuted"

Charles Woods, whose son, former Navy SEAL Tyrone Woods, was killed at Benghazi, met soon after his son's death with Obama, Vice President Joe Biden, and Secretary of State Hillary Clinton. Of his encounter with Hillary Clinton, Woods said, "I do appreciate her taking the time from her schedule to meet with the four families. While we were in the pod over there with our family she came over shook my hand and I reached out and hugged her shoulder. Her countenance was not good. And she made the statement to me that first of all she was sorry and then she said 'We will make sure the person who made that film is arrested and prosecuted.'"[18]

Clinton was referring to the producer of the video that Obama administration officials were blaming for the Benghazi massacre. Consulting his diary notes several years later, Woods emphasized that Hillary was quite clear in blaming the filmmaker for the massacre: "I gave Hillary a hug and shook her hand. And she said we are going to have the film maker arrested who was responsible for the death of my son. She said—'the filmmaker who was responsible for the death of your son.' She wasn't saying 'the failed foreign policy that I was responsible for.' It wasn't her taking the blame for it." Referring to his diary, Woods said, "It says we are going to place the responsibility [for] the death of your son on the filmmaker."[19]

Pat Smith, the mother of foreign service officer Sean Smith, who was also killed at Benghazi, echoed Woods' charges, recalling that Clinton had told her the massacre took place "because of the video."[20]

Soon, the president of the United States would double down on this remarkable assault on one of the nation's founding principles.

"The future must not belong to those who slander the prophet of Islam"

On September 25, 2012, thirteen days after the Benghazi jihad massacre, Barack Obama addressed the United Nations General Assembly and intoned, "The future must not belong to those who slander the prophet of Islam. But to be credible, those who condemn that slander must also condemn the hate we see in the images of Jesus Christ that are desecrated, or churches that are destroyed, or the Holocaust that is denied."[21]

Obama's attempt to balance his statement by calling on Muslims to condemn the desecration of images of Christ and the destruction of churches (Muslims are responsible for the vast majority of these acts), as well as Holocaust denial (rife in the Islamic world) did not mitigate the fact that saying "the future must not belong to those who slander the prophet of Islam" was nothing less than an embrace of the Sharia blasphemy prohibition on criticism of Muhammad. And it is worth noting that "slander" in Sharia law is a much broader category than non-Muslims may intuit. Islamic law defines slander as "mentioning anything concerning a person that he would dislike"—even if it is true.[22]

Administration officials began to move against such "slander." The first victim of this initiative was Nakoula Basseley Nakoula (a.k.a. Sam Bacile, a.k.a. Mark Basseley Youssef), the Coptic Christian from Egypt who had produced the Muhammad video that the administration had scapegoated for the Benghazi attack. Two days after Barack Obama told the world that "the future must not belong to those who slander the prophet of Islam," Hillary Clinton made good on her promise to Charles Woods: Nakoula was arrested.

Unable to have him arrested for violating Sharia blasphemy law, Hillary got him on a technicality. In 2010 Nakoula had been sentenced to twenty-one months in prison for check fraud; one condition of his probation was that he was only to go on the Internet with the permission of his probation officer.[23] *The Innocence of Muslims* being on YouTube was taken as evidence that Nakoula had violated the terms of his probation, and he was duly arrested, charged with eight counts of probation violation and put in jail without the opportunity of being freed on bail. He was declared to be a "danger to the community."[24] He served a year in prison.[25]

A SCAPEGOAT FOR FREE SPEECH

· · ·

Four years after his ordeal began, Nakoula was living in a homeless shelter, too notorious to get work, and understandably bitter. "I don't believe in democracy anymore," he declared. "I don't think there is such a thing as freedom of speech."[26] Journalist Kenneth Timmerman, who wrote a book about the scapegoating of Nakoula entitled *Deception: The Making of the YouTube Video Hillary and Obama Blamed for Benghazi*, has pointed out, correctly, that the filmmaker was "the first victim of Islamic Sharia blasphemy laws in the United States."[27]

American city streets are crowded with people who have committed probation violations more serious than Nakoula's. The Obama administration made a conscious decision to blame *The Innocence of Muslims*, and hence Nakoula, for the Benghazi massacre and subsequent copycat unrest in other Muslim countries. In light of Hillary Clinton's statements to Charles Woods and Pat Smith, it was difficult to escape the conclusion that Nakoula was arrested and imprisoned for making the video.

Nakoula had indeed violated Sharia blasphemy laws. But his speech was protected by the First Amendment of the Constitution—or it should have been. The Obama administration seemed more interested in enforcing the former than the latter.

The administration's attempts to bring two vastly different legal systems—Sharia law, which punishes speech critical of Islam, and American law, with its constitutional guarantee of free speech—more into line with each other would continue.

"A U.S. attorney in Tennessee is reportedly vowing to use federal civil rights statutes to clamp down on offensive and inflammatory speech about Islam"

While Obama's Justice Department never did move to officially criminalize criticism of Islam, Obama-appointed officials occasionally acted as if it had done so. In May 2013, Bill Killian, the Obama-appointed U.S. attorney for the Eastern District of Tennessee, gave another indication of how the First Amendment might be "tailored in an appropriate way" so as to preclude speech that the administration considered insulting to Muslims. Killian declared, "We need to educate people about Muslims and their civil rights, and as long as we're here, they're going to be protected."[28]

No problem with that. Everyone's civil rights deserve protection. Killian explained, "This is an educational effort with civil rights laws, as they play into freedom of religion and exercising freedom of religion. This is also to inform the public what federal laws are in effect and what the consequences are."[29]

But according to Byron Tau of Politico, this "educational effort" was needed because of "a recent controversy where a local Tennessee politician posted a photo of a man aiming a shotgun at the camera with the caption 'How to wink at a Muslim.'"[30] Killian asked rhetorically, "If a Muslim had posted 'How to Wink at a Christian,' could you imagine what would have happened?"[31]

What would have happened? Probably nothing—or perhaps another "outreach" program against "Islamophobia." Even the Left-leaning Politico picked up on the fact that there was more to Killian's initiative than an attempt to keep people from issuing threats on social media. According to Tau, "A U.S. attorney in Tennessee [Killian] is reportedly vowing to use federal civil rights statutes to clamp down on offensive and inflammatory speech about Islam."[32] But who would decide what was offensive? And what would the penalty be for offending Muslims or Islam?

The problem with Killian's initiative was that neither he nor the Obama administration—nor the OIC, for that matter—ever drew any distinction between genuinely threatening speech (which the "How to wink at a Muslim" shotgun photo may arguably have been) and honest analysis of how jihadists use the texts and teachings of Islam to justify violence and supremacism. On the contrary, they conflate criticism of Islam and even accurate reporting of facts about it (which the First Amendment protects) with threats of violence (which it does not) smearing as "hateful" all examination of the motives and goals of the jihad terrorists who have vowed to destroy the United States and conquer the free world.

Killian's "educational effort" took place on June 4, 2013, when he, FBI Special Agent Kenneth Moore, and Zak Mohyuddin of the American Muslim Advisory Council hosted an event called "Public Disclosure in a Diverse Society" in the town of Manchester, Tennessee. My American Freedom Defense Initiative colleague Pamela Geller and I called for a protest of an event that was clearly designed to intimidate

NO COMMENT

. . .

Politico's Tau reported that the Justice Department did not respond "to a question about what guidelines it draws concerning offensive speech and Islam, or whether the department believes that civil rights statutes could be used to stifle criticism of Islam."[33]

Americans into being afraid to criticize the elements of Islam that give rise to violence and supremacism—and patriots turned out in numbers far beyond what we expected.

Nearly two thousand protesters assembled at the Manchester Convention Center to register their disapproval of this attempt to silence criticism of jihad and Islamic supremacism and to stigmatize the critics. When the event started, the room was filled way beyond capacity, with people filling the aisles and standing in the doorways—while many hundreds more continued to rally outside and wait for news of what was going on inside.

News reports focused on the protesters' rudeness to the speakers, but this rudeness was borne of their awareness of what Killian, Moore, and Mohyuddin were clearly trying to do. Predictably, each of the three spoke at length about hate crimes and hate speech. Each assumed that the only possible reason anyone might harbor any suspicions toward Muslims was race prejudice or discomfort caused by cultural differences—not the very real jihad terror attacks that Muslims have perpetrated on American soil. All three speakers expatiated at length about how "inflammatory" speech could violate civil rights laws, how Arab and Muslim children were being taunted in school, and how Tennesseans should be more welcoming.

Of course the protesters were not there to defend the taunting of Muslim schoolchildren. Nor because they hated foreigners, or to defend sending people violent threats. The protesters turned out in such unexpectedly high numbers because they knew that truthful and accurate commentary on Islam's violent teachings had been deemed "inflammatory" by both Muslim groups and the Obama regime—leaving law enforcement and counter-terror officials, not to mention the public at large, unable to examine the motives and goals of jihad terrorists, or to defend adequately against them.

The choice of rural Tennessee, rather than some higher-profile area, for an event such as "Public Disclosure in a Diverse Society" was odd. Did the Justice Department and the U.S. Attorney's office think that their new suggestion that civil rights laws could be used to silence criticism of Islam would escape notice if it were held in a place that is usually outside the relentless gaze of the mainstream media? Did they hope to float a trial balloon and see if their anti-free speech initiative would be met with indifference and complacency in Manchester, Tennessee, which might be an indication that it wouldn't encounter serious resistance in Nashville or Dallas or New York or Washington, either?

Whatever the reason for their choice of venue may have been, their efforts failed in Manchester, Tennessee. But the foes of freedom of speech were not about to give up.

"The spread of false information or inflammatory or threatening statements about the perpetrators or the crime itself reduces public safety and may violate federal law"

In the summer of 2016, an Obama-appointed federal prosecutor in Idaho didn't even bother to go to war against the First Amendment. He simply behaved as if it didn't exist.

Three Muslim migrant boys whose families had been settled in a Twin Falls, Idaho, apartment complex brutally sexually assaulted a five-year-old girl who was their neighbor. Dissatisfied with the response from government and law enforcement, some Twin Falls residents began a petition:

> On behalf of the residents of Twin Falls, Idaho, we are presenting this petition in an attempt for justice for a local five year old girl. This little girl, as stated in the news, was raped, and urinated on by three Syrian refugee boys of the ages 8, 11, and 13. The boys took her at knife point into a laundry room and proceeded to take part on the previous stated actions which was videotaped by the eldest boy. The father was also caught on tape high fiving the

boys for their actions. The incident as well as the video was submitted to the police department. However, due to a language barrier, and the ages of the children involved, this case is being sealed. Many people in this community are in awe, and outraged that no consequences are being served to these boys nor their parents for this vile incident.[34]

Twin Falls County Prosecutor Grant Loebs almost immediately disputed this scenario on numerous particulars: "There was no gang rape, there was no Syrian involvement, there were no Syrian refugees involved, there was no knife used, there was no inactivity by the police. I'm looking at the Drudge Report headline: 'Syrian Refugees Rape Little Girl at Knifepoint in Idaho'—all false."[35]

Because this horrifying story involved Muslim migrants and took place at a time when the nation was embroiled in controversy over the wisdom (or lack thereof) of Obama's plan to flood the nation with Syrian refugees, it immediately became politicized. The Spokane, Washington, *Spokesman-Review* trumpeted Loebs's disputing of details in a story with the headline "False story on social media charges Syrian refugees raped Idaho girl."[36] The mainstream and leftist media eagerly retailed the false story angle, making the story not about rape, but about xenophobia. Amanda Marcotte's piece in Salon was entitled, "No, Syrian refugees didn't rape a child in Idaho: Right-wing urban legend shows how ugly anti-refugee movement has become."[37] Jezebel was even more sensationalistic: "Right-Wing News Sites Are Circulating a Fake Story About Syrian Refugees Raping a Child in Idaho."[38]

Loebs himself, in a lengthy Slate magazine piece that portrayed the entire case as an example of xenophobia and racism in the age of Donald Trump's presidential candidacy, lamented, "I'm a lifelong conservative Republican, and the behavior of the right-wing alternative press on this is atrocious. All of this makes this so much more difficult for this child to recover from this."[39]

Yet it was Loebs, not Twin Falls residents, "right-wing news sites," "the right-wing alternative press," or the "anti-refugee movement," that was materially distorting the facts of the case to fit a preferred narrative. While the attackers were not Syrian, they were Muslim refugees from Sudan and Iraq, and Loebs got other details wrong as well: the incident was in fact a gang rape, and the perpetrators did have a knife. The victim's mother recounted, "This is what my daughter has told me: that they grabbed her at knifepoint and forced her into the laundry room and told her that if she tried to leave, they would kill her. The seven-year-old boy took her clothes off. She tells me he put his private in her mouth and peed in her mouth, and put it in her private, and then peed all over her. And she said they recorded her, too.... She also told the emergency room CARES doctor that they had a knife as well, and they found on her neck a cut. Then the day after, they claimed it was a scratch, when in fact it looked like a cut."[40]

The girl's father saw part of the video of the attack made by one of the Muslim migrant boys: "I watched the 8-year-old boy push my daughter up against a wall and pull her pants down and his pants down; he then attempted to penetrate her from behind. She was able to run away and crouch in a corner shaking in fear while the boy danced around naked laughing at her. I stopped watching after that."[41]

An eyewitness gave a similar account of the incident:

This happened three weeks ago around 3:30. I was sitting on my porch patio and I looked over and saw this boy taking pictures with a camera. He was from Africa or somewhere overseas, standing outside the laundry room taking pictures of kids in the laundry room. I found them in there. I knew there was something going on because the boy (with the phone camera) was acting funny, he was taking pictures but he was telling the two younger boys what to do....

The door was cracked enough for him to see the pictures he was taking. I opened that door and I almost fainted when I saw what was going on and here I'm a nurse. What a pitiful thing for a poor little girl to go through.

The worst thing was the way they peed all over her clothes and on her too, and I thought that was one of the meanest things I've ever saw done.... The little girl had no clothes on. The boys took them off.[42]

In this overheated atmosphere of charge and counter-charge, Wendy J. Olson, the Obama-appointed U.S. Attorney for Idaho, chose to warn Twin Falls residents (and others interested in the case) that speech about the case could be a crime: "The spread of false information or inflammatory or threatening statements about the perpetrators or the crime itself reduces public safety and may violate federal law."[43]

The U.S. Attorney's primary concern appeared to be not justice for the five-year-old rape victim, but protecting the Muslim migrants. She also asserted, "We have seen time and again that the spread of falsehoods about refugees divides our communities."[44]

STICKS AND STONES MAY BREAK MY BONES, BUT WORDS WILL NEVER HURT ME

"There is no First Amendment exception for 'inflammatory' statements; and even false statements about matters of public concern, the Supreme Court has repeatedly held, are an inevitable part of free debate."

—Eugene Volokh, the Gary T. Schwartz Professor of Law at UCLA[46]

Legal scholar Eugene Volokh noted correctly that Olson's warning looked like "an attempt to chill constitutionally protected speech through the threat of federal prosecution."[45]

Challenged on First Amendment grounds, Olson backtracked, issuing a second statement in which she claimed that "many in the press, public and online bloggers" were "misinterpreting," her statement: "The statement was not intended to and does not threaten to arrest or prosecute anyone for First Amendment protected speech." She now claimed that she had issued her warning in response to threats that Twin Falls officials had supposedly received: "I issued the statement because public officials in Twin Falls have received threats. Certain threatening or harassing communications may violate federal law and will be investigated. I am also concerned that intentionally false and inflammatory rumors are creating an unsafe environment in Twin Falls."[47]

Volokh commented, "Most of us agree that 'inflammatory' statements are bad, as is spreading false information about alleged criminal and alleged governmental wrongdoing (of course, as we understand what's true and false, and as we define 'inflammatory'). But having the government threaten federal prosecution for such speech is worse."[48]

But in the Obama administration, that was the way the wind was blowing.

A U.S. Attorney in eastern Tennessee and another in Idaho—it was bad enough for two prominent attorneys in the Department of Justice to exhibit such a scanty understanding of the importance of the freedom of speech. It was much more disturbing when the Attorney General of the United States demonstrated that she, too, was in the number of these First Amendment–light officials.

"Now obviously this is a country that is based on free speech, but...."

On December 3, 2015, the day after two Muslims murdered fourteen people at a Christmas party in San Bernardino, California, Attorney General Loretta

Lynch gave an address at the tenth anniversary dinner of Muslim Advocates, the group that had been responsible for the Obama administration's removal of all mention of Islam and jihad from counter-terror training materials.

Despite the attack the previous day, Lynch was preoccupied not with jihad violence and how to stop it, but with what she claimed was an "incredibly disturbing rise of anti-Muslim rhetoric."[49]

Lynch said that her "greatest fear as a prosecutor, as someone who is sworn to the protection of all of the American people" was the prospect that "rhetoric will be accompanied by acts of violence."[50]

Certainly direct calls for violence are not protected speech; they are criminal acts that deserve to be treated as such. But Lynch was concerned not only about incitement to violent crimes, but also about speech that "edged toward violence": "Now obviously this is a country that is based on free speech, but when it edges towards violence, when we see the potential for someone lifting that mantle of anti-Muslim rhetoric—or, as we saw after 9/11, violence directed at individuals who may not even be Muslims but perceived to be Muslims, and they will suffer just as much—when we see that we will take action."[51]

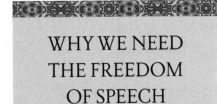

WHY WE NEED THE FREEDOM OF SPEECH

• • •

"Whoever would overthrow the liberty of a nation must begin by subduing the freeness of speech."

—Benjamin Franklin[57]

Lynch did not explain how the Justice Department would evaluate whether or not any particular example of "anti-Muslim rhetoric" "edge[d] toward violence," but she did not seem to be referring to speech directly inciting violent crimes: "When we talk about the First Amendment we [must] make it clear that actions predicated on violent talk are not American. They are not who we are, they are not what we do, and they will be prosecuted."[52]

"My message not just to the Muslim community but to all Americans is 'We cannot give in to the fear that these backlashes are really based on.'"[53]

Superficially, it was reasonable enough to say that speech inciting violence would be prosecuted. But the attorney general's words were ambiguous enough to suggest that the Obama administration would prosecute speech criticizing Islam if it were deemed capable of moving someone to commit an act of violence. That was how many understood her words, including Illinois Congressman–turned-radio host Joe Walsh.

Walsh published a video in which he said, "I think Islam has a real freaking problem, all right? There is a cancer in Islam, and if they're not going to learn to assimilate, I don't want them in this country." Then he challenged the Attorney General: "You got a problem, Loretta Lynch, with me saying that? Then throw me in jail. I think Islam is evil. I think Islam has a huge problem. I think most Muslims around the world are not compatible with American values. I don't want them here."[54]

Walsh wasn't alone in thinking Lynch's words an attack on the freedom of speech. Former New York Governor George Pataki, who was running for President at the time, tweeted on December 4, 2015, "We must declare war on radical Islam. @LorettaLynch I'm not edging toward violent speech, I'm declaring we kill them. Go ahead, arrest me."[55]

Neither Walsh nor Pataki was prosecuted. But the Obama administration had yet again made it clear: defending the freedom of speech was not high on its priority list.

Hillary Clinton vs. the freedom of speech

Hillary Clinton promised more of the same. During a December 2015 Democratic presidential candidates' debate she claimed that the Islamic State (ISIS) was "going to people showing videos of Donald Trump insulting Islam and Muslims to recruit more radical

HOW WE CAN LOSE IT

• • •

"I believe there are more instances of the abridgment of the freedom of the people by gradual and silent encroachments of those in power than by violent and sudden usurpations."

—James Madison[56]

jihadists."[56] She was swiftly proven wrong: an Islamic State video featured Barack Obama ("liar") and Bill Clinton ("fornicator"), but never mentioned Trump. More disquieting than its inaccuracy, however, was the clear implication of Hillary's claim: that the Democratic Party's 2016 candidate for President of the United States was, like her predecessor, a foe of the freedom of speech.

Hillary's point in claiming that the Islamic State was using "videos of Donald Trump insulting Islam and Muslims to recruit more radical jihadists" was that if we all stopped insulting Islam and Muslims—or saying and doing things that she or they claim insult Islam and Muslims—then the jihad recruitment will lose its impetus. It was the same argument that the Obama administration had made after the Benghazi jihad massacre, with Clinton's own carefully worded statements adding to the impression that the attack had been all about a Muhammad video.

The message was always the same: if we only could learn to stay quiet, we would be okay.

Chapter Four

THE "HATE SPEECH" SCAM

The groundwork for the shocking U.S. government campaign to curtail the freedom of speech was laid by the popularization of the concept of "hate speech." The most ominous development in the American public discourse over the last few decades has been the general acceptance of the idea of "hate speech"—with the assumption that it is a readily identifiable category of speech, and that it is not entitled to First Amendment protection.

I first encountered the belief that "hate speech" is not protected by the First Amendment in May 2014 after a talk I gave at Cal Poly University in San Luis Obispo, California. During the question-and-answer period, I spoke about assaults on the freedom of speech, saying, "You all are here in this university, and only one point of view is allowed…and only one perspective is acceptable. And that is a symptom of the problem I am discussing.... Just ponder what might happen if you end up holding a point of view that is one of those that is not allowed. Do you really want to be in that position? Or would it be better to live in a society where all points of view were allowed, and freedom of speech were open, and ideas would live and die on the basis of their truth, not on the basis of who in power found them acceptable or unacceptable?"[1]

When asked what ideas I thought were not allowed to be discussed at Cal Poly, I responded that my entire perspective on Islam and jihad, as represented in my books on jihad, the Qur'an, and Muhammad, was not allowed at Cal Poly or at most other American universities, and if discussed at all, was only brought up to be cursorily dismissed.

Then one young woman said, "I just want to say that I'm actually in a class on Islam right now, and some of the points of view that you have expressed were discussed in an open forum. We openly discussed them and came to the conclusion that there's a difference between freedom of speech and hate speech, which is a term that you've been intermixing throughout this lecture, and hate speech is not freedom of speech. It's not constitutionally protected."

When I asked her what hate speech was, she said, "Hate speech is speech that threatens or harms, without any factual content that actually expresses a valuable idea." When I asked her who should be entrusted with the authority to determine that certain speech was threatening or harmful and devoid of any factual content that actually expresses a valuable idea, she said that was a question for the judicial system. I pointed out that the very concept of "hate speech" was a tool in the hands of the powerful to silence the powerless. To that she retorted, "That's a Hobbesian argument against the powerful."

She was right about one thing. I don't trust the very powerful United States government—or any government—to shield me from certain types of speech that it considers unacceptable. No free person should, in the

United States or anywhere else. Unfortunately, however, this young woman at Cal Poly is not alone. While there is no foundation in First Amendment jurisprudence for the notion that "hate speech" falls outside the protection of the Constitution, there are many who believe that it should—or even that it already does. Some of them are in positions of considerable power and influence.

STICKS AND STONES MAY BREAK MY BONES, BUT WORDS WILL NEVER HURT ME

"There's no fine line between 'free speech' and 'hate speech': Free speech is hate speech; it's for the speech you hate—and for all your speech that the other guy hates. If you don't have free speech, then you can't have an honest discussion."

—Mark Steyn[2]

"There is no hate speech exception to the First Amendment"

On May 6, 2015, three days after our Muhammad Art Exhibit and Cartoon Contest in Garland, Texas, which was designed to show that at least some Americans were determined to defend the freedom of speech, CNN anchorman Chris Cuomo, who was sharply critical of the event, was challenged on Twitter: "Too many people are trying to say hate speech (doesn't equal) free speech."[3]

Cuomo, who actually has a law degree, responded, "It doesn't. Hate speech is excluded from protection. Don't just say you love the Constitution…read it."[4]

Cuomo was widely ridiculed for this claim, but his confusion was understandable. No less an authority than the National Constitution Center, an organization which by its very name suggests expertise about the document, has asserted, "Over the time since 1791, when the Bill of Rights was ratified, the Supreme Court has given its blessing to an entire governing edifice that regulates First Amendment rights: the laws of libel and defamation, limits on publishing secret military strategy, regulation of 'obscene' and 'indecent' expression, and limits on 'hate speech.'"[5]

This is actually not the case. There is no basis in the Constitution, or in the numerous Supreme Court decisions interpreting it up to now, for the claim that there is any exclusion of "hate speech" from First Amendment protection. The closest that the authoritative interpretation of the Constitution has come to a prohibition of "hate speech" is the exclusion of "fighting words" from the First Amendment right to the freedom of speech.

"Fighting words," according to the Supreme Court in its unanimous 1942 decision in *Chaplinsky vs. New Hampshire*, are those that "by their very utterance inflict injury or tend to incite an immediate breach of the peace"— that is, they are likely to lead directly to the outbreak of violence. This is, said the Court, one of the "well-defined and narrowly limited classes of speech the prevention and punishment" of which "have never been thought to raise any constitutional problem."

Cornered by Constitutionalists, Chris Cuomo referred to this doctrine in his own defense: "Of course the First Amendment does not expressly mention hate speech among its six protections in its text. I meant to refer to the relevant case law about the (First Amendment) to see what is protected. There you quickly find that hate speech is almost always protected. The keyword is 'almost.' Hate speech can be prohibited; that is why I keep citing the *Chaplinsky* case and the fighting words doctrine."[6]

But what is generally considered nowadays to be "hate speech"—as far as the Left is concerned, practically any statement that deviates from the Democratic Party platform—does not constitute "fighting words." The mere expression of conservative or counter-jihad sentiments cannot reasonably be taken as a direct incitement to violence. Said James Weinstein of Arizona

State University's Sandra Day O'Connor Law School, "The fact that something is hate speech or not is irrelevant for First Amendment analysis."[7]

Yet even in debunking this notion, legal scholar Eugene Volokh notes its popularity: "I keep hearing about a supposed 'hate speech' exception to the First Amendment, or statements such as, 'This isn't free speech, it's hate speech,' or 'When does free speech stop and hate speech begin?' But there is no hate speech exception to the First Amendment."[8]

> ## STICKS AND STONES MAY BREAK MY BONES, BUT WORDS WILL NEVER HURT ME
>
>
>
> "Hateful ideas (whatever exactly that might mean) are just as protected under the First Amendment as other ideas. One is as free to condemn Islam—or Muslims, or Jews, or blacks, or whites, or illegal aliens, or native-born citizens—as one is to condemn capitalism or Socialism or Democrats or Republicans."[9]
>
> —Eugene Volokh, the Gary T. Schwartz Professor of Law at UCLA

Michael Herz, co-director of the Floersheimer Center for Constitutional Democracy at the Benjamin N. Cardozo School of Law at Yeshiva University, noted that aside from the "fighting words" exception, "the overwhelming understanding is that 'hate speech' is constitutionally protected in the United States. Indeed, that protection makes this country different from most other countries in the world."[10]

"The internet is a place for free speech, not hate speech"

The sad fact that other countries do not value or protect the freedom of speech as the United States does bodes ill for Americans in an increasingly globalized environment. In May 2016, actions by the European Union opened up the possibility that, because of prohibitions on online "hate speech," it could become illegal to oppose jihad terror on the Internet.

Late that month, the European Union concluded an agreement with Facebook, Twitter, YouTube, and Microsoft on strategies to combat online "hate speech."[11] The social media giants, according to the Associated Press, "committed to 'quickly and efficiently' tackle illegal hate speech directed against anyone over issues of race, color, religion, descent or national or ethnic origin. The sites have often been used by terrorist organizations to relay messages and entice hatred against certain individuals or groups."[12]

Vera Jourova, the European Union commissioner responsible for "justice, consumers and gender equality," explained the new initiative in terms that should have moved Chris Cuomo to applaud: "The internet is a place for free speech, not hate speech."[13] She added that the new rules would "ensure that public incitement to violence to hatred has 'no place online.'"[14]

But incitement to violence was not all that the social media giants were planning to stamp out: Karen White, Twitter's European head of public policy, declared, "We remain committed to letting the Tweets flow. However, there is a clear distinction between freedom of expression and conduct that incites violence and hate."[15]

But "clear" is precisely what the distinction is not. The problem with both Jourova's and White's statements is that they assume that "hate speech" can be identified objectively, when actually it is a subjective judgment based on one's own political preconceptions. And given the years-long insistence from leftists and Islamic supremacists that any honest discussion of jihad and its sources in the texts and teachings of Islam constitutes "hate speech," these new rules could mean the end of opposition to jihad terror on the Internet.

"Robert Spencer must be shot head"

Consider, for example, what Twitter does *not* consider to be "hate speech." A Muslim named Obaid Karki, @stsheetrock on Twitter, runs a website headed "Obaid Karki St.Sheetrock's Painfulpolitics Offensive Comedy Hepcat" and another called "Suicide Bombers Magazine."[16] He posted this on one of them in late May 2016, just before the European Union and the social media sites announced their new agreement: "Robert Spencer mustn't [be] featured but lynched from his scrotum along with Zionists scumbags, Pamela Geller, Pat Condell, Daniel Pipes, Debbie Schlussel and JIHAD-WATCH Jackass duo Baron Bodissey & Geert Wilders for inspiring Anders Behring Breivik to [kill] innocent students in 2011."[17]

Neither Bodissey or Wilders actually runs Jihad Watch—I do. And although he mentioned me in his insane manifesto, I didn't inspire the mad Norwegian mass killer Anders Breivik to do anything. But what is interesting about Karki's loony message is that he posted this call for me and others to be lynched on Twitter.[18]

Twitter supposedly has a policy against death threats. "The Twitter Rules" say, "Violent threats (direct or indirect): You may not make threats of violence or promote violence, including threatening or promoting terrorism."[19] So I duly reported this one—but as of this writing, it has not been taken down. After reporting Karki's tweet (which he posted along with variants several times on Twitter), I received this message from Twitter: "Thank you for letting us know about your issue. We've investigated the account and reported Tweets for violent threats and abusive behavior, and have found that it's currently not violating the Twitter Rules (https://twitter.com/rules)."

This had happened before. On May 12, 2014, Karki tweeted, "Robert Spencer must be arrested and lynched along the Zionists Dumbasses Daniel Pipes, Geert Wilders and JIHADWATCH…"[20] On September 18, 2013,

Karki tweeted, "Robert Spencer must be shot head not only for comparing Alnoor 24:35 to Corinthians 11:14–15 satanically but for…"—that is, for comparing a passage in the Qur'an to a passage from the Bible.[21]

Calling for me to be "lynched" and "shot" was not "hate speech" as far as Twitter is concerned. Meanwhile, the antipathy of both Twitter and Facebook to conservatives is well established. William Hicks of Heat Street pointed out, "Whatever's going on in that boiler room where miserable editors toil over the trending topics, we do know that Facebook routinely shuts down pages and blocks users simply for stating right-of-center opinions."[22] Ian Tuttle of *National Review* noted in June 2016, "It's no secret that social-media companies lean left."[23] It's therefore a very real question: will our social media masters use their new censorship initiative to shut down foes of jihad terror, while allowing jihadis and their sympathizers to speak freely?

It could happen. In some ways it is happening already.

"The EU is quite candid: it is applying a political lens to their censorship"

The free speech news site Epoch Times reported last March that "while Twitter says it is making strong efforts to shut down terrorist accounts, activists say that not only is the microblogging company not taking down the accounts that matter, but it has even been shutting down accounts of users trying to report terrorists."[24]

And Facebook, immediately after the agreement with the European Union was concluded, began moving aggressively against foes of jihad terror and mass Muslim migration in the West. Nina Rosenwald, the president and founder of the conservative think tank Gatestone Institute, on June 2, 2016 recorded Facebook's haste to implement the new speech regulations: "On Tuesday, the European Union (EU) announced a new online speech code to be enforced by four major tech companies, including Facebook and

YouTube. On Wednesday, Facebook deleted the account of Ingrid Carlqvist, Gatestone's Swedish expert."[25]

Carlqvist's crime, according to Rosenwald, was to take note of real crimes by Muslim migrants: "Ingrid had posted our latest video to her Facebook feed—called 'Sweden's Migrant Rape Epidemic.'"[26] In that video, said Rosenwald, "Ingrid calmly lays out the facts and statistics, all of which are meticulously researched."[27] Rosenwald added that the video was adapted from a "research paper that Gatestone published last year. The video has gone viral—racking up more than 80,000 views in its first two days. But the EU is quite candid: it is applying a political lens to their censorship.... "[28]

Carlqvist was not the only target of the social media censorship. On June 12, 2016, in the immediate aftermath of the jihad massacre at the Pulse gay nightclub in Orlando, Florida, moderators at the social media site Reddit, the fourteenth most visited website in the United States, banned users solely for the offense of posting articles that took note of the fact that the shooter, Omar Mateen, was a Muslim.[30] That same day, Facebook deleted Pamela Geller's Stop Islamization of America group, which had fifty-five thousand members. Facebook's notice to Geller explained, "The group 'Stop Islamization of America' has been removed because it violated our Terms of Use. Among other things, groups that are hateful, threatening or obscene are not allowed. We also take down groups that attack an individual or group.... "[31] Facebook did not elucidate on how it distinguished being "hateful" from responding to a genuine threat, or attacking "an individual or group" from identifying the source of that threat. At the same

BIG BROTHER IS WATCHING YOU

"...the EU...now has teams of political informants—with the Orwellian title of 'trusted reporters'—to report any cases of 'xenophobia' or 'hate speech' to Facebook for immediate deletion."

—Nina Rosenwald, president of the Gatestone Institute[29]

time, Facebook also banned Geller from posting for thirty days, without specifying what exactly she had written that the social media giant found so offensive.[32]

After an outcry, the Stop Islamization of America group was restored, as were Geller's posting privileges, but a precedent had been set, and it would be reinforced.[33] Just days after the SIOA group was banned and then reinstated, Facebook banned the page of a gay magazine, *Gaystream*, after it published an article by David Berger, its editor-in-chief, criticizing German gay activists and leftists for ignoring the Islamic root causes of the Orlando jihad massacre. Berger wrote, "Whoever had thought the culmination of masochism and Islam-appeasement by left-green professional homosexuals was already achieved, will now be mistaken: it becomes even more masochistic and perverse."[34]

Facebook—again without any specific explanation of what it found so offensive—deleted not only the magazine's page, but Berger's personal page as well.[35] In the new world order delineated by the European Union and its social media allies, criticism of the Left's blindness to Islamic jihad terror was out of bounds. *National Review* enumerated more instances of social media censorship of conservatives around the same time, including the case of videogame developer Mark Kern, who was suspended from Twitter for writing, "I don't see why mosques with radical leanings should be excluded from surveillance when the rest of us get our emails collected by the NSA."[36] The administrator of a pro–Donald Trump Facebook group was banned for arguing that Trump was not anti-Muslim but anti-ISIS.[37]

In early February 2017, they came for me.

On February 7, 2017, referrals to my website, Jihad Watch, from Facebook numbered 23,783, and from Twitter, 1,718. These numbers were generally representative: referrals from Facebook for several years up to that point had averaged between 15,000 and 20,000 a day, and 1,500 to 2,000 a day from Twitter. But on February 10, 2017, those numbers dropped suddenly and precipitously, with only 2,923 referrals from Facebook and 295 from Twitter. That's around where they have held since then: on March 20, 2017, there were 1,954 referrals from Facebook and 241 from Twitter.[38]

Did thousands of people who used to click through to Jihad Watch articles from Facebook and Twitter suddenly lose interest on February 10, 2017? Of course not. What happened on that day was that Facebook and Twitter began to censor Jihad Watch as "hate speech," in accordance with the assurances they had given to the European Union.

Now, I do not accept and will never accept the idea that reporting on jihad activity and Sharia oppression constitutes "hate speech." But that is the longstanding claim of the Organization of Islamic Cooperation (OIC) and Muslim groups in the West, and it has been uncritically adopted by the Left, with which Facebook and Twitter are so firmly aligned.

This only underscored the necessity to boycott and disempower these social media platforms. If Facebook and Twitter shut out the truth, then we have to shut out Facebook and Twitter.

"I am stunned that the policy that YouTube developed for the express purpose of fighting Islamic State propaganda is now being used to silence critics of radical jihad"

In July 2016, YouTube also invoked "hate speech" criteria, which supposedly it had developed as a tool to use against jihad recruiting videos, to delete a video critical of non-violent Muslim Brotherhood efforts to advance Sharia in the West. Jim Hanson, executive vice president of the Center for Security Policy, whose CounterJihad subsidiary produced the video, commented, "I am stunned that the policy that YouTube developed for the express purpose of fighting Islamic State propaganda is now being used to silence critics of radical jihad. Instead of counteracting radical propaganda online, these policies are now being used to silence the very speech that

SOCIAL MEDIA IS WATCHING YOU

· · · · · · · · · · · · · · · · · · ·

"YouTube's removal of CounterJihad's factual analysis of the threat of ISIS and radical Islam is a devastating blow against credible counter-terrorism efforts. No company or individual can legitimately say they support free speech and at the same time set up blockades against the very people doing the work necessary to counter the ideology. There is no other way to look at this."

—Muslim reformer Shireen Qudosi, commenting on Facebook's perverse censorship of critics of jihad[40]

YouTube said it wanted—speech that challenges ISIS."[39]

In late July 2016, popular radio host Michael Savage posted on his Facebook page a news article about a Muslim migrant in Reutlingen, Germany, murdering a pregnant German woman. Shortly thereafter, Facebook deleted his page temporarily and sent him this notice: "You recently posted something that violates Facebook policies, so you're temporarily blocked from using this feature."[41] Which of Facebook's policies had Savage violated? Apparently he had posted "hate speech." In response, Savage told his radio audience that Facebook founder Mark Zuckerberg "doesn't care about the audience of conservatives. He'd rather you all drop dead and go home."[42]

Zuckerberg, said Savage, was a "classless citizen who enjoys all the benefits of America, enjoys all of the wealth that America has given him, and he stabs America in the back by siding with the Islamic terrorist nations of Iran and Saudi Arabia. That's why he would ban me from posting an article, which I didn't write, incidentally. It was a link an article about a Muslim in Germany, about a week ago, who cut a nine-month pregnant woman to death in the street. Zuckerberg found that offensive and anti-Islamic."[43]

Likewise in September 2016, Tim Selaty Sr., founder of the Tea Party Community, had his Facebook page, "Ban Sharia Law," removed by Facebook for supposedly violating its "Community Standards." The page had been up for two years and had gained ten thousand "likes." But the new arbiters of what was acceptable speech and what wasn't clearly didn't like it at all.[44]

Those arbiters didn't bother to wait for legislation. They were behaving as if "hate speech" were an objectively verifiable category already enshrined in American law.

The most notorious victim of this censorship and the Left's increasing hostility to free speech and free discourse was the gay conservative gadfly Milo Yiannopoulos. On July 19, 2016, Twitter permanently banned Milo, as he is universally known, after he got into a public spat on the social media platform with actress Leslie Jones, who then claimed that she was inundated with racist and sexist tweets from Milo's followers. This was after Twitter had temporarily suspended Milo several times for statements its censors found offensive (including remarks critical of Islam and jihad terror), and after it had stripped him of the blue checkmark that was supposedly simply an indication that a particular Twitter account had been verified as actually belonging to the prominent person whose name it bears—up until that time it had not been advertised or regarded as a sign of Twitter's approval.

Milo responded to his permanent suspension from Twitter by noting how inhospitable it had become to conservatives while providing a ready platform for Islamic jihadists:

> With the cowardly suspension of my account, Twitter has confirmed itself as a safe space for Muslim terrorists and Black Lives Matter extremists, but a no-go zone for conservatives.
>
> Twitter is holding me responsible for the actions of fans and trolls using the special pretzel logic of the left. Where are the Twitter police when Justin Bieber's fans cut themselves on his behalf?
>
> Like all acts of the totalitarian regressive left, this will blow up in their faces, netting me more adoring fans. We're winning the culture war, and Twitter just shot themselves in the foot.

This is the end for Twitter. Anyone who cares about free speech has been sent a clear message: you're not welcome on Twitter.[45]

Just a few weeks before this ban, Milo had skewered the Left's peculiar logic in being so eager to censor critics of Islam:

Liberals consider everyone that is not a straight white male to be on a pyramid of victimhood. Various minorities shift places on this pyramid. For example, white gay men have recently dropped quite close to the bottom. (I think I'm partly responsible for that!)

For unknown reasons, liberals have put Muslims at the very top of this pyramid.

That is why Muslims can act and speak with impunity against others groups like gays, Jews, and women—they have been placed at the pinnacle of the victim pyramid.

The major flaw of liberal logic, with apologies to the term logic, is that in this case the top of the victim pyramid is intent on murdering and abusing the entire rest of the pyramid![46]

"Facebook, Twitter, and YouTube have notoriously censored speech that they deem critical of Islam, thereby effectively enforcing blasphemy laws here in the United States"

As Milo pointed out the Left's hypocrisy and the self-defeating character of its unwillingness to criticize Islam, there was pushback in the courts as well. On July 13, 2016, the American Freedom Law Center (AFLC) filed a federal lawsuit in the U.S. District Court for the District of Columbia, on behalf of Pamela Geller's American Freedom Defense Initiative (AFDI), of which I am vice president, challenging Section 230 of the Communications

Decency Act (CDA), which grants Facebook, Twitter, and YouTube immunity from lawsuits, and thus makes it impossible to challenge their consistent bias against foes of jihad terror and tolerance of jihad terror activity.

Section 230 of the CDA explicitly immunizes Facebook, Twitter, and YouTube from challenges to anything they do to "restrict access to or availability of material that" that they deem "obscene, lewd, lascivious, filthy, excessively violent, harassing, or otherwise objectionable, whether or not such material is constitutionally protected."[47]

Robert Muise, AFLC co-founder and senior counsel, noted that "Section 230 of the CDA confers broad powers of censorship upon Facebook, Twitter, and YouTube officials, who can silence constitutionally protected speech and engage in discriminatory business practices with impunity by virtue of this power conferred by the federal government in violation of the First Amendment."[48]

David Yerushalmi, AFLC co-founder and senior counsel, added, "Facebook, Twitter, and YouTube have notoriously censored speech that they deem critical of Islam, thereby effectively enforcing blasphemy laws here in the United States with the assistance of the federal government. It has been the top agenda item of Islamic supremacists to impose such standards on the West…. Facebook, Twitter, and YouTube are falling in line, and we seek to stop this assault on our First Amendment freedoms."[49]

That assault was ongoing. Barack Obama's intention to turn over control of the Internet to an international body in October 2016 presaged the across-the-board enforcement of the censorship that Facebook and Twitter were already beginning to implement.

On October 1, 2015, the United States' National Telecommunications and Information Administration (NTIA) transferred authority over the Internet's domain name system (DNS) to a global governing body. Drew Johnson, national director of Protect Internet Freedom, remarked, "The biggest concern is that countries who don't value internet freedom, who silence online speech

WHY WE NEED THE FREEDOM OF SPEECH

. . .

"If there's one American belief I hold above all others, it's that those who would set themselves up in judgment on matters of what is 'right' and what is 'best' should be given no rest; that they should have to defend their behavior most stringently.... As a nation, we've been through too many fights to preserve our rights of free thought to let them go just because some prude with a highlighter doesn't approve of them."

—Stephen King[55]

and censor the web, will be able to directly shape internet policy.... Down the road, ICANN [the Internet Corporation for Assigned Names and Numbers] could very easily decide to transfer oversight of '.mil' domain names used by the Pentagon or to assign '.gov' domain names used by top federal officials to hostile countries. There's a threat that Russia or China could ultimately have say over America's most sensitive websites."[50]

Russia or China—or Saudi Arabia or Iran. Civil liberties advocate Ryan Hagemann of the Niskanen Center warned that "the United States will be handing over more geopolitical power over the Internet to states like Russia and Iran."[51]

Republican senator Ted Cruz of Texas was determined not to let Obama "give away the Internet," and introduced legislation to stop him.[52] "Russia, and China, and Iran don't have a First Amendment," he said. "They don't protect free speech, and they actively censor the Internet. ICANN could do the same thing, putting foreign countries in charge of what you can say online, prohibiting speech that they disagree with."[53]

Cruz got nowhere, and the transfer went ahead as planned. As his efforts failed, former UN Ambassador John Bolton lamented, "It didn't happen. I don't know why. I don't know whether the Republican leadership in the Senate and the House were not receptive to it. It's inconceivable to me, inconceivable, that we're about to let this happen, because it is completely correct that once we let go, we are never going to get it back."[54]

U.S. control over the Internet was gone. Coming, in all likelihood, were "hate speech" restrictions on the Internet.

Chapter Five

"PEER PRESSURE AND SHAMING" TO REIN IN FREE SPEECH

"I do solemnly swear that I will faithfully execute the Office of President of the United States, and will to the best of my ability, preserve, protect and defend the Constitution of the United States, and fight against negative stereotypes of Islam wherever they appear. So help me Allah."

Is that the oath of office Barack Obama took?

On June 4, 2009, Obama went to al-Azhar in Cairo, the foremost institution in Sunni Islam, to make an address that was designed to herald a new era of friendship between Muslim countries and the United States. In that address, he said, "I have known Islam on three continents before coming to the region where it was first revealed. That experience guides my conviction that partnership between America and Islam must be based on what Islam is, not what it isn't. And I consider it part of my responsibility as President of the United States to fight against negative stereotypes of Islam wherever they appear."[1]

It was a curious statement. Obama did not explain where in the Constitution he found any responsibility conferred upon the president to fight against negative stereotypes of Islam. Nor did he ever make any similar remark about having a responsibility to fight against negative stereotypes of Judaism, Christianity, Hinduism, Buddhism, or any other religion.

"And together we have begun to overcome the false divide that pits religious sensitivities against freedom of expression"

A presidential responsibility to fight against negative stereotypes of Islam—and Islam alone—is difficult to square with the First Amendment. "Negative stereotypes" are not exempt from freedom of speech protection. But the Obama administration appeared determined to find ways to square the circle—to make the freedom of speech that is guaranteed in the Constitution somehow compatible with a government campaign to protect Muslims from the criticism that they find offensive, and that their religion asserts should be against the law. Hillary Clinton, then Secretary of State, attempted to finesse the logical contradiction in an address at the Center for Islamic Arts and History in Istanbul on July 15, 2011, with the OIC's Secretary General Ekmeleddin Ihsanoglu present.

Clinton began with an anecdote from the Balkan wars of the 1990s that illustrated, she said, "what incitement to violence and hatred can lead to."[2] By way of contrast, she recalled how fifteen years before she and Ihsanogulu had engaged in a memorable "conversation...talking about the imperative for us to move beyond these differences and how much the three great monotheistic religions have in common, especially our respective commandments to love our neighbors and to seek peace and understanding."[3]

To try to build harmony with Muslim nations, Clinton said, "in established democracies, we are still working to protect fully our religious diversity, prevent discrimination, and protect freedom of expression." She went on to "applaud the Organization of Islamic Conference and the European Union for helping pass Resolution 16/18 at the Human Rights Council." Revealing that the U.S. delegation had actively worked for the Resolution's passaged, Clinton said, "I was complimenting the secretary general on the OIC team in Geneva. I had a great team there as well. So many of you were part of that effort."[4]

Resolution 16/18—which, as we have seen, called for the nations of the world to ban "defamation of religion"—was an attempt to reconcile the irreconcilable opposition between the freedom of speech and the cherished Islamic belief that blasphemy should be a crime. Clinton expressed confidence that such "religious sensitivities" and free expression were perfectly compatible: "And together we have begun to overcome the false divide that pits religious sensitivities against freedom of expression, and we are pursuing a new approach based on concrete steps to fight intolerance wherever it occurs. Under this resolution, the international community is taking a strong stand for freedom of expression and worship, and against discrimination and violence based upon religion or belief."[5]

Clinton claimed that "the resolution calls upon states to protect freedom of religion, to counter offensive expression through education, interfaith dialogue, and public debate, and to prohibit discrimination, profiling, and hate crimes, but not to criminalize speech unless there is an incitement to imminent violence."[6]

"We are focused on promoting . . . old-fashioned techniques of peer pressure and shaming, so that people don't feel that they have the support to do what we abhor"

But without criminalizing speech, how could Muslims' fragile religious sensitivities be safeguarded from inevitable offense?

In addressing this question, Clinton first lamented that "in the United States, I will admit, there are people who still feel vulnerable or marginalized as a result of their religious beliefs. And we have seen how the incendiary actions of just a very few people, a handful in a country of nearly 300 million, can create wide ripples of intolerance. We also understand that, for 235 years, freedom of expression has been a universal right at the core of our democracy."[7]

To smooth out those "ripples of intolerance" without moving to directly criminalize the freedom of expression, Clinton explained that "we are focused on promoting interfaith education and collaboration, enforcing anti-discrimination laws, protecting the rights of all people to worship as they choose, and to use some old-fashioned techniques of peer pressure and shaming, so that people don't feel that they have the support to do what we abhor."[8]

That was an ominous phrase: "old-fashioned techniques of peer pressure and shaming." In the absence of any easy way to get around the First Amendment and actually criminalize speech, Clinton was declaring her intention, and presumably the policy of the Obama administration, to stigmatize speech, to the extent that people would be afraid to cross what Ihsanoglu had called "red lines that should not be crossed."

Even before Clinton spoke these fateful words, these techniques she recommended had been used by media and academic elites, whose agenda was difficult to distinguish from that of the Obama administration. When Swedish artist Lars Vilks drew Muhammad as a dog in 2007 and al-Qaeda put a $100,000 bounty on his head, CNN's Paula Newton condemned not al-Qaeda but Vilks, who, she said, "should have known better because of what happened in Denmark in 2005, when a cartoonist's depictions of the prophet sparked violent protests in the Muslim world and prompted death threats against that cartoonist's life."[9]

And in May 2008, when the Netherlands-based Iranian avant-garde artist Sooreh Hera received death threats for her provocative depictions of

Muhammad and his son-in-law Ali as homosexuals, she was rebuked by John Voll, associate director of the Saudi-funded Prince Alwaleed bin Talal Center for Muslim-Christian Understanding at Georgetown University. Voll asked rhetorically: "Can you imagine what would happen if John McCain used the n-word about Obama while campaigning? There are consequences. Free speech is not absolute."[10]

Soon people with a great deal more power than reporters and academics would be doing everything they could to make it clear to those exercising their free speech in ways that offended Muslims that the freedom of speech was "not absolute." With the election of Barack Obama and his appointment of Hillary Clinton to head the Department of State, the idea that they "should have known better" would become de facto American government policy.

"Those who flirt with hate speech against Muslims should realize they are playing directly into the hands of al-Qaeda and the Islamic State"

General David Petraeus—the former commander of CENTCOM who had resigned as CIA director amidst a scandal—helped delineate the red lines that should not be crossed in a May 2016 *Washington Post* piece entitled "Anti-Muslim Bigotry Aids Islamist Terrorists."

Petraeus wrote that he was "increasingly concerned about inflammatory political discourse that has become far too common both at home and abroad against Muslims and Islam, including proposals from various quarters for blanket discrimination against people on the basis of their religion."[11]

By "proposals from various quarters for blanket discrimination against people on the basis of their religion," Petraeus meant presidential candidate Donald Trump's proposed temporary moratorium on Muslim immigration—but the language also applied to other speech that Muslims might find offensive.

Petraeus didn't just oppose Trump's proposed moratorium as a matter of policy; he was saying that even to speak them at all was damaging: "The ramifications of such rhetoric could be very harmful—and lasting."[12] He claimed that simply expressing such thoughts might "compound the already grave terrorist danger to our citizens."[13]

How could mere words do that? Petraeus explained, "Those who flirt with hate speech against Muslims should realize they are playing directly into the hands of al-Qaeda and the Islamic State. The terrorists' explicit hope has been to try to provoke a clash of civilizations—telling Muslims that the United States is at war with them and their religion. When Western politicians propose blanket discrimination against Islam, they bolster the terrorists' propaganda."[14]

Petraeus didn't address the problem that Trump's immigration moratorium was meant to deal with: the general didn't offer any alternative suggestion as to how jihad terrorists could be prevented from entering the United States. In a classic shaming move, he just dismissed the proposal and "hate speech against Muslims" in general because, he charged, such speech would enrage Muslims and make more of them join the jihad against America.

"This stunt that he is talking about pulling could greatly endanger our young men and women in uniform who are in Iraq, who are in Afghanistan"

Petraeus was just following the line of the Obama administration. When nondenominational Florida pastor Terry Jones announced plans to burn several hundred copies of the Qur'an at an "International Burn-a-Koran Day" on September 11, 2010, the Obama administration was appalled. Obama himself said on *Good Morning America*, "If he's listening, I just hope he understands that what he's proposing to do is completely contrary to our values [as] Americans."[15] What values were those? Not the values of the First Amendment, which protects both free speech and religious exercise—but doesn't protect believers from offense by others' exercise of *their* freedom of speech and religion. It does not do so because it could not do so. It is impossible to protect any group's "right" not to be offended without infringing on the free speech rights of others who disagree with them.

But many on both sides of the aisle agreed with Obama. The 2008 Republican Vice Presidential nominee, Sarah Palin, said that the Qur'an-burning that Jones had planned was "antithetical to American ideals."[16] Secretary of State Hillary Clinton called it "disgraceful."[17]

Displaying the inverted sense of causality that had become conventional wisdom in Washington, Obama declared that Jones could endanger American troops: "I just want him to understand that this stunt that he is talking about pulling could greatly endanger our young men and women in uniform who are in Iraq, who are in Afghanistan."[18]

General Petraeus, at that time commander of the International Security Assistance Force in Afghanistan, also chimed in, warned that burning the Qur'an "could endanger troops and it could endanger the overall effort in Afghanistan."[19]

THE OLD GOOD COP–BAD COP ROUTINE

The upshot of General Petraeus's argument was that we must not say things to which Muslims might object, because this would just make more of them become jihadis. His prescription for minimizing the jihad against the West was essentially for the West to practice self-censorship in order to avoid offending Muslims. It's the same argument that we've seen before, and it makes a certain perverse sense. After all, if we pre-emptively adopt Sharia blasphemy law, jihadis won't have to impose it on us via terror.

Jones even received a private phone call from Defense Secretary Robert Gates pressuring him to rescind his call to burn the Quran. Pentagon press secretary Geoff Morrell issued a statement, "Secretary Gates reached out to Pastor Jones this afternoon. They had a very brief phone conversation during

AN END RUN AROUND THE FIRST AMENDMENT

. . . .

Obama threatened that Jones could be "cited for public burning." If he had been, then laws intended to promote public safety and clean air would have been used as a patently obvious fig leaf. The real crime for which he would have been punished (just as the filmmaker Nakoula was jailed, supposedly for violating probation): defying Islamic blasphemy laws.[21]

which the Secretary expressed his grave concern that going forward with the Quran burning would put at risk the lives of our forces around the world, especially those in Iraq and Afghanistan, and he urged the Pastor not to proceed with it."[20]

In reality it was not Jones or any action of his, but rather Muslims willing to commit violence in response to it, that were the danger to American troops. But Obama and Petraeus deflected all responsibility for jihadis' actions onto Jones himself.

Obama warned, "You know, you could have serious violence in places like Pakistan or Afghanistan. This could increase the recruitment of individuals who'd be willing to blow themselves up in American cities, or European cities."[22]

General Ray Odierno agreed, saying, "This feeds right into what they want."[23] The idea here was that Muslims, enraged by the burning Qur'ans, would see the United States as an enemy of Islam, and join the jihad. If we didn't burn Qur'ans, then presumably they would see the United States as favorably disposed toward Islam and Muslims and refrain from joining jihad groups.

The problems with this reasoning were legion. In the first place, if these Muslims were so easily set against the United States, they would probably seize upon some other provocation to join jihad groups even if no Qur'ans were burned. Whether or not Qur'ans went up in smoke, they would hardly become reliable allies of the United States.

"A small number of individuals, who have been extremely disrespectful to the holy Quran"

Jones canceled his September 11, 2010 event, but in April 2011, he went ahead and burned a copy of the Qur'an. After Muslims rioted in Afghanistan, the administration demonstrated that its grasp on the freedom of speech had not improved in the intervening seven months. Officials passed up a chance to explain the necessity and importance of the freedom of speech, and its protection under the U.S. Constitution.

General Petraeus declared that the Qur'an-burning was "hateful, it was intolerant and it was extremely disrespectful and again, we condemn it in the strongest manner possible."[24]

Obama, as he had done the previous September, warned that the Qur'an-burning would endanger American troops in Afghanistan and elsewhere. He issued a statement saying that he hoped "the Afghan people understand that the actions of a small number of individuals, who have been extremely disrespectful to the holy Quran, are not representative of any of the countries of the international community who are in Afghanistan to help the Afghan people."[25]

The media took Jones's responsibility for the violence for granted. ABC News reported, "U.N. Staffers Killed in Afghanistan Over Terry Jones Koran Burning, Police Say."[26] The *Christian Science Monitor* published an article purporting to explain "Why Terry Jones Quran burning spurred two days of deadly

COUNTERPRODUCTIVE COUNTERTERRORISM

There is always the possibility that Muslims worldwide may see the American anxiety to prevent Qur'an-burning and other insults to Islam as signs that Americans are weak—and ripe for defeat. In that case, the administration's efforts to prevent the Qur'an-burning could have ended up having the opposite effect from the one intended—increasing jihad recruitment.

Afghan protests."[27] The *New York Times* equated the burning of a book with mass murder: "Afghans Avenge Florida Koran Burning, Killing 12."[28] Mark Potok of the hard-Left Southern Poverty Law Center charged that Jones bore "moral responsibility for the deaths…of at least a dozen people in Afghanistan, after mobs enraged by his March 20 burning of the Koran stormed a United Nations building and killed men and women inside."[29]

Jones rightly disclaimed responsibility: "We do not feel responsible. We feel more that the Muslims and radical Islam uses that as an excuse. If they didn't use us as an excuse, they would use a different excuse."[30] Indeed. Jones was not forcing anyone to riot and murder. Those who chose to kill other human beings to avenge his insult to their scriptures were the only ones who could rightly be held accountable for the deaths.

But this would not be the end of the administration's attempts to rein in Jones's exercise of his First Amendment rights. Two years later, with Jones offering public support for the Muhammad video that the Obama administration was disingenuously blaming for the Benghazi jihad attack, Joint Chiefs of Staff chairman General Martin Dempsey also called Jones. Dempsey's spokesman Colonel Dave Lapan said, "In the brief call, Gen. Dempsey expressed his concerns over the nature of the film, the tensions it will inflame and the violence it will cause. He asked Mr. Jones to consider withdrawing his support for the film."[31]

STICKS AND STONES MAY BREAK MY BONES, BUT WORDS WILL NEVER HURT ME

Because of the First Amendment, Jones couldn't be stopped by law. But the Obama administration did its level best to stop him by shaming him with the prospect of being responsible for the deaths of American troops in Afghanistan. No one was willing to stand up and denounce the Muslims who would kill over an insult to their religion as irrationally violent, authoritarian, and supremacist—and responsible for their own actions.

Everyone seemed to agree that if Muslims rioted over something an American said or did, the fault lay entirely with the American. It was always and in every case the responsibility of Americans to conform their behavior to Muslim sensibilities, so as not to set them off.

"You can't say that we're going to apply the First Amendment to only those cases where we are in agreement"

Only New York City Mayor Michael Bloomberg demonstrated a grasp of what was really at stake. When Jones announced his initial plans to burn a Qur'an in September 2010, Bloomberg said, "I happen to think that it is distasteful." But he added that "the First Amendment protects everybody, and you can't say that we're going to apply the First Amendment to only those cases where we are in agreement."[32]

Virtually everyone else seemed to have forgotten that.

I opposed Jones's Qur'an-burnings, but not for the reasons Obama, Petraeus, Gates, Dempsey or anyone else articulated. I oppose all book-burning. I'd prefer that the contents of the Qur'an, and the ways that jihadists use those contents to justify violence, be known.

But under the free speech regime established by the First Amendment, I can't make Jones conform his speech to my beliefs. Jones is free to do what he wants to do. Obama and Petraeus would have done better to tell the Afghans that in America we have freedom of speech, and that we put up with expression of beliefs that we dislike without trying to kill the speaker.

He would have done better to tell them that their murderous rage over any burning of the Qur'an was an outrageous overreaction, and that mass murder was a heinous crime, far dwarfing any crime they thought Jones was committing.

The idea that in wartime one should be careful not to do anything that the enemy is likely to respond to with irrational and even murderous

COUNTERPRODUCTIVE COUNTERTERRORISM

In the case of Pastor Terry Jones, no less a figure than the president of the United States showed that he had imbibed and was now propagating the idea that if Muslims don't like what we say, we must stop saying it; otherwise, they have a legitimate excuse to become violent. In reality, this argument will only encourage them to become violent—after the Jones incidents, they have proof that violence works.

anger may seem tactically wise at first glance. But ultimately, it is a recipe for surrender. One is already accepting the enemy's worldview and perspective and working to accommodate it, instead of working on various fronts—not just the military one—to show why it is wrong and should be opposed.

Of course, to that Obama and his ilk would likely respond, *We are not at war with Islam or the Qur'an, and so to burn the book is a needless provocation.*

This ignores the fact that, as we have already seen, the Organization of Islamic Cooperation (OIC) and other Muslim groups, many of them *not* engaged in violent jihad, are already waging a war against the freedom of expression.

Without approving of the Qur'an-burning, Obama and Petraeus should have defended Jones's freedom of expression, and used the burning as a teaching moment in Afghanistan. Obama could and should have said, *We are going to defend our free society no matter what you bring against us. The United States will always defend American citizens who are exercising their Constitutional freedoms.*

The course of action that Obama and his generals actually took instead will never bring peace; it is a recipe for setting the world on fire.

"Not only protected speech—
it is core political speech"

Meanwhile, with the Obama administration taking such an obviously dim view of the freedom of speech, other authorities nationwide didn't consider themselves particularly bound to uphold it, either. One major free speech battle began when the American Freedom Defense Initiative, of which I am a co-founder, attempted to run ads in the New York City subway system that read: "In any war between the civilized man and the savage, support the civilized man. Support Israel. Defeat Jihad."

Arguing erroneously that the ad referred to all Muslims—rather than Palestinian jihadis and their supporters who had behaved with manifest savagery—as savages, New York City's Metropolitan Transit Authority (MTA) refused to run the ad, despite the fact that it had already run in other cities. But in July 2012, Judge Paul A. Engelmayer of the U.S. District Court for the Southern District of New York ruled that in refusing to run the ad, the MTA had violated the First Amendment. The ad, he wrote, was "not only protected speech—it is core political speech," and consequently "is afforded the highest level of protection under the First Amendment."[33]

The MTA was not moved by this ruling to become an energetic defender of the First Amendment. In 2015, when the Council on American-Islamic Relations (CAIR) ran a series of ads attempting to portray the Islamic concept of jihad as entirely peaceful and benign, AFDI devised a series of ads featuring genuine quotes from Muslim spokesmen about jihad, including one from a music video that had run on Hamas's al-Aqsa TV channel: "Killing Jews is worship that draws us closer to Allah."[34]

The MTA refused to run that ad as well, arguing that it could incite Muslims to kill Jews. But Judge John G. Koeltl of the U.S. District Court ruled, "While the court is sensitive to the M.T.A.'s security concerns, the defendants have not presented any objective evidence that the 'Killing Jews advertisement' would be likely to incite imminent violence.... The defendants underestimate the tolerant quality of New Yorkers, and overestimate the potential impact of these fleeting advertisements."[35]

Having lost once again on free speech grounds, but determined not to run any more AFDI ads, the MTA tried its final gambit: in April 2015, it banned *all* political ads on city subways and buses.[36] The ban was specifically directed at AFDI, as the *New York Post* made clear in reporting when the ban was upheld up in court the following March: "An appeals court judge has upheld a previous ruling that the MTA's policy of refusing all political and religious ads in the transit system is legal, meaning the agency can continue to reject controversial posters by firebrand Pamela Geller and the anti-Muslim American Freedom law Center—for now."[37] (The American Freedom Law Center represented AFDI in these court battles.)

A double standard was revealed, however, in October 2015, when U.S. District Judge Colleen McMahon ruled that the MTA had to run ads for *The Muslims Are Coming!*, a satirical film mocking "Islamophobia"—while leaving the ban on political ads in place. The movie, the judge argued, was not political.[38] But as Pamela Geller, my AFDI co-founder, said, "Make no mistake. *The Muslims Are Coming!* ad is political. And no, the movie is not about the Muslim invasion of Europe. This 'movie' is nothing but agitprop for Islam under the guise of—you guessed it—making lame jokes about 'Islamophobia.' If that's comic, no one is laughing."[39] *The Muslims Are Coming!* reflected the favored political views of the day, so its ads could run.

Other cities, including Boston, Washington, D.C., Chicago, and Miami followed New York's example in banning political ads. This facially neutral prohibition of political advertising, in reality instituted precisely to avoid running AFDI ads, came to be known as "the Geller ban." It was enforced by private companies as well as public entities, and always selectively.

Geller noted in November 2015 that Boston's Massachusetts Bay Transit Authority (MBTA) was running "yet another series of Jew-hating ads, one after another, while refusing no less than three pro-Israel, counter-jihad campaigns from AFDI."[40]

And in February 2016, the national billboard company Lamar Advertising ran an anti-Israel ad on an interstate highway near Chicago's O'Hare International Airport.[41] Criticized for running the ads, Lamar invoked the freedom of speech:

> We have received a large number of social media comments and hundreds of telephone calls concerning a billboard in Chicago sponsored by the Seattle Mideast Awareness Campaign (SEAMAC). The advertisement suggests that people should "Boycott Israel Until Palestinians Have Equal Rights." It is important to understand that this is a message from SEAMAC and not Lamar Advertising. Lamar has been in the billboard business for over 100 years and we have developed a strong commitment to supporting the First Amendment right of advertisers who wish to use our medium to promote legal products and services or to convey noncommercial messages such as the one in Chicago. We do not accept or reject copy based upon agreement or disagreement with the views presented. We think SEAMAC has a right to present their views and would also support the right of those who disagree with SEAMAC. We welcome your comments.[42]

Commented Pamela Geller, "'We do not accept or reject copy based upon agreement or disagreement with the views presented.' Really? For the past nine months, AFDI has submitted various ads to 15 cities. All were rejected, yet every ad was fact-based.... 'We think SEAMAC has a right to present their views and would also support the right of those who disagree with

WHY WE NEED THE FREEDOM OF SPEECH

· · ·

"Once a government is committed to the principle of silencing the voice of opposition, it has only one way to go, and that is down the path of increasingly repressive measures, until it becomes a source of terror to all its citizens and creates a country where everyone lives in fear."

—Harry Truman[45]

SEAMAC.' But apparently Lamar does not believe that AFDI has any such right."[43]

By September 2016, Geller noted, San Francisco was "the last city where the 'Geller ban' is not in effect. We've seen this where we tried to run ads in response to some fallacious ads that the Jew-haters are running, whether it's SEAMAC or American Muslims for Palestine or some other nefarious group that is running blood libel against Israel." She observed that the ban on political ads, which was essentially a ban on AFDI ads, was "a ban on the truth, in accordance with Sharia."[44]

Chapter Six

"IS THAT BEING RACIST?": AMERICANS LEARN SELF-CENSORSHIP

"Peer pressure" and "shaming" also worked by means of charges of "racism" and "Islamophobia." Nidal Malik Hasan, the U.S. Army major who murdered thirteen people and wounded thirty at Fort Hood on November 5, 2009, owed his career advancement to his colleagues' fears of being labeled racist, xenophobic, or prejudiced against Muslims. Hasan's behavior had caused concerns for years before his attack. In 2007, according to AP, he gave a presentation to coworkers "questioning whether the U.S.-led war on terror was actually a war on Islam. And students said he suggested that Shariah, or Islamic law, trumped the Constitution and he attempted to justify suicide bombings."[1]

Then in December 17, 2008, Hasan emailed jihad terror mastermind Anwar al-Awlaki and asked him whether Sergeant Hasan Akbar, a Muslim soldier in the U.S. military who had killed two of his commanding officers

91

with a grenade attack in Kuwait, should be considered a martyr. He added (spelling and grammar as in the original), "I realize that these are difficult questions but you seem to be one of the only ones that has lived in the u.s. has a good understadning of the the Qur'an and Sunna and is not afraid of being direct."[2]

Law enforcement officials knew that Hasan was corresponding with Awlaki, but they did nothing. The FBI agent who was monitoring Hasan's emails asked the agency's Washington Field Office (WFO) why it didn't act, and was told: "WFO doesn't go out and interview every Muslim guy who visits extremist websites"—suggesting that numerous Muslims in the United States were visiting such sites. Hasan, it added, was "politically sensitive for WFO."[4] It did not explain why.

Despite Hasan's pro-jihad statements, his superior officers praised his "outstanding moral integrity" and "unique insights into the dimensions of Islam" in a March 2009 evaluation, saying that his "moral reasoning" could be of "great potential interest and strategic importance to the U.S. Army."[5] Four months later another evaulation noted that Hasan had "a keen interest in Islamic culture and faith and has shown capacity to contribute to our psychological understanding of Islamic nationalism and how it may relate to events of national security and Army interest in the Middle East and Asia." Hasan, the evaluation said, has "great potential as an Army officer."[6]

HE DIDN'T HAVE TO TWIST HIS ARM

In one email U.S. Army Major Nidal Hasan made the argument to terror mastermind Anwar al-Awlaki that Hamas's practice of firing rockets into Israeli civilian areas was justified: "Hamas and the Muslims hate to hurt the innocent but they have no choice if their [sic] going to have a chance to survive, flourish, and deter the Zionist enemy. The recompense for an evil is an evil. So, to claim that these rocket attacks go against the spirit of Islam is false."[3]

Why did his superiors continue to praise and promote Hasan, ignoring all the warning signs? Surely we don't need Army officers who defend suicide bombing and put Sharia law above the Constitution?

THEY GOT THAT ONE RIGHT

. . . .

Among Major Nidal Hasan's "unique skills," according his supervisors in the Army: "Islamic studies."

The actions of Hasan's superior officers simply reflected the prevailing military culture at the time (and today), which can be summed up in Mohamed Atta's words: *Just stay quiet and you'll be okay.* They knew, without having to be told, that to take action against a Muslim officer in the U.S. military—even one who had raised as many red flags as Hasan had—would make them vulnerable to charges of "bigotry" and could mean the end of their careers. Because he was an Arab and a Muslim, Hasan was as "politically sensitive" for his colleagues in the Army as he was for the FBI agents in the Washington Field Office who did nothing though they knew a U.S. Army officer was corresponding with a known recruiter of terrorists. These Americans all stayed quiet, and they did end up more more okay than the airline passengers on 9/11. At least they kept their lives. But they would have to carry the weight of Hasan's mass murder to their graves. Their politically correct silence had a high human cost.

"Should I call someone or is that being racist?"

A similar massacre had been averted in 2006, when one young American decided to brave the risk and do the "racist" thing: report a jihad plot and save lives. In 2005 and 2006, five Muslims were plotting to commit jihad mass murder at the U.S. Army base in Fort Dix, New Jersey.[7]

But their plot was foiled by their desire to watch their favorite jihad videos on DVD rather than VHS. They went to Circuit City and asked the young clerk, Brian Morgenstern, to transfer their VHS tapes to the new format. While Morgenstern was doing the job, he became alarmed about what he saw on the tapes. Finally he asked another Circuit City employee, "Dude, I just saw some really weird s—. I don't know what to do. Should I call someone or is that being racist?"[8] (Ironically, the jihad plotters were white European Muslims from the former Yugoslavia.)

Morgenstern decided to be "racist," and the plot was foiled. But his question showed how much power political correctness has to silence Americans—to intimidate them from taking action even when they are faced with obvious evidence of jihad threats. This is a kind of "peer pressure" and "shaming" that grows ever more aggressive. Americans are internalizing Islamic blasphemy law.

Instances of this self-censorship can be found all over. In January 2017, I was asked by The Hill, an online political publication, to write a piece about rumors that actress Lindsay Lohan had converted to Islam. In the piece, I included quotations from the Qur'an denying equality of rights to women, calling for them to be beaten when disobedient, and the like, and wondered whether Lohan was familiar with such material.

It was a minor piece about a minor celebrity, but it caused the foes of freedom major agitation. The day it was published, leftists and Islamic supremacists tweeted angrily at The Hill, outraged that they had published the "racist" "hatemonger," Robert Spencer.

What was "racist" or "hateful" about the actual article they did not and could not say, because there wasn't really anything racist or hateful about it.[9] But The Hill's editor Bob Cusack demonstrated that he was thoroughly susceptible to peer pressure and shaming, and pulled the article from The Hill after it had been up for about a day.[10]

"Curt Schilling's tweet comparing Muslims to Nazis is even worse than it sounds"

Increasingly, those who dare to cross red lines and say anything perceived to be "racist" face abusive criticism, ostracism, and possibly even professional ruin—as baseball star-turned-sports announcer Curt Schilling discovered in August 2015.

Schilling ran afoul of the guardians of acceptable opinion, and was subjected to "old-fashioned techniques of peer pressure and shaming," for posting a meme on Twitter that read, "It's said only 5–10% of Muslims are extremists. In 1940, only 7% of Germans were Nazis. How'd that go?"

Schilling quickly deleted this tweet, something that only reinforced the impression that it was a horrible thing to say, and that Schilling had realized that.

The headline in the *Washington Post* was reasonably accurate: "Curt Schilling compares Muslim extremists to Nazis in deleted tweet." But other outlets were heavier on outrage than on accuracy. "Curt Schilling compares Muslims to Nazis in baffling deleted tweet," said *USA Today*.[11] SB Nation was even more hysterical: "Curt Schilling tweets, deletes awful meme about Muslims and Nazis."[12] The liberal website Vox dramatically informed readers, "Curt Schilling's tweet comparing Muslims to Nazis is even worse than it sounds." That was the headline of a hit piece by Max Fisher.[13] In fact Schilling had said nothing of the sort. He had compared Nazis not to Muslims in general but to a small minority of "extremists" in the Muslim population.

But Schilling had transgressed against America's unwritten, but nonetheless frightfully draconian, speech codes. He had to be shamed.

Fisher professed ignorance of Schilling's illustrious baseball career, thereby semaphoring that he was a good leftist elitist, ignorant of brutish and bourgeois athletic achievements: "Curt Schilling, whom [sic] Wikipedia

MUCH ADO ABOUT (ALMOST) NOTHING

. . . .

Back in 2005, a group called the Free Muslims Coalition held what it dubbed a "Free Muslims March Against Terror" in Washington, D.C. The announcement of the rally invited people of all faiths to join in: "Please join us and help us send a message to the terrorists and extremists that their days are numbered. Also, join us in sending a message to the people of the Middle East, the Muslim world and all people who seek freedom, democracy and peaceful coexistence that we support them."[20] This was intended to be a massive event. Free Muslims stated, "Since we announced the Rally nearly 30 organizations have endorsed it and more are on the way. Among the list of speakers are several Congressmen and Senators. We want to remind everyone that this rally is open to people of all backgrounds. We hope to have the endorsements of at least 100 organizations and places of worship."[21] In the run-up to the event, there was enthusiastic national and international publicity. It ended up drawing a crowd of about fifty people, many of them non-Muslims.[22]

informs me is a former baseball star and current ESPN commentator, sent a tweet on Tuesday that seems to have emerged straight from the internet nether-void of racist email forwards."[14]

Where was the racism? What race are "extremist Muslims"? What race are Muslims in the aggregate? What race is Islam? Or did Fisher mean that Schilling's tweet was racist against Germans?

But Fisher's woolly logic was typical of the firestorm that engulfed Schilling; he was removed from ESPN's coverage of the Little League World Series.

Schilling himself was repentant and apologetic, but it did no good: he had to be subjected to "old-fashioned peer pressure and shaming," and so he was.

What exactly was so offensive about Schilling's tweet? Was it that he had compared "extremist Muslims" to Nazis? Surely that couldn't have been it. The Islamic State hasn't murdered six million Jews, but it certainly would if it could, and meanwhile its gleeful bloodlust, sex slavery, terrorizing of non-Muslims, and all the rest of it made the comparison reasonable.

Or was Schilling "insensitive" for daring to suggest that peaceful Muslims weren't doing much to rein in their violent coreligionists? There is ample evidence to support that contention: A Muslim rally on the National Mall to condemn ISIS in July 2016 drew only a "small crowd" of Muslims—thousands fewer than expected.[15] In July 2015, Muslims in Ireland held a demonstration against the Islamic State—for which fewer than fifty people showed up.[16] And in October 2014 in Houston, a rally against the Islamic State organized by the Council on American-Islamic Relations (CAIR) drew a grand total of ten people.[17] In August 2013 in Boston, about twenty-five Muslims rallied against "misperceptions" that Islam was violent.[18] About the same number showed up in June 2013 at a progressive Muslim rally in Toronto to claim that their religion had been "hijacked."[19]

Contrast those paltry showings to the thousands of Muslims who have turned out for rallies against Muhammad cartoons, and against Israel. In the aftermath of the jihad massacre of Muhammad cartoonists in January 2015, eight hundred thousand Muslims in Chechnya protested—not against the massacre, but against Muhammad cartoons. There were similar protests in Iran, Pakistan, Ingushetia, and elsewhere.[23] Ten thousand Muslims in Pakistan protested, also against *Charlie Hebdo*'s Muhammad cartoons, not against the murders of the cartoonists who had drawn them.[24] In Australia, a thousand Muslims rallied against *Charlie Hebdo* and the freedom of speech.[25] In Kyrgyztsan, a thousand Muslims rallied, chanting, "I am not Charlie, I love my Prophet."[26]

But given a chance to show how Muslims overwhelmingly rejected "extremism," only a handful showed up.

The savaging and demonization of Curt Schilling was disquieting proof of how effective Hillary's "old-fashioned peer pressure and shaming" could be: anyone and everyone who dared to speak a word against jihad terror

UNHOLY ALLIANCE

. . .

The push to enact Sharia blasphemy law via political correctness went hand in hand with the Left's campaign to shame and silence the critics of its own agenda. After Schilling posted a series of tweets criticizing the idea of allowing "transgender women" (men claiming to be women) to use women's restrooms, ESPN fired him.[27] No one concerned about "intolerance" and "bigotry" shed a tear.

would inevitably be mauled in the public square, and charged with racism, bigotry, and "Islamophobia"—despite the fact that everyone, including the leading Muslim groups in the United States, was supposed to be against jihad terror. No one, no matter how previously beloved, was exempt from this tactic: Schilling was the hero of two World Series champion teams and a widely respected figure, but that did not save him from the "peer pressure and shaming" buzzsaw.

And Schilling, unprepared for the onslaught, backed down immediately, thereby reinforcing the usefulness of this tactic.

The ultimate result was to inhibit honest speech about the jihad threat. The establishment media and other elites who had piled onto Schilling preened themselves on their tolerance, open-mindedness, and bold stand against bigotry. But in reality their enforcement of the politically correct narrative about Islam advanced goals that were anything but tolerant.

The concerted initiative by the OIC and other Islamic entities to impose Islamic blasphemy law on the West was only aided and abetted by the West's increasing willingness to censor its own.

"Free speech . . . becomes its own kind of fanaticism"

Speaking three months after Islamic jihadists massacred the *Charlie Hebdo* Muhammad cartoonists in their Paris offices, renowned *Doonesbury* cartoonist Garry Trudeau spoke out strongly against the murdered cartoonists as he received a lifetime achievement award from the George Polk Awards in journalism. By drawing Muhammad, he said, the murdered cartoonists had "wandered into the realm of hate speech." He laid blame at the feet of the concept of free speech itself. "Free speech," he proclaimed, "becomes its own kind of fanaticism."[28]

Criticized for his attack on the freedom of speech, Trudeau attempted to clarify his remarks in an interview with Chuck Todd on *Meet the Press*. He insisted that he was not blaming the Muhammad cartoonists for their own deaths, and admitted that he "should have made it a little clearer that I was as outraged as the rest of the world at the time. I mourn them deeply."[29]

But then Trudeau made the bizarre claim that it's "not really for us to decide" whether or not Muhammad could be criticized or mocked—a deference he had never accorded to the many objects of his mockery in *Doonesbury* over the years.[30] "I mean, we, as societies, collectively decide what's untouchable. But I don't have the right to decide what is sacred and holy and profane for someone else. All societies come to a consensus about that."[31] What consensus had ever been established for the mockery of Christianity and other religions in the West, he did not explain.

Trudeau insisted that he wasn't losing his satirical edge: "I certainly wouldn't draw pictures of the prophet. However, I've done many cartoons satirizing in the specific: terrorists, the Taliban, Al Qaeda, the P.L.O.... and have never received any blow-back from the Muslim community. They understand that I'm separating out the two."[32]

Presumably Trudeau wouldn't draw pictures of Muhammad because he believes that he doesn't "have the right to decide what is sacred and holy and profane for someone else." But that's not what's at issue. There is no question that Muhammad is sacred and holy to Muslims. The question is whether or not that fact obligates anyone else. If I believe something is sacred and holy, does that oblige you to respect it too? Trudeau would apparently say yes. I doubt, however, that he would say the same thing about what Christians hold sacred. I don't remember him condemning *Piss Christ* or the dung-encrusted painting of the Virgin Mary that was exhibited in New York a few

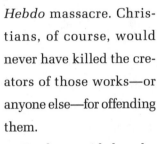

STICKS AND STONES MAY
BREAK MY BONES, BUT WORDS
WILL NEVER HURT ME

· ·

"The responsibility for violence lies with those who perpetrate it."
—Salman Rusdie[34]

years before the *Charlie Hebdo* massacre. Christians, of course, would never have killed the creators of those works—or anyone else—for offending them.

Trudeau said that the *Charlie Hebdo* cartoonists were "not at all to blame," but undercut that statement by saying, "I didn't agree with the decisions they made that brought a world of pain to France."[33]

In fact it was the jihad mass murderers, not *Charlie Hebdo*, who had "brought a world of pain to France." If they had not been willing to commit mass murder in the service of Sharia blasphemy laws, France would not have experienced any pain at all. Trudeau was saying that the proper response to a thug who threatens to kill you unless you shut up is to submit and obey. That would be to install a thugocracy, allowing those who will kill the most people the most ruthlessly the right to rule. Trudeau's ill-thought-out condemnation of the *Charlie Hebdo* cartoonists was helping to pave the way for that thugocracy.

"A hideous crime was committed, but was it a freedom-of-speech issue for PEN America to be self-righteous about?"

PEN International describes itself as a "global literary network" that works "to defend and promote freedom of expression, and to remove barriers to literature."[35] Its U.S. branch, PEN America, proclaims that it "stands at the intersection of literature and human rights to protect open expression in the United States and worldwide. We champion the freedom to write, recognizing the power of the word to transform the world. Our mission is to unite writers and their allies to celebrate creative expression and defend the liberties that make it possible."[36]

That is exactly what PEN intended to do when it decided in April 2015 to give its annual Freedom of Expression Courage award to two members of the *Charlie Hebdo* staff who had not been murdered in January's jihad massacre at its offices: the magazine's editor in chief, Gerard Biard, and staff member Jean-Baptiste Thoret.

But six PEN members—writers Peter Carey, Michael Ondaatje, Francine Prose, Teju Cole, Rachel Kushner, and Taiye Selasi—took umbrage. Sniffed Carey, "A hideous crime was committed, but was it a freedom-of-speech issue for PEN America to be self-righteous about? All this is complicated by PEN's seeming blindness to the cultural arrogance of the French nation, which does not recognize its moral obligation to a large and disempowered segment of their population."[37]

"Cultural arrogance." In Carey's view, the French, and *Charlie Hebdo* in particular, manifested "cultural arrogance" by persisting in saying and doing things that offended the sensibilities of Muslims, who deserved to be protected from such offenses in France and elsewhere in the West because they were "disempowered."

Deborah Eisenberg, another writer dissatisfied with PEN's decision of award recipient, was similarly solicitous of Muslim

IT ALL DEPENDS ON WHOSE OX IS BEING GORED

Apparently it did not cross Peter Carey's mind that that the jihad attackers were displaying a "cultural arrogance" of their own by murdering the cartoonists in the service of Islam's blasphemy law, to which the cartoonists did not subscribe. Or if it did, he waved the thought away in light of the putative victim status of Muslims in France and the West in general.

feelings: "What I question is what PEN is hoping to convey by awarding a magazine that has become famous both for the horrible murder of staff members by Muslim extremists and for its denigrating portrayals of Muslims. *Charlie Hebdo*'s symbolic significance is unclear here."[38]

It was left to someone who well understood the importance of the freedom of speech, and the necessity for free societies to defend it, to explain that significance. Salman Rushdie—whose novel *The Satanic Verses* inspired a death fatwa from the Ayatollah Khomeini in 1989 and who ever since has been a symbol of the resistance to attempts to impose Islamic blasphemy law on the world—declared, "It is quite right that PEN should honour [the *Charlie Hebdo* staff's] sacrifice and condemn their murder without these disgusting 'buts.'"[39] Rushdie dismissed the six PEN dissenters Carey, Ondaatje, Prose, Cole, Kushner, and Selasi as "Six Authors in Search of a bit of Character" and declared that they were "horribly wrong.... If PEN as a free-speech organisation can't defend and celebrate people who have been murdered for drawing pictures, then frankly the organisation is not worth the name. What I would say to both Peter and Michael and the others is, I hope nobody ever comes after them."[40]

Rushdie waved aside the claim that Muslims in France were "disempowered" and thus should be sheltered from mockery and criticism: "This issue has nothing to do with an oppressed and disadvantaged minority. It has everything to do with the battle against fanatical Islam, which is highly organised, well funded, and which seeks to terrify us all, Muslims as well as non Muslims, into a cowed silence. These six writers have made themselves the fellow travellers of that project. Now they will have the dubious satisfaction of watching PEN tear itself apart in public."[41]

Carey said that he wrote to PEN's president "to say that I did not wish to have my name, without my knowledge or prior approval, publicly linked to a political position I did not hold."[42] That political position was apparently the idea that Islam, like all other belief systems and ideas, can be criticized, found wanting, rejected, and even mocked.

Carey, like many leftists today, apparently believes that the freedom of expression should only be accorded to those with whom he agrees. The rest can be forcibly silenced, even murdered, without protest—as long as the thugs and murderers are members of a victim class duly recognized by the Left.

> ## STICKS AND STONES MAY BREAK MY BONES, BUT WORDS WILL NEVER HURT ME
>
> "If we only endorsed freedom of speech for people whose speech we liked that would be a very limited notion of freedom of speech. It's a courage award, not a content award."
> —PEN president Andrew Solomon, reiterating a basic principle that was quickly vanishing from the contemporary discourse[44]

Andrew Solomon, the president of PEN, hastened to assure the world that the PEN did "not agree with the content of what they expressed, it expressed admiration for that commitment of free speech."[43]

In a letter to PEN trustees, Solomon noted that "in addition to provoking violent threats from extremists, the *Hebdo* cartoons offended some other Muslims and members of the many other groups they targeted." He assured them that despite having offended Muslims, *Charlie Hebdo*'s intent was not to "disempower" them: "Based on their own statements, we believe that *Charlie Hebdo*'s intent was not to ostracise or insult Muslims, but rather to reject forcefully the efforts of a small minority of radical extremists to place broad categories of speech off limits—no matter the purpose, intent, or import of the expression. There is courage in refusing the very idea of forbidden statements, an urgent brilliance in saying what you have been told not to say in order to make it sayable. At PEN, we never shy away from controversy nor demand uniformity of opinion across our ranks."[45] He wasn't going to cancel the award: "We will be sorry not to see those who have opted out of the gala, but we respect them for their convictions."[46]

The "peer pressure" Hillary Clinton had advocated using against those who insulted Islam was in heavy play. Two hundred four other writers quickly joined the six in protesting the award to *Charlie Hebdo*, making it clear that they found Carey's arguments against *Charlie Hebdo*'s supposed "cultural arrogance" more compelling than the defense of free speech by Rushdie and Solomon. In a letter explaining their position, they asserted that there was "a critical difference between staunchly supporting expression that violates the acceptable, and enthusiastically rewarding such expression."[47]

This was a fine distinction indeed. But what it all boiled down to was that, as far as hundreds of the most prominent writers in America were concerned, Carey was right: issues of political power and the lingering effects of colonialism were more compelling than the freedom of speech. As they explained,

> In the aftermath of the attacks, *Charlie Hebdo*'s cartoons were characterized as satire and "equal opportunity offense," and the magazine seems to be entirely sincere in its anarchic expressions of principled disdain toward organized religion. But in an unequal society, equal opportunity offence does not have an equal effect.
>
> Power and prestige are elements that must be recognized in considering almost any form of discourse, including satire. The inequities between the person holding the pen and the subject fixed on paper by that pen cannot, and must not, be ignored.
>
> To the section of the French population that is already marginalized, embattled, and victimized, a population that is shaped by the legacy of France's various colonial enterprises, and that contains

a large percentage of devout Muslims, *Charlie Hebdo*'s cartoons of the Prophet must be seen as being intended to cause further humiliation and suffering.

Our concern is that, by bestowing the Toni and James C. Goodale Freedom of Expression Courage Award on *Charlie Hebdo*, PEN is not simply conveying support for freedom of expression, but also valorizing selectively offensive material: material that intensifies the anti-Islamic, anti-Maghreb, anti-Arab sentiments already prevalent in the Western world.[48]

Freedom of expression was just fine—unless it was "anti-Islamic." Most if not all of the signatories to this letter considered "anti-Islamic" speech to be on par with the worst racist and anti-Semitic discourse. The renowned writer Joyce Carol Oates explained on Twitter, "PEN honors & defends 'freedom of expression' but not all 'expression'—it is selective. Not antisemitic, for instance. Seems reasonable."[49] She added, "To some, cartoons depicting black women as monkeys are just so offensive we resent 'award'. But would defend freedom of expression. If we are 'offended' we can just look away, not censor. But we are reluctant to give 'award.' (Realize others disagree)."[50]

Were cartoons of Muhammad really akin to racist and anti-Semitic speech? One key difference: Islamic jihadis were proudly raping, killing, and committing other atrocities in the

THE JOYOUS SIDE OF JIHAD?

Joyce Carol Oates was anxious to find the positive side of Islamic jihad, tweeting a few months later, "All we hear of ISIS is puritanical & punitive; is there nothing celebratory & joyous? Or is query naïve?"[51] "Naïve" was putting it mildly. But Oates's solicitude for the Islamic State's public image illustrated the general leftist tendency to wave aside the atrocities of Islamic jihadis, dismissing any discussion of them as racism and bigotry.

name of Islam, while the victim groups to which the dissenting writers likened Muslims contained no violent global movements openly declaring their will to destruction and conquest. Not all Muslims were responsible for this violence, of course, but to place Islam beyond criticism because Muslims were supposedly being discriminated against in France and other Western countries was to ignore, as Rushdie put it, "the battle against fanatical Islam, which is highly organised, well funded, and which seeks to terrify us all, Muslims as well as non Muslims, into a cowed silence."

In all their explanations of their position, the writers who condemned PEN's award to *Charlie Hebdo* never did address that reality. "Peer pressure and shaming," rather than reasoned discourse, were the order of the day, as the writers who protested PEN's award signaled to the world that they were in the camp of virtue, the one that did not offend "disempowered" Muslims, not with those who supposedly stood for "racism" and were busy reviving colonialist oppression.

Nor were these writers singular. In the immediate aftermath of the *Charlie Hebdo* massacre, *Variety* worried that "the Charlie Hebdo carnage will likely fuel the racism and anti-Islam sentiment which has been on the rise in France. It will also certainly boost the popularity of far-right (Front national) party leader Marine Le Pen, who is expected to run for President in 2017."[52]

Variety's message to its readers was clear: The real tragedy of the *Charlie Hebdo* massacre wasn't the murder of the cartoonists, or the existential threat to free speech. It was the danger that the bloody attack would awaken people to the jihad threat—an awareness that the magazine could see only in terms of "racism and anti-Islam sentiment" and a boost for the "far-right" Marine Le Pen. Given those priorities, it made sense to decry the massacre while simultaneously denouncing the cartoonists. That was what all the cool people, the intelligentsia, the best and the brightest were doing.

One writer was not susceptible to the peer pressure. The Netherlands-based Iranian dissident Afshin Ellian, author of a book entitled *Freedom of Speech under Attack*, who has received death threats for his writings about Islam, insisted that "whenever a society applies self-censorship out of fear from terrorism, freedom dissipates." He decried the boycott of the PEN award to *Charlie Hebdo*, noting that at the same time the jihadis struck in the *Charlie Hebdo* offices, they also murdered Jews at the Hyper Cacher kosher supermarket in Paris. "If you start with saying they shouldn't make the cartoons," Ellian declared, "you may as well say they shouldn't write novels. After all, what have the Jews done? Why are *they* killed? Would the writers say they shouldn't have been Jews? A writer who cannot tolerate such a prize is not worthy of the name 'writer.'"[53]

Indeed.

"The screening of this film in its present state would greatly offend our local Muslim believers as well as any foreign Muslim visitor to the museum"

Truth was no defense against peer pressure and shaming. In April 2014, Muslim groups protested against the screening of a seven-minute film entitled "The Rise of Al Qaeda" at the National September 11 Memorial Museum in New York City. Sheikh Mostafa Elazabawy, the imam of Masjid Manhattan, huffed, "The screening of this film in its present state would greatly offend our local Muslim believers as well as any foreign Muslim visitor to the museum. Unsophisticated visitors who do not understand the difference between Al Qaeda and Muslims may come away with a prejudiced view of Islam, leading to antagonism and even confrontation toward Muslim believers near the site."[54]

This was an extraordinary complaint in light of the fact that the film in no way conflated al-Qaeda with Muslims in general. All it did was use the words "jihad" and "Islamist." Nevertheless, Akbar Ahmed, a noted Islamic scholar at American University, insisted that many visitors to the museum were "simply going to say Islamist means Muslims, jihadist means Muslims. The terrorists need to be condemned and remembered for what they did. But when you associate their religion with what they did, then you are automatically including, by association, one and a half billion people who had nothing to do with these actions and who ultimately the U.S. would not want to unnecessarily alienate."[55]

Ahmed did not address the fact that it was the terrorists, not the 9/11 Memorial Museum, who were responsible for "associat[ing] their religion with what they did." (Mohamed Atta, for example, reminded himself in a note found in a checked suitcase that didn't make it onto the hijacked plane, "Increase your mention of God's name. The best mention is reading the Qur'an. All scholars agreed to this. It is enough for us, that [the Qur'an] is the word of the Creator of Heaven and Earth, Who we are about to meet.")[56] Ultimately, the museum stood firm about the film, but it did remove the term "Islamic terrorism" from its website.[57]

The episode was illuminating: even to note the obvious fact that the 9/11 hijackers identified themselves as Muslims and explained that they were doing what they did because of Islam was offensive to other Muslims. To take note of the hijackers' Islamic self-identification was unacceptable. And with judicious use of shaming, offenders could be brought into compliance.

"I'm pretty sure the first amendment extends to bacon"

Offenses to Muslims could be trivial as well as great: Muhammad Syed, the president of Ex-Muslims of North America (EXMNA), found that out in June 2016 when he went to the bakery inside the Wegman's grocery store in Fairfax, Virginia, to order a cake to celebrate the third anniversary of the organization's founding. According to EXMNA, "the request included a picture of the Ex-Muslims of North America (EXMNA) name and logo, with a caption of 'Congratulations on 3 years!'"

A Wegman's associate, however, refused to make the cake, dubbing it "offensive" and explaining, "My employees may not know what this stands for, Ex-Muslims of North America, and I don't have enough time and people to educate them on what it is." Muslim employees hadn't actually complained about the cake, but the associate said that the store couldn't "put them in that situation."

EXMNA's President declared, "I'm shocked by the denial. There is nothing about our name or logo that can be considered offensive to any reasonable individual. There are some, however, who take our very existence as an affront to their faith, and to them I have only this to say: We have every right to exist and be proud of who we are, and we won't back down. Ex-Muslims around the world are persecuted and threatened, even by their own family and friends. We assumed that here, in the United States, we could go about our business without disruption. Unfortunately, even respectable businesses would rather turn away a persecuted group than risk offence."[58] After a firestorm of criticism, Wegman's backed down and apologized to Syed and EXMNA.[59]

The owners of Sneakers Bistro in Winooski, Vermont, likewise ran into the buzz saw of genuine or feared Muslim offense when they put up a sign advertising "Sneakers Bacon." A Muslim woman took to the online Winooski Front Porch Forum to register her offense, claiming that the sign was offensive to people who didn't eat pork. Sneakers took the sign down. One Winooski resident who was unhappy with that decision said about the complaining Muslim, "I respect her religion and her right to believe what she wants but I'm pretty sure the first amendment extends to bacon and the selling of it."[60]

Pretty sure, yes, but these days you can't be certain. In August 2016, when a group called "Wyoming against Islam, Americans for a secure Wyoming" held a "Ban Islam" rally in Gillette, Wyoming, and burned a Qur'an, local

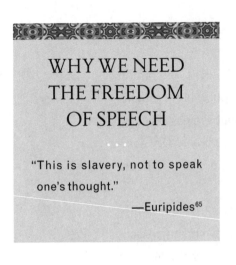

WHY WE NEED THE FREEDOM OF SPEECH

• • •

"This is slavery, not to speak one's thought."

—Euripides[65]

television station KCWY 13, reported fastidiously, "Members of 'Wyoming against Islam' burned a Quran during the rally, but news 13 will not show that out of respect for Muslims."[61]

Respect? Or fear? When it came to Muslims and Islam in America, it was increasingly difficult to tell the difference. In 2009, Yale University Press published an account of the Danish Muhammad cartoon controversy, *The Cartoons That Shook the World* by Danish author Jytte Klausen. While the book contained numerous illustrations, it did not contain any of the cartoons of Muhammad that were the actual subject of the book.[62]

According to the *New York Times*, "John Donatich, the director of Yale University Press, said by telephone that the decision was difficult, but the recommendation to withdraw the images, including the historical ones of Muhammad, was 'overwhelming and unanimous.' The cartoons are freely available on the Internet and can be accurately described in words, Mr. Donatich said, so reprinting them could be interpreted easily as gratuitous."[63]

Pundit Christopher Hitchens was appalled: "The capitulation of Yale University Press to threats that hadn't even been made yet is the latest and perhaps the worst episode in the steady surrender to religious extremism—particularly Muslim religious extremism—that is spreading across our culture."[64]

By 2009, that surrender was already established by abundant precedents. Americans were learning self-censorship, and the portion of the public discourse that was de facto under Islamic blasphemy law rather than the First Amendment would only continue to grow.

Chapter Seven

"IRRESPONSIBLY PROVOCATIVE": THE EROSION OF FREE SPEECH FROM RUSHDIE TO GELLER

The campaign to compel the West to abandon free speech gained critical momentum in the wake of the publication of the Danish cartoons. But the Islamic jihad against the free speech in the West had been declared earlier, on February 14, 1989, when Iran's Supreme Leader, the Ayatollah Ruhollah Khomeini, issued this fatwa against novelist Salman Rushdie for his novel *The Satanic Verses*, which Khomeini believed insulted Islam and Muhammad:

> In the name of Him, the Highest. There is only one God, to whom we shall all return. I inform all zealous Muslims of the world that the author of the book entitled *The Satanic Verses*—which has been compiled, printed, and published in opposition to

Islam, the Prophet, and the Koran—and all those involved in its publication who were aware of its content are sentenced to death.

I call on all zealous Muslims to execute them quickly, wherever they may be found, so that no one else will dare to insult the Muslim sanctities. God willing, whoever is killed on this path is a martyr.

In addition, everyone who has access to the author of this book, but does not possess the power to execute him, should report him to the people so that he may be punished for his actions.

May peace and the mercy of God and his blessings be with you.

Ruhollah al-Musavi al-Khomeini, 25 Bahman 1367.[1]

Khomeini's fatwa followed the banning of *The Satanic Verses* in India upon its publication in September 1988 and the burning of the book by Muslims in two English cities. When the U.S. edition was published in February, international protests began. On February 12, 1989, protesters stormed the American cultural center in Islamabad, Pakistan; five people were killed when police opened fire on the demonstrators.[2]

The American Embassy in Islamabad immediately abandoned the United States' fundamental founding principle, assuring protesters that "the U.S. government in no way supports or associates itself with any activity that is in any way offensive or insulting to Islam or any other religion."[3] It said nothing about the First Amendment or the freedom of speech. The next day, February 13, the day before Khomeini's fatwa, there were anti-Rushdie riots in Srinagar, India; three people were killed and sixty wounded.[4]

Rushdie was prepared at least to some degree for what might happen. Not long before Khomeini's fatwa was published, the novelist wrote, "A powerful tribe of clerics has taken over Islam. These are the contemporary

Thought Police."[5] On the day the fatwa was issued, Rushdie made his last public appearance for many years at a memorial service for the British writer Bruce Chatwin. Word of the death sentence spread quickly among the mourners, and travel writer Paul Theroux whispered to Rushdie, "Your turn next. I suppose we'll be back here for you next week. Keep your head down, Salman."[6]

A state-funded Iranian charity offered $3 million to Iranians or $1 million to foreigners who murdered Rushdie.[7] The writer quickly went into hiding, with his protection paid for by the British government at a cost approaching £1 million a year.[8]

Soon thereafter, Rushdie offered an apology of sorts, along with a sly appeal to the Muslims calling for his head to respect the realities of a world in which people disagreed on fundamental issues of conscience: "As author of *The Satanic Verses*, I recognize that Muslims in many parts of the world are genuinely distressed by the publication of my novel. I profoundly regret the distress that the publication had occasioned to sincere followers of Islam. Living as we do in a world of many faiths, this experience has served to remind us that we all must be conscious of the sensibilities of others."[9]

Khomeini was neither mollified nor inclined to pay his respects to pluralism. In response to rumors that the death sentence would be lifted if Rushdie apologized, Khomeini's office issued a statement:

> The imperialist foreign media falsely allege that the officials of the Islamic Republic have said that the sentence of death on the author of *The Satanic Verses* will be retracted if he repents. His Excellency, Imam Khomeini, long may he live, has said: "This is denied 100 per cent. Even if Salman Rushdie repents and becomes the most pious man of all time, it is incumbent on every Muslim to employ everything he has, his life and wealth, to send

him to Hell." His Excellency the Imam added: "If a non-Muslim becomes aware of Rushdie's whereabouts and has the ability to execute him quicker than Muslims, it is incumbent on Muslims to pay a reward or fee in return for this action."[10]

This invitation to non-Muslims to murder Rushdie was significant: Khomeini was inviting non-Muslims to share Muslim sensibilities regarding Rushdie's alleged offense, and trying to induce them to do so by the prospect of financial reward.

It would take years for this invitation to foreigners and non-Muslims to kill Rushdie to evolve into the "shaming," as Hillary Clinton would put it, of those who dared to decline to participate in the de facto implementation of Islamic blasphemy laws. Clinton's "peer pressure and shaming" imperative demonstrated that, in the two decades between the Rushdie fatwa and her endorsement of UNHRC Resolution 16/18, non-Muslims had become the principal enforcers of Sharia blasphemy laws in the West.

"I realised that my only survival mechanism was my own integrity"

Not so much shamed as terrified and demoralized, Rushdie kept seeking a way out. On December 24, 1990, he made his most imaginative attempt to quash the fatwa: he converted to Islam, issuing a statement saying that any character in *The Satanic Verses* who "casts aspersions...upon the authenticity of the holy Qur'an, or who rejects the divinity of Allah" did not have his support.[11] Muslim leaders dismissed his conversion because he did not withdraw *The Satanic Verses* from publication.[12] Later Rushdie recanted, explaining, "It was deranged thinking. I was more off-balance than I ever had been, but you can't imagine the pressure I was under. I simply thought I was making a statement of fellowship. As soon as I said it I felt as if I had ripped my own tongue out. I realised that my only survival mechanism was my own integrity. People, my friends, were angry with me, and that was the reaction I cared about."[13]

As the Islamic jihad against free speech gathered steam, integrity would be in increasingly short supply. Islamic jihadis never did kill Rushdie (at least not as of this writing), although they tried on several occasions; once a Muslim blew himself up in a British hotel room with a bomb that was meant for Rushdie. Jihadis did manage to murder Hitoshi Igarashi, who had translated *The Satanic Verses* into Japanese. Two other translators of the book, Ettore Capriolo (Italian) and Aziz Nesin (Turkish), and its Norwegian publisher, William Nygaard, were seriously injured in attacks; the attempt on Nesin's life left thirty-seven others dead. Many bookstores that dared to carry the book were firebombed.[14]

These attacks had their intended effect: fear and silence. The British government, while showing an admirable commitment to the freedom of speech by paying for Rushdie's protection, told him not to say anything that might anger the Islamic jihadis who were holding British hostages. British Airways banned him from its airplanes, afraid his presence would endanger airline employees.[15] French and Israeli publishing houses dropped their plans for translations of the book.[16]

Meanwhile, many hastened to demonstrate their willingness to accept Islamic blasphemy laws, or at best their dispiriting failure to grasp what was at stake. The Catholic Church seemed more upset with the blasphemy against Islam than with the death fatwa: the Vatican's semi-official *L'Osservatore Romano* harshly denounced Rushdie, and Cardinal Albert Decourtray of Lyons called *The Satanic Verses* an "insult to religion."[17] U.S. President George H. W. Bush temporized, "However offensive that book may be, inciting murder and offering rewards for its perpetration are deeply offensive to the norms of civilized behavior."[18] The Japanese government offered a stunningly weak observation: "Encouraging murder is not something to be praised."[19]

"It is our duty to form ranks behind him, and our duty to state to the world that if he is ever assassinated, it will become our obligation to stand in his place"

Some were robust in their defense of the freedom of speech. In many circles Rushdie was hailed as a hero, a living martyr for the freedom of speech. Writer Christopher Hitchens noted, "We risk a great deal by ceding even an inch of ground to the book-burners and murderers."[20] Egyptian Nobel laureate Naguib Mahfouz denounced Khomeini's fatwa as "intellectual terrorism"—although several years later, under pressure himself from Islamic hardliners (who ultimately stabbed and seriously injured him), he denounced Rushdie's book as "insulting" to Islam, but he still condemned the death sentence.[21] Novelist Norman Mailer was more bombastic, declaring his willingness to die for the freedom of speech, saying of Rushdie,

> It is our duty to form ranks behind him, and our duty to state to the world that if he is ever assassinated, it will become our obligation to stand in his place. If he is ever killed for a folly, we must be killed for the same folly.... For if one writer can be killed on a hit contract, and all concerned get away with it, then we may be better off being hit each of us, one by one, in future contracts, until our chiefs in the Western world may be finally aroused by the shocking spectacle of our willingness, even though we are selfish creative artists, to be nonetheless martyred in a cause.[22]

Some thought Mailer's words rang hollow. Andy Ross, whose Berkeley, California, bookstore was bombed, denounced Mailer for "spouting off right and left every time you turned on the TV. I mean, there he was probably sitting in a fancy penthouse somewhere, telling those of us who were actually out there on the front lines about how it's our moral responsibility to sell the book and if we don't, we are a bunch of cowards."[23]

But the fact that Mailer was willing to stand publicly with Rushdie was a good thing: not all members of the Western intelligentsia did so, and even in 1989, some in the West thought Rushdie deserved everything he got. When asked if the Iranians were within their rights to kill Rushdie, UCLA professor Georges Sabbagh, director of the university's Near East Studies Center, said simply, "Why not?"[24]

Pop star Cat Stevens, who had recently converted to Islam and taken the name Yusuf Islam, went even farther, saying of a burning effigy of Rushdie, "I would have hoped that it'd be the real thing."[25]

Natalie Merchant of the alternative rock band 10,000 Maniacs, which had had a hit with a version of Stevens' "Peace Train" in 1987, refused to play the song after Yusuf Islam expressed his support for the death sentence on Rushdie, and even had it removed from U.S. copies of the group's album *In My Tribe*.[27] When I saw 10,000 Maniacs in concert in 1989, Merchant told the crowd that she knew they wanted the group to play "Peace Train," but that they were no longer going to do so since "Cat Stevens has gone insane." The audience applauded wildly.

It may have been the high-water mark of pop culture support for the freedom of speech.

Meanwhile Kalim Siddiqui, director of the Muslim Institute in London, appearing with Yusuf Islam on a British television discussion of the Rushdie fatwa, expressed sentiments that would become increasingly common in the West. "I wouldn't kill him," he said of Rushdie, "but I'm sure that there are very many people in this country prepared at the moment. If they

NO LONGER RIDING THE PEACE TRAIN

. . .

"I might ring somebody who might do more damage to him than he would like. I'd try to phone the Ayatollah Khomeini and tell him exactly where this man is."[26]

—Yusuf Islam (the former Cat Stevens), explaining what he would do if he encountered Salman Rushdie could lay their hands on Rushdie, he would be dead. As a British citizen, I have a duty, if you like, a social contract with the British state, not to break British law. We are not a pacifist religion. We don't turn the other cheek. We hit back."[28]

Siddiqui did not explain how a book that contained material that he disliked constituted a "hit" severe enough to warrant "hit[ting] back" with violence. He took that for granted, and so did more and more people in the West in the decades following the Rushdie fatwa.

Nonetheless, over the years Rushdie was laden with honors. In June 2007, he was knighted for "service to literature." Amid worldwide Muslim protest, British Home Secretary John Reid defended the honor—and the principle of free speech: "We have a right to express opinions and a tolerance of other people's point of view, and we don't apologise for that."[29]

But there were already many people in the West apologizing for exactly that.

"There is no more Molly"

The announcement in the *Seattle Weekly* was laconic: "You may have noticed that Molly Norris' comic is not in the paper this week. That is because there is no more Molly."[30]

Molly Norris was still alive, but she would never be seen or heard from again, at least by that name, because of a chain of events that started with Comedy Central's satirical cartoon television show *South Park*. On April 14, 2010, the show, which had previously mocked Moses, Jesus, and Buddha, depicted Muhammad, the prophet of Islam, in a bear costume. The following day, the U.S. Islamic group Revolution Muslim issued a warning to South Park creators Matt Stone and Trey Parker: "We have to warn Matt and Trey that what they are doing is stupid, and they will probably wind up like Theo van Gogh for airing this show. This is not a threat, but a warning of the reality of what will likely happen to them."[31] A Muslim had murdered van Gogh on a street in Amsterdam in 2004 for the crime of criticizing the treatment of Muslim women under Islamic law in his film *Submission.*

Revolution Muslim member Younus Abdullah Muhammad explained that the warning to Stone and Parker "was intended in a principle that's deeply rooted in the Islamic religion, which is called commanding the good and forbidding the evil."[33] This principle apparently mandated killing those who were perceived to have insulted Muhammad and forbidding people to draw him, in accord with Sharia blasphemy restrictions.

Comedy Central backed down: the subsequent episode of *South Park* covered over the cartoon of Muhammad with a large "CENSORED" graphic; his name was bleeped over in the soundtrack. Stone and Parker noted, "After we delivered the show, and prior to broadcast, Comedy Central placed numerous additional audio bleeps throughout the episode." They revealed that Comedy Central was not streaming the original episode on its website, as it did with other episodes. The writers added, "In the 14 years we've been doing 'South Park' we have never done a show that we couldn't stand behind. We delivered our version of the show to Comedy Central, and they made a determination to alter the episode."[34]

Molly Norris was unhappy with Comedy Central's cowardice. On April 20, 2010, the same day the censored *South Park* episode ran, she posted on her website an image of a poster reading, "In light of the recent veiled (ha!) threats aimed at the creators of the television show South Park (for depicting Mohammed in a bear suit) by bloggers on Revolution Muslim's website, we hereby deemed May 20, 2010 as the first annual 'Everybody Draw Mohammed Day.'"[36]

> ## ANSWERING SPEECH WITH VIOLENCE
>
> - - -
>
> "If there is no check in the freedom of your words, then let your hearts be open to the freedom of our actions."[32]
>
> —telling quotation from Osama bin Laden included in the threat to *South Park* creators Matt Stone and Trey Parker

JETTISONING FREE SPEECH

• • •

The *South Park* episode's closing speech "about intimidation and fear...didn't mention Muhammad at all but it got bleeped too."[35]

—from Matt Stone and Trey Parker's statement on Comedy Central's censorship of their work

Interviewed on a Seattle radio show, Norris explained that she had called for "Everybody Draw Mohammed Day" because "as a cartoonist, I just felt so much passion about what had happened...it's a cartoonist's job to be non-PC."[37]

But Norris quickly made an about-face, posting on her website on April 26, "I am NOT involved in 'Everybody Draw Mohammd [sic] Day!'"[38] She added, "I made a cartoon that went viral and I am not going with it. Many other folks have used my cartoon to start sites, etc. Please go to them as I am a private person who draws stuff."[39]

It wasn't enough. "On the insistence of top security specialists at the FBI," the *Seattle Weekly* explained in September 2010, "she is, as they put it, 'going ghost': moving, changing her name, and essentially wiping away her identity. She will no longer be publishing cartoons in our paper or in *City Arts* magazine, where she has been a regular contributor. She is, in effect, being put into a witness-protection program—except, as she notes, without the government picking up the tab."[40] All this was necessary because of "the appalling fatwa issued against her this summer, following her infamous 'Everybody Draw Mohammed Day' cartoon."[41]

And that was that. Unlike in Rushdie's case, the threats against Norris never became front page news. Her cause did not become *célèbre*. Also unlike Rushdie, she had to foot the bill for her security measures: no government was rushing to her aid. The difference was not due entirely to the fact that Rushdie had already been an internationally notable writer at the time of the publication of *The Satanic Verses* and Norris was merely an obscure cartoonist for a local weekly; nor could it be attributed entirely to the fact that Rushdie's fatwa came from a head of state while Norris' was issued by a little-known gang of Muslim thugs.

The relative indifference to Norris' fate was in large part attributable to a weakening in the societal commitment to free speech between 1989 and 2010. During that time, it was increasingly accepted that the proper response to jihadis' threats over speech that offended them was to back down and give them what they wanted. That Islamic jihadists could force an American citizen into hiding for exercising her freedom of speech was bad enough; that her cause aroused only indifference from the media and the nation's leading officials was even worse.

As lost as Norris' identity was the fact that, as whimsical as it was, her "Everybody Draw Mohammed Day" announcement made a serious point: Islamic supremacists were threatening to murder people—Parker and Stone, European cartoonists Kurt Westergaard and Lars Vilks, and anyone else who dared to draw Muhammad. But what would happen if *everyone* decided to draw him? The thugs couldn't possibly kill us all, could they?

For her pains, Norris became a living (if invisible) illustration of how right her point was in the first place. It was precisely because not enough other people were willing to draw Muhammad, or to stand up for the free speech rights of those who did, that she was forced to disappear. By 2010, the Western political and media elites were falling over themselves to abandon the freedom of speech in the face of Muslim threats.

And it was only going to get much, much worse.

"Of course we have a right to draw what we want, but we also have an obligation not to be irresponsibly provocative"

On the evening of May 3, 2015, I was standing next to Pamela Geller at the venue of our just-concluded American Freedom Defense Initiative/Jihad

Watch Muhammad Art Exhibit and Cartoon Contest in Garland, Texas, when one of our security team ran in and told us that there had been a shooting outside. It is safe to say that if the jihadis had succeeded in their aims, we would both be dead.

Instead, as the audience was led to another area and the outside of the building was swept for bombs and additional jihadis, Geller and I were hurried to a safe room.

Since that day, Pamela Geller has never been safe; she is now the Islamic State's number one target in the United States.

ISIS quickly issued a communiqué on the Garland attack, including this fatwa against Geller:

> The attack by the Islamic State in America is only the beginning of our efforts to establish a wiliyah [administrative district] in the heart of our enemy. Our aim was the khanzeer [pig] Pamela Geller and to show her that we don't care what land she hides in or what sky shields her; we will send all our Lions to achieve her slaughter. This will heal the hearts of our brothers and disperse the ones behind her. To those who protect her: this will be your only warning of housing this woman and her circus show. Everyone who houses her events, gives her a platform to spill her filth are legitimate targets. We have been watching closely who was present at this event and the shooter of our brothers. We knew that the target was protected. Our intention was to show how easy we give our lives for the Sake of Allah.

All this was sensational enough, and the threat was reinforced by the subsequent jihadi attempts on Geller's life.

But the response of Western politicians and pundits was even more disturbing. This time, they were not nearly as disposed to defend the freedom of speech as they had been at the time of the Rushdie fatwa, or even the *Charlie Hebdo* massacre.

"Of course we have a right to draw what we want, but we also have an obligation not to be irresponsibly provocative," said Michael Coren, the ex-Catholic author of *Why Catholics Are Right*.[42]

"It's needlessly provocative," said New York Representative Peter King, whose hearings on Muslim radicalization in 2011 had themselves been widely termed "provocative."[43] King said he thought our event was "insulting someone's religion."[44]

Coren and King were expressing the dominant view. Other, more prominent voices soon piled on, including even voices on the Right such as Bill O'Reilly, Laura Ingraham, and Greta van Susteren (although Sean Hannity, Mark Steyn, *National Review*'s David French, Rich Lowry, and others robustly defended the freedom of speech, as did Megyn Kelly, with a bit less robustness). After being on the receiving end of a chorus of condemnation from the media, Geller was harshly questioned by CNN's Alisyn Camerota. Geller told Camerota, "The fact that we have to spend upwards of $50,000 in security speaks to how dangerous and how in trouble freedom of speech is in this country. And then we have to get on these news shows, and somehow we are, those that are targeted, those that were going to be slaughtered, are the ones who get attacked speaks to how morally inverted this conversation is."[45]

Two days after the event in Garland, future President Donald Trump thundered to Kelly, "I watched Pam earlier, and it really looks like she's just taunting everybody. What is she doing drawing Muhammad? I mean it's disgusting. Isn't there something else they could be doing? Drawing Muhammad?... They can't do something else? They have to be in the middle of Texas doing something on Muhammad and insulting everybody? What is she doing? Why is she doing it? It's probably very risky for her—I don't know, maybe she likes risk? But what the hell is she doing?"[46]

Trump should have known better. Once again it fell to Salman Rushdie to point out what was wrong with this way of thinking. As he explained, the free world had learned the "wrong lessons" from the death fatwa issued against him. "Instead of concluding we need to oppose these attacks on freedom of expression," Rushdie noted, "we believed we should calm them through compromises and ceding."[47]

Rushdie added, "If people weren't being killed right now, if bombs and Kalashnikovs weren't speaking today, the debate would be very different. Fear is being disguised as respect." He said that if he were threatened for insulting Islam today, "these people would not come to my defence and would use the same arguments against me by accusing me of insulting an ethnic and cultural minority."[48] Dozens of writers' opposition to the PEN award to *Charlie Hebdo* were living evidence of the accuracy of Rushdie's analysis.

The dominant line was essentially that if Pamela Geller and I had just left well enough alone, all would have been well. The police officer who was shot in the ankle by one of the jihadis would still be walking without difficulty, and the two jihadis, Ibrahim (formerly Elton) Simpson and Nadir Soofi, would still be breathing air.

But is it realistic to assume that if only we hadn't cooked up this cartoon exhibit, Simpson and Soofi would have been loyal, patriotic, law-abiding American Muslims? Their deadly rage over cartoons was hardly testimony to the compatibility of Islam and the U.S. Constitution.

The erroneous assumption behind the widespread condemnation of Muhammad cartoons is that to make America compatible with Islam, all we have to do is give just a little. What non-Muslims have to give up is the right to draw and publish cartoons of Muhammad. And surely that's not so great a sacrifice. Why insist on being gratuitously "provocative"?

The problem with this rosy little scenario is that the jihadis are already "provoked."

Ibrahim Simpson wasn't "radicalized" by our cartoon contest.

Long before it took place, he was in touch with jihad terrorists who encouraged him to carry out a jihad attack.[49] If he hadn't opted to attack our heavily guarded event, he might have chosen a softer target, as did his fellow Islamic State–inspired jihadists Amedy Coulibaly, who murdered four Jews in the Hyper Cacher kosher supermarket in January of 2015, and Man Haron Monis, who took hostages (of who two were subsequently killed) in the Lindt Chocolat Café in Sydney, Australia, the previous month.

ONCE YOU HAVE PAID HIM THE DANEGELD YOU NEVER GET RID OF THE DANE

But why poke a stick in their eye? Isn't sponsoring cartoon contests and drawing Muhammad just adding fuel to the fire—quite unnecessarily? We have to stand up for our right to draw Muhammad precisely because the jihadis have threatened to kill those who do so, and made good on that threat in January in the Paris offices of the *Charlie Hebdo* satirical magazine. To stop drawing Muhammad in the face of these threats and violence will only send the signal that threats and violence work—and that will bring even more threats and violence.

The reality is that if the gunmen hadn't been "provoked" by the Muhammad cartoons, they would have been "provoked" by something else. What had the Jews in Hyper Cacher done to "provoke" the Muslims? They dared to be Jews. What had the people in the Lindt Chocolat Cafe done to "provoke" the Muslims? Dared to be non-Muslims.

What's more, the Islamic State, to which Simpson pledged allegiance before his attack, is already "provoked," as we have seen in abundance by their repeated threats against the United States and Europe, by the very existence of nations and peoples not subject to Islamic governance.

In the face of this threat, is avoiding being "provocative" really going to accomplish anything?

When the Islamic State boasts of the West's societal and cultural weakness, is it really wise to give them another example of it?

Drawing Muhammad is a crime in Islamic law, not in American law. To refrain from doing so is to accept the authority of Islamic law even over non-Muslims—which is exactly what the jihadis are trying to assert. No wonder they think we're weak.

Representative King was arguably correct that drawing Muhammad is "insulting someone's religion," although the straight-faced depictions of Muhammad marrying a nine-year-old and ordering the murders of his enemies in Islamic texts don't offend Muslims—only drawings of these events do. Many in the West, especially Christians, have said that non-Muslims shouldn't go around gratuitously insulting Muslims' religion. And after all, even though Christianity doesn't mandate death for blasphemy, it still frowns upon it.

Cartoons of Muhammad are not necessarily offensive in themselves; they're mostly only offensive from a Muslim perspective—that of Sharia blasphemy law. This is particularly true of the winning cartoon in our contest, which merely lampoons the idea of threatening people with death, and killing them, for drawing Muhammad. Accepting that these images are insulting requires accepting the premises of Sharia.

And Sharia forbids a great many other things that non-Muslims must not do on pain of offending Muslims: building new houses of worship or repairing old ones, holding authority over Muslims, and more.

Once we begin granting the premise that non-Muslims should not offend Muslims, we are going to end up curtailing a great many more of our behaviors besides drawing cartoons.

It is not an offensive act, but ultimately an act in defense of Western civilization to show Islamic jihadists that their violent threats will not cow me, and that I will not allow violent intimidation to rule the day, and that I will not offend them in a larger sense by treating them as if they were demented children who cannot control their actions and must necessarily kill in the face of being offended.

It was the murderous jihadis who made drawing Muhammad the flash point of the defense of free speech, not Pamela Geller and I. It is they who, by their determination to murder non-Muslims who violate their religious law on this point, have made it imperative that free people signal that they will not submit to them. If we give in to the demand that we conform to this Sharia principle, there will be further demands that we adhere to additional Sharia principles. It is ultimately a question of whether we will submit to Sharia, or stand up for freedom.

At Garland we were standing. In the aftermath, it is clear that a huge segment of the Western political and media elites are ready, if not eager, to kneel, not daring to "provoke" their new masters.

Our stand for the freedom of speech earned us the opprobrium of the elites—and not just those on the Left, but Donald Trump, Bill O'Reilly, Laura Ingraham, and others. If, God forbid, anything does happen to Pamela Geller, we can be sure that the talking heads will look soulfully into the cameras and say something that slyly implies that she had it coming.

The world rallied to proclaim "Je suis Charlie" after the massacre of Muhammad cartoonists in Paris in January. But when those jihadis targeted our Muhammad cartoon event five months later, few were saying "Je suis Pamela Geller." What's the difference? The *Charlie Hebdo* cartoonists were reliably leftist, while Geller is identified with the Right. Conservative pundits and politicians may not defend free speech as robustly as they should, but the Left is positively hostile to our First Amendment freedom of expression.

And now it is clear: the leftist intelligentsia would rather see the freedom of speech restricted, and Sharia censorship imposed, than stand with someone whose opinions they find unacceptable.

Those who understand that the freedom of speech, and free society in general, cannot possibly survive the imposition of censorship to avoid offending a group that reacts with murderous violence to being offended were indeed saying *Je suis Pamela Geller* at the time of the ISIS fatwa against her. But they were very, very, few, and regarded by mainstream analysts as being on the fringe of American political discourse.

The defense of the freedom of speech had become a fringe issue.

"The important thing is that this fatwa is as fresh as ever for Muslims"

Over the years Salman Rushdie gradually emerged from hiding and eventually resumed regular public appearances, although the fatwa remained in force. In 2012 Hassan Sanei, the leader of the Iranian charity that placed the original bounty on Rushdie's head, increased that bounty to two million dollars. He lamented that if only Rushdie had been killed, later perceived insults to Islam would not have materialized: "Surely if the sentence of the Imam had been carried out, the later insults in the form of caricatures, articles and the making of movies would not have occurred. I am adding another $500,000 to the reward for killing Salman Rushdie and anyone who carries out this sentence will receive the whole amount immediately."[50]

Sanei shouldn't have bothered. The Western media was already eagerly becoming Sharia-compliant. The reaction to the Danish cartoons and Molly Norris going into hiding had demonstrated that. The feeble response to the *Charlie Hebdo* massacre and above all to the fatwa against Pamela Geller would make it even clearer. Western media had been tested in their commitment to the freedom of speech, and failed the test. The Iranian mullahs had won without having to dirty their hands with Salman Rushdie's blood.

On February 14, 2014, the twenty-fifth anniversary of the day Khomeini pronounced the death sentence on Rushdie, a senior Muslim cleric in Iran, Ahmad Khatami, declared during a Friday sermon, "The important thing is that this fatwa is as fresh as ever for Muslims. Faithful Muslims are looking for an opportunity to implement Imam's fatwa."[51]

DEFENDING THE FREEDOM OF SPEECH:
MY SPEECH AT THE GARLAND, TEXAS, MAY 3, 2015, MUHAMMAD CARTOON EVENT THAT WAS ATTACKED BY JIHADIS

Geert Wilders mentioned that the PEN Writers Association that was founded in order to defend the freedom of expression is giving an award to the *Charlie Hebdo* cartoonists—Pamela spoke about this as well—and that 145 of the members of PEN, including some very prominent writers—Joyce Carol Oates, who you may've heard of, and some others—have pulled out. Because they say that it is manifesting cultural arrogance. They said that the French manifested cultural arrogance in drawing Muhammad and allowing *Charlie Hebdo* to draw Muhammad.

They don't seem concerned about the cultural arrogance of the assassins who murdered these cartoonists in the name of a blasphemy law that the cartoonists did not hold. They didn't care about that imposition of one culture over another; they only cared that the French were following their own long tradition of free expression.

Now, that's a terrible thing for an organization that's designed to defend the freedom of expression. It's a terrible descent. And it bespeaks a descent in our whole culture in general.

You will see around the room—you probably have already noticed as you were coming in—that we have some of the entries into the cartoon contest blown up. And we also have interspersed some historical images of Muhammad.

Now, it's very noteworthy—take a look as you're going out this evening—take a look at some of these, because you'll find them very interesting. Some of them are ancient Persian images made by Muslims. And nobody got killed. Nobody got death threats. Nobody was called a racist. They depict Muhammad cursing women in hell, they depict Muhammad beheading the Qurayza Jews, of which he massacred between 600 and 900, according to his earliest biographer. These are depictions by Muslims of Muhammad.

Some of them you'll see, his face is covered. But in some of them, he's just depicted as he is in the cartoons that are more contemporary.

Even more important, there are some images you will find from earlier centuries in the West, when we did have more cultural confidence. Dante Alighieri, the author of "The Divine Comedy"—it's a three-part allegory, one of the greatest poems in Western civilization, the great Italian poem. And he goes into hell and then into purgatory, and then into heaven.

And in hell, he meets all these people who've been damned to hell. One of them is Muhammad. Because Dante was a Christian. And he viewed Muhammad as somebody who had tried to turn people away from the truth faith and was thus condemned.

His depiction of Muhammad in hell was made into a fresco which is on the wall of a church in Italy. It's been there for centuries. Now it's under armed guard. It was never under armed guard in the 17th century, the 18th century, the 19th century. Only now.

Why is that? Because now Muslims are, in the first place, much more present in the West than they were. But they're a much more aggressive presence in the West. And that is an aggression fueled in large part by our own cultural weakness.

A very good friend of mine told me right before I left for this event that—you're just poking them in the eye, you're trying to provoke them. You know, why are you doing that? You're the one that's being offensive. And this was a friend, you know, and I was kind of taken aback. And I had to stop and think—well, what exactly is wrong with that?

And what's wrong with that is that this is only offensive because Muslims have made it offensive. This is only something, as Geert Wilders said, that needs armed guards because Muslims will kill you for drawing Muhammad. It would never be offensive otherwise.

Consider this—the murderers of the *Charlie Hebdo* cartoonists had an accomplice. And as they were murdering the cartoonists, the accomplice went to a kosher supermarket in Paris and murdered four Jews. What have they done? They didn't draw Muhammad. How did they offend Muslims? They offended Muslims by being Jewish.

Okay, so we have to not draw Muhammad, because that'll poke them in the eye and offend them. And then we have to not be Jewish, because that will poke them in the eye and offend them. And then what? Okay, I guess pork and alcohol are right out. Okay, and then what? Take—humor, yes.

And the Islamic State—the Islamic State is beheading people and taking sex slaves, and subjugating the Christians under the hegemony of the Islamic law. And they're doing it all on the basis of Koranic directives. And so that's all Islamic. So I guess we can't say a word about that. Because that would poke them in the eye and offend Muslims.

And you see, step by step by step, we're ending up going in the direction of accepting Islamic law. And every Western media outlet that refused to publish the Muhammad cartoons was accepting Islamic blasphemy law.

And so I'd say it's time for a little cultural self-assertiveness. In the 19th century, they didn't have these problems. There's the famous story that I'll close with from the British Raj, the British colonization of India. And in India, the Hindus—not the Muslims, but the Hindus—had the practice of sati, where the widow, the wife of a man who had just died, would be thrown upon his funeral pyre and be burnt to death. And the British outlawed it.

And the Hindu delegation came to General Sir Charles Napier, who was the governor general of the area, and they said to him—you can't outlaw this, this is our culture. And he said—oh, it's your culture, oh. Well then, very well. You live out your culture. But we also have a culture. And our culture is that men who force women to throw themselves on fires will be hanged by the neck until dead.

So you live out your culture, and then we'll live out ours.

In the West, we should be saying exactly that. Yeah, okay, you're going to kill for people who draw Muhammad? Then we will protect people who draw Muhammad. And we will hunt you down and kill you for trying to kill people for drawing Muhammad.

The freedom of speech is not an end in itself. The freedom of speech was put into the Constitution as our fundamental protection against tyranny. If the governing authority or any power that rules in whatever way—and as Pamela noted, you want to know who rules over you, then find out who you cannot criticize. The people who have the clout, the people who have the power—if they are able to silence by the rule of law, by the force of law, those whose opinions they don't like, then a free society is dead. Then they can do whatever they wish unopposed, and dissent is impossible.

And that's what this is all about. This is not about insulting Muslims or offending Muslims or poking them in the eye, or even about drawing Muhammad, ultimately. It's just that that's where they're making the line, and that's where we're going to stand. And we're going to stand against tyranny and for freedom.

WHY WE NEED THE FREEDOM OF SPEECH

. . .

"Two things form the bedrock of any open society—freedom of expression and rule of law. If you don't have those things, you don't have a free country."

—Salman Rushdie[52]

Whether or not Rushdie is ever killed, the fatwa against him is indeed as fresh as ever. Our freedom of speech, on the other hand, is fading. In the years between the Rushdie fatwa of 1989 and the Geller fatwa of 2015, the United States had surrendered almost completely on the principle of free speech—without most people even realizing that it had happened.

Chapter Eight

"CAN'T WE TALK ABOUT THIS?": THE DEATH OF FREE SPEECH IN EUROPE

I n majority-Muslim countries, restrictions on certain kinds of speech and expression are routine. In January 2007 in Qatar, a man went to the Saudi-owned Jarir Bookstore and bought a Winnie the Pooh book for his daughter, only to find that someone had carefully gone through every page and blacked out the title character—lest any young Muslim's developing Islamic sensibilities be offended by the sight of a cartoon of an animal deemed unclean by Islamic law.[1]

This kind of thing happens even in Muslim countries that are widely reputed to be moderate. In Malaysia in 2014, KHL Printing Company, the local printer of the *International New York Times*, blackened out images of the faces of pigs in two photos. A KHL employee explained, "This is a Muslim country so we covered the pigs' eyes. We usually do that for the *International New*

York Times—also for pictures of cigarettes, weapons, guns and nude pictures."[2]

Such censorship has long been taken for granted in Muslim countries. But now it has arrived in Europe.

"When this great writer resorts to outrageous stigmatization of Islam, the limits of what is tolerable are breached"

The Satanic Verses is not the only book that Islamic supremacists hate. In June 2002, the Islamic Center of Geneva called for *The Rage and the Pride*, Italian journalist Oriana Fallaci's masterpiece of righteous anger after the September 11 jihad attacks, to be banned. Swiss Muslim leader Hani Ramadan, grandson of Muslim Brotherhood founder Hassan al-Banna, claimed that Fallaci was "insulting the Muslim community as a whole with her shameful words."[3]

Compliant Swiss authorities tried to have Fallaci extradited to Switzerland to face trial, but failed.[4]

> ## THE FUNDAMENTAL THINGS DON'T APPLY (AS TIME GOES BY)
>
> . . . .
>
> "Freedom of expression is and will remain a fundamental right...but when this great writer [Fallaci] resorts to outrageous stigmatization of Islam, the limits of what is tolerable are breached."
> —the Movement Against Racism and for Friendship between Peoples (MRAP) in France[5]

But authorities in her native Italy attempted to put Fallaci—seventy-five years old and dying of cancer—on trial for "defaming Islam." The complaint came from an Italian convert to Islam with the improbable name of Adel Smith. Smith, president of the Muslim Union of Italy, was never charged with defaming Christianity though he had referred to a crucifix as a "miniature cadaver" during his efforts to have depictions of Christ on the Cross removed from Italian schools.[6]

Smith also demanded that Christians deny aspects of their faith that offended his Islamic sensibilities: He called for the destruction of Giovanni da Modena's fifteenth-century fresco *The Last Judgment* in the cathedral of San Petronio in Bologna, Italy, because that priceless expression of medieval Christianity depicts the Muslim Prophet Muhammad in hell.[7] And in the mother of all frivolous lawsuits, in February 2004 Smith brought suit against Pope John Paul II and Joseph Cardinal Ratzinger, who later became Pope Benedict XVI, for offending Islam by expressing in various writings the opinion—utterly unremarkable from two Christian leaders—that Christianity is preferable to other religions, including Islam.[8]

Smith's suit against Fallaci was hardly less frivolous, but he was able to find a judge willing to play along. Judge Armando Grasso of Bergamo, Italy, ruled that *The Force of Reason*, Fallaci's brilliant follow-up to *The Rage and the Pride*, contained eighteen statements "unequivocally offensive to Islam and Muslims," and that therefore she had to be tried.[9] Smith exulted at Grasso's decision: "It is the first time a judge has ordered a trial for defamation of the Islamic faith. But this isn't just about defamation. We would also like (the court) to recognize that this is an incitement to religious hatred."[10]

Fallaci remarked of the indictment, "When I was given the news, I laughed. Bitterly, of course, but I laughed. No amusement, no surprise, because the trial is nothing else but a demonstration that everything I've written is true."[11] The trial was set for June 2006, but Fallaci, by then living in New York City, made no plans to attend, saying in June 2005, "I don't even know if I will be around next year. My cancers are so bad that I think I've arrived at the end of the road. What a pity. I would like to live not only because I love life so much, but because I'd like to see the result of the trial. I do think I will be found guilty."[12] At a preliminary hearing in June 2006, a judge ruled that Fallaci should indeed stand trial, and set that trial for December 18 of that year.[13] Fallaci died on September 15, 2006, in Florence.

After her death, the European intelligentsia demonstrated just how much they appreciated Fallaci and her stand for the freedom of speech. The obituary in the *Guardian* termed her "notorious for her Islamophobia."[14] The British sociologist Chris Allen, in his 2013 book *Islamophobia*, criticized her for "inferring that Islam should not be in 'our' lands what with it being indeterminably Other."[15] Another book published that same year blamed Fallaci for helping create and reinforce "an anti-Islamic Zeitgeist that has developed and reinvented the assortment of stereotypes about the 'migration question' and generated a specific xenophobia against Muslims."[16] In 2014, an attempt to name a street in Rome after Fallaci ran afoul of two Italian leftist political parties, the Democratic Party (PD) and the Left Ecology Freedom (Sel), which complained that her writings contained "religious hatred."[17]

Clearly the real religious hatred in Europe was coming from other quarters. But no matter how much hostility European Muslims expressed towards non-Muslim culture in general and Christianity in particular, they appeared to be immune from charges that they were engaging in "hate speech."

"Allah weet het beter"

In May 2002, a Dutchman named Volkert van der Graaf shot dead the Dutch politician Pim Fortuyn. Although the mainstream media described van der Graaf as an "animal rights activist," the killer himself explained that he "did it for Dutch Muslims," in view of Fortuyn's outspoken criticism of Islam and opposition to mass Muslim immigration into the Netherlands.[18]

Fortuyn's friend Theo van Gogh, a prominent Dutch intellectual and great grand-nephew of the famous painter, did not share van der Graaf's solicitude for Muslims in the Netherlands. After Fortuyn's death, he became a prominent critic of Islam, penning a book, *Allah Weet Het Beter* (*Allah Knows*

Better), in 2003, and a film, *Submission*, in 2004, which graphically illustrated the plight of women under Islamic law by showing near-naked women with Qur'an verses (in the original Arabic) written on their bodies.

In post-Rushdie Europe, it was perhaps inevitable that van Gogh would receive death threats over *Submission*, but he waved them away, saying that the film itself was "the best protection I could have. It's not something I worry about."[19]

And so it happened on a street in Amsterdam on November 2, 2004. A devout Muslim named Mohammed Bouyeri spotted van Gogh riding on his bicycle, took out a gun, and opened fire. When van Gogh fell to the ground, Bouyeri came running up and began to behead him. In his death throes, van Gogh spoke his last words—words that, if the West surrenders entirely to the global jihad and adopts Islamic blasphemy laws, will serve as the epitaph to free societies: "Can't we talk about this?"[20]

> ## IT'S A REAL MYSTERY
>
> Studiously ignoring the facts of Theo van Gogh's murder, engaging in self-censorship, and foreshadowing what was to become the default response of officials to every jihad attack in the West, Dutch Prime Minister Jan Peter Balkenende announced that "nothing is known about the motive" of the murderer.[22]

The answer was no, but Bouyeri said nothing. His only reply was to stab van Gogh with his bloody knife, attaching a note to the filmmaker's body with the blade. The note contained quotations from the Qur'an and threats to others in the Netherlands whom Bouyeri deemed to have offended Islam. Van Gogh's collaborator on *Submission*, the Somali ex-Muslim Ayaan Hirsi Ali, later recounted, "The letter was addressed to me," telling her that van Gogh had been "executed" for his blasphemous film, and that she would soon be "executed" as well, for her apostasy.[21]

At his trial, Bouyeri flaunted his certainty of his own righteousness. Clutching a copy of the Qur'an, he declared, "I did what I did purely out my beliefs. I want you to know that I acted out of conviction and not that I took his life because he was Dutch or because I was Moroccan and felt insulted.... If I ever get free, I would do it again.... What moved me to do what I did was purely my faith. I was motivated by the law that commands me to cut off the head of anyone who insults Allah and his prophet."[23] He even told van Gogh's grieving mother, "I don't feel your pain. I don't have any sympathy for you. I can't feel for you because I think you're a non-believer."[24]

"Freedom of speech is a cornerstone of the EU's order"

In the face of this horrific attack on the freedom of speech, some Western officials came to the defense of this core principle of any free society. Amsterdam mayor Job Cohen declared, "We will show loud and clear that freedom of speech is important to us."[26]

Two years later, European Commission spokesman Johannes Laitenberger would say, "[F]reedom of speech is a cornerstone of the EU's order as is the freedom and respect of all religions and beliefs, be it Christianity, Islam, Judaism, Buddhism or laicism."[27]

The battle was on: it was free expression versus *Allah weet het beter.* But the "Allah knows better" faction was making steady advances all over Europe.

If the freedom of speech was really a cornerstone of the EU's order, it had a funny way of showing it. In January 2009, Austrian politician Susanne Winter was fined €24,000 ($31,000) for opining that "in today's system" Muhammad would be classified as a "child molester" for marrying a six-year-old girl and consummating the marriage when she was nine, and for criticizing what she called an "Islamic immigration tsunami."[28]

SHUT UP, HE EXPLAINED

Testifying in 2007 at the trial of seven accused jihad terrorists, Bouyeri was asked how a Muslim should respond to someone who insults Islam. He replied, "Off with his head. Slaughter him."[25]

The truth was no defense. It didn't matter in the least that Islamic tradition itself says Muhammad "married Aisha when she was a girl of six years of age, and he consummated that marriage when she was nine years old."[29] He was at that time fifty-four years old. Islamic tradition also depicts Aisha herself recounting that she was six when Muhammad married her and nine when he took her into his household:

> My mother, Umm Ruman, came to me while I was playing in a swing with some of my girl friends. She called me, and I went to her, not knowing what she wanted to do to me. She caught me by the hand and made me stand at the door of the house. I was breathless then, and when my breathing became normal, she took some water and rubbed my face and head with it. Then she took me into the house. There in the house I saw some Ansari [recent Muslim converts] women who said, "Best wishes and Allah's Blessing and a good luck." Then she entrusted me to them and they prepared me (for the marriage). Unexpectedly Allah's Messenger came to me in the forenoon and my mother handed me over to him, and at that time I was a girl of nine years of age.[30]

But none of that mattered at the trials of Winter and another Austrian, human rights activist Elisabeth Sabaditsch-Wolff. In November 2009, Sabaditsch-Wolff gave a seminar about Islam at a political academy known as the Freedom Education Institute. A socialist magazine in Austria called *NEWS* secretly recorded two of her lectures and then had her charged with hate speech.[31]

There was just one problem: Sabaditsch-Wolff hadn't actually engaged in any "hate speech"; her lectures were largely made up of quotations from the Qur'an and other Islamic sources. But even when it became clear that the charge was baseless, Judge Bettina Neubauer didn't dismiss the case, instead she simply suspended the hearings until January 18, 2011—at which point Neubauer told Sabaditsch-Wolff that she was now being charged not only with hate speech, but with "denigration of religious beliefs of a legally recognized religion."[32] Sabaditsch-Wolff was duly found guilty of the latter charge.[33]

Sabaditsch-Wolff was guilty, Neubauer explained, because she had said that Muhammad, the prophet of Islam, "had a thing for little girls."[34] This constituted denigration because while Muhammad consummated his marriage with a nine-year-old girl when he was fifty-four, Islamic sources did not record that he ever showed any interest in other prepubescent girls, and also had adult wives at the same time, so it was false and defamatory to say that he was a pedophile.

Sabaditsch-Wolff was fined 480 ($625) plus the costs of the trial; she vowed to continue to appeal the verdict to the European Court for Human Rights.[35] Her conviction, she said, was "a black day for Austria." The Vienna Federation of Academics called Neubauer's decision 'politically and sentimentally motivated justice" that meant "the end of freedom of expression in Austria."[36]

"I am standing in the dock for the second time. Because I dare to criticize Islam"

The freedom of speech isn't in much better health anywhere else in Europe. In the Netherlands, politician Geert Wilders, leader of the Party for Freedom, was tried in 2010 for inciting hatred and discrimination against Muslims. The charges were based on his short film *Fitna*, which vividly illustrated how Islamic terror attacks were in line with passages of the Qur'an, and also on statements by Wilders criticizing Muhammad and Islam and comparing the Qur'an to *Mein Kampf*. In January 2009, the Amsterdam appeals court ordered the prosecution of Wilders for "inciting hatred and discrimination, based on comments by him in various media on Muslims and their beliefs. The court also considers appropriate criminal prosecution for insulting Muslim worshippers because of comparisons between Islam and Nazism made by Wilders."[37]

With an Orwellian twist, the court claimed that democracy itself mandated the prosecution of Wilders: "In a democratic system, hate speech is considered so serious that it is in the general interest to…draw a clear line."[38]

Wilders asserted, more accurately, that the prosecution was an "attack on the freedom of expression," and observed that "participation in the public debate has become a dangerous activity. If you give your opinion, you risk being prosecuted."[39]

Abdelmajid Khairoun, chairman of the Dutch Muslim Council (NMO), was happy with the prosecution, complaining that "Muslim youngsters who make anti-semitic remarks are prosecuted but Wilders' anti-Islamic remarks go unpunished."[40]

Wilders based his defense on the truthfulness of his words; he submitted a list of desired witnesses that included van Gogh's killer, Mohammed Bouyeri, as well as Britain-based jihad leader Anjem Choudary, Iranian Ayatollahs Ahmad Jannati and Mohammad Yazdi, Islamic scholar

STICKS AND STONES MAY BREAK MY BONES, BUT WORDS WILL NEVER HURT ME

. . . .

"People must know that I, a democratically elected politician who does not employ violence and the like, am being put on trial for speaking my mind and for making a movie [*Fitna*] that simply quotes the Koran itself. There must only be one outcome for this trial, and that is a full acquittal—and if not, Europe will pay a heavy price.… Many of our politicians in Europe are simply afraid; they are appeasers.… There is a lot of fear and a lot of political correctness, and the only way to deal with this is to stand up and not be afraid and not allow yourself to be intimidated."

—Geert Wilders in a 2010 interview[41]

Hans Jansen, ex-Muslim Wafa Sultan, and me. The court disallowed most of these witnesses, frustrating Wilders's attempt to use his prosecution to place Islam and jihad on trial.[42]

Nonetheless, on June 23, 2011, Wilders was acquitted on all charges; Judge Marcel van Oosten appeared somewhat grudging about the verdict, calling Wilders's statements "gross and denigrating," but saying that they were "acceptable within the context of public debate."[43]

Wilders, describing himself as "incredibly happy," commented, "It's not only an acquittal for me, but a victory for freedom of expression in the Netherlands. Now the good news is that it's also legal to be critical about Islam, to speak publicly in a critical way about Islam and this is something that we need because the Islamisation of our societies is a major problem and a threat to our freedom and I'm allowed to say so."[44]

But the thought police were not through with Wilders. He was put on trial again in March 2016 for saying that there should not be more but fewer Moroccans in the Netherlands. Prosecution spokeswoman Ilse de Heer asserted that this new prosecution of Wilders was different from the earlier one because this time Wilders had "targeted a specific race, which is considered a crime.... That is the difference now."[45]

Wilders was found guilty of "inciting discrimination."[46]

Lars Hedegaard, writer, free speech activist, and president of the Danish Free Press Society, was also put on trial for "hate speech" for noting in a December 2009 interview that there were high rates of child rape and wife-beating among Muslims. Although this was true, Hedegaard was charged under Article 266b of the Danish penal code, which mandates a fine or imprisonment for up to two years for anyone who "publicly or with the intent of public dissemination issues a pronouncement or other communication by which a group of persons are threatened, insulted or denigrated due to their race, skin color, national or ethnic origin, religion or sexual orientation."[48]

DEFENDING THE FREEDOM OF SPEECH: OPENING STATEMENT BY GEERT WILDERS AT HIS 2016 TRIAL

Mr President, Members of the Court,

For more than eleven years, I have been living under death threats. Every day, I am reminded of this. Even today. This morning, I was driven here in a convoy of armored cars, with sirens, flashing lights, and surrounded by bodyguards. And not only today, but every day.

I will be brought home in the same way. Home is a safe-house. My office is a shielded room. And when I have to stand in court, it is here, in a bunker at Schiphol.

For more than eleven years already, I have been paying a heavy price. And I think that you as well as I know why. I am paying that price for the same reason as why I am standing in the dock for the second time. Because I dare to criticize Islam and mention the Moroccan problem.

"Freedom is the power that we have over ourselves," said the great Dutch jurist Hugo Grotius. His statue stands at the entrance of the Supreme Court in The Hague. Hugo Grotius is the symbol of Dutch law. But once he was on trial himself. He was sentenced to life because he had fought on the side of Johan van Oldenbarnevelt for Dutch freedoms. But Grotius escaped in a coffin and fled to Antwerp.

Sometimes I wish that I could escape myself. But I know that I cannot. I would have to pay a price which I do not want to pay. I would have to shut up. And I cannot. I do not want that. And I will not do it. Freedom of expression is the only freedom I still have.

And, forgive me, I will never give it up.

So here I stand again.

And I honestly think it is a disgrace that I have to stand here.

Millions of people in this country and abroad think so, too.

I do not ask for your compassion. But now that I am forced to stand here, I ask of you that you give me what I am entitled to: a fair trial. I ask that Lady Justice be blindfolded.

And I fear this will not be the case.

As my lawyer explained, over half of the legal complaints lodged against me proved to be false when they were investigated. People thought they were voting in elections, instead of pressing charges. Or they did not know my name. Or they were illiterate or did not recognize their signature. Or they said they did not feel discriminated against, even though it said so in their complaint. I hope that you will never be accused of something that you did not do. Or they got assistance from mosques or Labor politicians. Or they were told by the police that the officers also felt uncomfortable with Wilders' statements. Or they were told by the mosque administration that they had to fill out the forms the police was going to bring.

Mr President, Members of the Court, this is nothing but deception, manipulation, intimidation, ignorance, it is a scam. It is incredibly shocking.

And that the prosecutor just said that this nothing to worry about is a disgrace.

Because in front of you stands a politician.

And he is being prosecuted because he has voiced a political opinion.

Why did I speak about fewer Moroccans?

The honest answer is because I want fewer Moroccans in the Netherlands.

The Netherlands has a huge Moroccan problem. It is my job as a democratically elected representative of the people to honestly identify the problems in our country.

How and why do I want to get fewer Moroccans in our country has already been written down in the PVV election platform since 2006: We want to stop immigration from non-Western immigrants, and therefore also of Moroccans, to promote voluntary repatriation, and to denaturalize criminals with a dual nationality and expel them from the Netherlands. And before, during and after the contested election night, I have repeatedly explained this in front of many cameras and microphones.

I did not say "All Moroccans must leave the country" or "Moroccans are no good," but I advocated "fewer Moroccans". Because that is my opinion, that is what I want, and what many millions of Dutch want together with me.

The Public prosecutor is trying to catch me, but he is selectively shopping.

If I would have advocated fewer Syrians, then I would not be standing here today. Or I would not stand here alone, but together with Prime Minister Rutte and almost all the government leaders in Europe. Because today they all want to get fewer Syrians.

The Public Prosecution is also applying double standards. And there are many examples of this.

How quiet was it when, earlier, politicians from the Labor Party spoke about Moroccan c*nts (Mr Oudkerk), about humiliating Moroccans (Mr Spekman) and about Moroccan boys who have an ethnic monopoly on nuisance (Mr. Samson). Why were they not being prosecuted?

And how quiet was it when a Turkish member of the Dutch Parliament (Mr Öztürk) compared me with a tumor and said "One has to fight him," and likened me to Hitler. Where were the mayors then who spoke shame of it and led processions of people going to press charges?

Where was the Public Officer's press spokesperson when a Labor Party chairman (Mr Den Hertog) said that he hopes that I die of a heart attack, but that if a bullet is needed then it would have to big enough to engrave from the grateful people on it?

Where was the outrage of the Prime Minister when a D66 member (Mr Mohammed) said he would put a bullet through my head and cut me open and feed me to the pigs?

And why was there no prosecution of the former police commissioner of Amsterdam, Mr Van Riessen, who said about me, and I quote: "Basically one would feel inclined to say: let's kill him, just get rid of him now and he will never surface again." End of quote.

Where were the preprinted declaration forms then?

What a duplicity. What a selective indignation.

And when someone is taken to court, such as the Moroccan rapper who said that he, and I quote, "hates these fucking Jews even more than the Nazis", end of quote, then he is acquitted, because then suddenly his words are covered by freedom of speech.

These double standards and this hypocrisy by both politicians and the Public Prosecutor turn this trial into a political trial. The leader of the largest opposition party, who proves too strong to defeat in Parliament, must be neutralized. That is a disgrace and I hope you will not allow yourselves to be taken advantage of.

Because the problems of which I speak will not go away by keeping silent about them.

Silence is not an option.

Silence is cowardly.

Silence is betrayal.

If I, as the political leader of my party, during an election gathering of my party, am not allowed to say what has been written down in my party platform for a decade, then this is absolute madness and then one has to convict me.

My opinions will not change. And one will not be able to silence me.

I have been deprived of my freedom for over eleven years and the only freedom I still have is my freedom of speech. Nobody will be able to rob me of it.

But obviously, I hope that you will leave the political and public debate to the political and public debate, that you will not turn this courtroom into a political forum, and that you acquit me.

On August 24 last year, in the television program "Looking into the Soul", I heard one of your fellow penal judges, Mr Hermans, say that voting for the PVV is—I quote—a "huge contra-indication to the profession of judge." Excuse me that this worries me.

And I am even more worried because, of all people, it happened to be one of you three, Mrs Van Rens, who on August 17 last year in the television program "Looking into the Soul" criticized political views of my party, which is allowed of course. She said that she opposes minimum sentences and expelling illegal immigrants. But she said even more. Mrs Van Rens also criticized the judicial decision during my previous trial to approve our objection to the court. She said she did not understand that the objection was assigned by fellow judges because, and I quote: "there was no proper basis in penal law to allocate the objection."

Mr President, Members of the Court, there has been only one single judge in the Netherlands who has openly criticized the judicial decision in favor of me. Only one. And she is exactly the judge opposite me in court today.

Madam Judge, I hope you understand that I am saying this and that I do not find this very reassuring. It would do you credit if you would withdraw from this case and I strongly call on you to do so.

Mr President, Members of the Court.

I conclude.

I meant what I have said, I spoke on behalf of millions of Dutch, I retract nothing and have no regrets. I have said what I think and I will continue to do so. Always.

But I hate no one, I do not incite any hatred and I abhor everything that has to do with discrimination.

That is the truth. Only in a dictatorship, speaking the truth is a crime.

And only in a dictatorship, the opinion of millions of people is criminalized.

I stand here before three judges, but actually it should be the 17 million Dutch who should judge my political expressions.

So I ask you: Let freedom of expression prevail.

Let the Netherlands remain a free country.

Acquit me.

Thank you very much.[47]

Hedegaard's legal ordeal went on for several years, with his persecutors claiming that his remarks suggested that all Muslims were child molesters and wife beaters. He was acquitted in January 2011, but prosecutors appealed, and a superior court found him guilty in May 2011. His case made it all the way to the Danish Supreme Court, where Hedegaard delivered an eloquent defense of the freedom of speech in connection with Islam.

In April 2012, the Danish Supreme Court acquitted Hedegaard on a technicality. While declaring that his statements did indeed violate Danish law, the court ruled that Hedegaard had not been proven to have made them "publicly," as he wasn't aware that his remarks would be published. Hedegaard was "pleased that the Supreme Court has handed down a judgment in accordance with the evidence that was presented in the District Court and High Court," but he noted the ominous implications: "This judgment cannot be interpreted as a victory for freedom of speech. Article 266b, under which I was charged, remains unchanged. It remains a disgrace to any civilized society and is an open invitation to frivolous trials. Thus, we still have no right to refer to truth if we are indicted under this article."[50]

DEFENDING THE FREEDOM OF SPEECH: LARS HEDEGAARD'S SPEECH BEFORE THE DANISH SUPREME COURT

Honourable Supreme Court,

My attorney has presented juridical arguments to the effect that I must be acquitted and I shall refrain from elaborating.

However, allow me to express my quiet bafflement that somebody can claim that it has been my intention to accuse every last Muslim father in the world of abusing his children—particularly in light of the fact that I have carefully explained that it was never my intention to disseminate such an absurd contention.

For precisely that reason, I would have welcomed an opportunity to review the statements I now stand accused of having uttered before they were placed on the Internet. If the interviewer had fulfilled this basic journalistic obligation, I would have demanded that my remarks be corrected so as to reflect my true opinions and the prosecutor could have saved the trouble of dragging me through the courts.

I am even more baffled at one of the claims about my person that has been circulated in connection with this case, namely that I am a racist. I have never been, I am not now and I shall never be a racist. On the contrary, all my life I have opposed racist attitudes, by which I mean hatred towards and denigrating speech about people due their descent, skin colour or other so-called racial characteristics—in other words, antipathy against or ill treatment of people due to circumstances over which they have no control.

Islam is not a race and therefore criticism of Islam cannot be racism.

Islam, which lurks behind this entire case, has been described from a variety of viewpoints. Some say that it is a religion, others that is an all-encompassing ideology that contains a religion, still others emphasise its cultural norms, its culturally transmitted customs and practices. Some even maintain that Islam is so multifaceted that it is impossible to describe it.

But regardless of one's approach, it must be clear that Islam is not a hereditary human attribute.

If our Western freedom means anything at all, we must insist that every grown-up person is responsible for his or her beliefs, opinions, culture, habits and actions.

We enjoy political freedom and we enjoy freedom of religion. This implies a largely unlimited right to disseminate one's political persuasion and religious beliefs. That is as it should be. But the price we all have to pay for this freedom is that others have a right to criticise our politics, our religion and our culture.

Islamic spokesmen have the freedom to advocate their concept of society, which implies the introduction of a theocracy governed by god-given laws, i.e. sharia, the abolition of man-made laws and by implication freedom of expression and democracy. They are free to think that women are inferior to men as concerns their rights and their pursuit of happiness. They are even entitled to disseminate such opinions.

I cannot recall a single instance in this country where an Islamic spokesman has been prosecuted for saying that, of course, sharia will become the law of the land once the demographic and political realities make it possible. This despite the fact that we have several examples of, e.g., imams who have openly declared that the imposition of theocracy is a religious duty incumbent on all believers.

In return, these theocrats and sharia-advocates must accept the right of those who believe in democracy, free institutions and human equality to criticise Islam and to oppose its dissemination and the atavistic cultural norms practiced by some Muslims.

It is this right—I would even say duty—to describe, criticise and oppose a totalitarian ideology that I have tried to exercise to the best of my ability.

My speech and my writings have had no other purpose than to alert my fellow citizens to the danger inherent in the Islamic concept of the state and the law.

I have made no secret of the fact that I consider this fight for our liberties to be the most important political struggle of our time.

I would not be able to live with my guilty conscience if—out of fear of public condemnation and ridicule—I refrained from telling the truth as I see it.

And regardless of the outcome of this trial, I intend to continue my struggle for free speech and against totalitarian concepts of any stripe.[49]

"Destroying our country"

The persecutions of Fallaci, Wilders, Winter, Sabaditsch-Wolff, and Hedegaard were the highest-profile free speech cases in Europe, but there were others:

France: Michel Houellebecq, a novelist, was prosecuted but ultimately acquitted in 2002 for saying that Islam was "the stupidest religion" and that the Qur'an was "badly written."[51] Even literary criticism was apparently now "hate speech."

France: Brigitte Bardot, the film legend, was charged with "inciting racial hatred" for making statements critical of Muslims and Islam and was found guilty no fewer than five times. In June 2008, she was given a fine of 15,000 euros (around $23,000) for observing that Muslims in France were "destroying our country."[52] No one seems to have dared to point out that what was really destroying the country were fines of that size for speech that was considered beyond the bounds of acceptable discourse.

France: Marine Le Pen, leader of the National Front party, was accused in 2010 of "inciting discrimination, violence or hatred toward a group of people based on their religious beliefs" after she compared the de facto enforcement of Sharia law in areas of France to the German occupation during World War II: "If you want to talk about the occupation, let's talk about that, by the way, because here we are talking about the occupation of our space. It's an occupation of entire stretches of territory, of neighborhoods where religious law is applied. This is an occupation. Sure, there are no armored vehicles, no soldiers, but it's still an occupation, and it weighs on the inhabitants." For that she faced a stiff fine and a jail term, but in December 2015 she was acquitted on the grounds that she hadn't meant to refer to all Muslims. The Collective Against Islamophobia in France, one of the groups that had filed complaints against Le Pen, groused, "This acquittal shows, once again, the legitimization and normalization of Islamophobia and of the hate speech that conveys it."[53] In reality, it was a rare victory—rare in contemporary Europe, that is—for the freedom of speech.

France: In 2010, writer Renaud Camus gave a speech about how multiculturalism was a Trojan Horse for the French people. He was convicted of "Islamophobia" and fined 4,000 euros.[54]

France: Marie Laforêt, a singer and actress, was prosecuted in 2011 over a job advertisement she placed on an Internet website. The ad said that "people with allergies or orthodox Muslims" need not apply—because she owned a dog. Dogs are considered unclean under Islamic law.[55]

The Netherlands: Gregorius Nekschot, a satirical cartoonist, was arrested in 2008 for cartoons that Dutch authorities thought were offensive to Muslims. The charges were thrown out in 2010, but Nekschot, weary of the ordeal, stopped drawing cartoons.[56]

Denmark: Jesper Langballe, a Member of Parliament, was convicted of hate speech in 2010 for noting (correctly) that among Muslim families honor killings and sex abuse are disturbingly common. Truth is no defense in Denmark.[57]

Finland: Jussi Kristian Halla-aho, a politician, was charged in 2009 with "incitement against an ethnic group" and "breach of the sanctity of religion" for saying that Islam was a religion of pedophilia—a reasonable assertion in light of the facts that Muhammad did consummate his marriage with a nine-year-old when he was fifty-four and that his example is the model for normative Muslim behavior.[58]

Those who dared to speak out against jihad terror and Islamic supremacism in Europe didn't face challenges only from legal authorities and Islamic jihadists. There was also self-censorship on the part of publishers. The French translation of ex-Muslim Hamed Abdel-Samad's book *Der Islamische Faschismus: Eine Analyse* (*Islamic Fascism: An Analysis*) was dropped at the last minute by its publisher, Piranha, not just because of threats, but because the book would aid the "extreme right."[59] And in Germany, novelist Gabriele

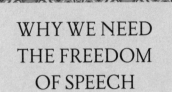

WHY WE NEED THE FREEDOM OF SPEECH

• • •

"To view the opposition as dangerous is to misunderstand the basic concepts of democracy. To oppress the opposition is to assault the very foundation of democracy."

—Aung San Suu Kyi[63]

Brinkmann lost the publisher of her novel *Wem Ehre Geburt* (*To Whom Honor Gives Birth*) because the book could be seen as "insulting to Muslims."[60]

"I believe that respecting the sensitivities of people of different religions or cultures is a step forward towards integration"

Special accommodation of Muslim sensibilities has become the cultural norm in Europe. Often, Muslims don't even need to complain: the solicitude for their feelings has been so thoroughly inculcated in the European populace that it regularly trumps free speech. In November 2015 in Italy, a school headmaster, Marco Parma of the Garofani school in Rozano, seeing offense to Muslims in a hallowed Christian practice, canceled the school's annual Christmas carol concert. Explained Parma, "I believe that respecting the sensitivities of people of different religions or cultures is a step forward towards integration," he said. "This is a multiethnic school."[61]

What about the sensitivities of Italians who wanted to sing Christmas carols? Parma didn't address them, but in the storm of indignation that followed, Parma was forced to resign. By the next summer, however, as Muslim migrants flooded into Italy, attitudes had changed—at least among some Italians. In the summer of 2016, even Christian prayer in a Christian church were deemed offensive to Muslims. Members of the Catholic charity Caritas told parishioners at St. Anthony church in Ventimiglia not to recite the rosary aloud, but to pray in silence so as not to offend the Muslim migrants who were being housed at the church.[62]

It was clear who was in charge.

Chapter Nine

CATHOLICS AGAINST FREE SPEECH

Europe was still reeling from the battle over the *Jyllands-Posten* Muhammad cartoons when the enemies of free speech opened another front in their war. Pope Benedict XVI, who had granted Oriana Fallaci her first private audience as pope and delighted her with what she believed was his comprehensive understanding of the threat mass Muslim migration posed to European civilization and the free world, unwittingly touched off international riots with remarks he made about Islam. On September 12, 2006 in Regensburg, Germany, the Pope delivered a thoughtful, carefully argued, and nuanced address about faith, reason, violence, and the relationships between the three; in the course of it, he quoted the fourteenth-century Byzantine emperor Manuel II Paleologus dismissing Islam in brusque terms: "Show me just what Muhammad brought that was new, and there you will find things only

THE OLD GOOD COP– BAD COP ROUTINE

"...we are hopeful that such statements and such positions would not be stated in order to not allow tension and distrust and recriminations to brew between the Muslim as well as the West."[4]

—Egyptian Foreign Minister Ahmed Aboul Gheit on the pope's Regensburg address, expressing in a more sophisticated way the same message Bouyeri had expressed by murdering Theo van Gogh: no, we can't talk about this, the West must simply submit to Islamic sensibilities

evil and inhuman, such as his command to spread by the sword the faith he preached."[1]

Benedict then argued that violence was incompatible with the divine nature: "God is not pleased by blood—and not acting reasonably is contrary to God's nature. Faith is born of the soul, not the body. Whoever would lead someone to faith needs the ability to speak well and to reason properly, without violence and threats.... To convince a reasonable soul, one does not need a strong arm, or weapons of any kind, or any other means of threatening a person with death."[2]

Mohammed Bouyeri would have disagreed.

Egypt's Foreign Minister, Ahmed Aboul Gheit, fumed, "This was a very unfortunate statement and it is a statement that shows that there is a lack of understanding of real Islam."[3]

In the midst of condemnations of Pope Benedict after his Regensburg address, European Commission spokesman Johannes Laitenberger unexpectedly came out strongly for the freedom of speech, saying, "Reactions which are disproportionate and which are tantamount to rejecting freedom of speech are unacceptable.... "[5] In fact the EU spokesman offered the pope more support than many of his fellow Christian clergy.

The Coptic Pope, Shenouda III, spoke out against Pope Benedict, declaring that "any remarks which offend Islam and Muslims are against the teachings of Christ."[6] He was speaking as the head of an Egyptian Church that had suffered over thirteen centuries of persecution, discrimination, and harassment from Muslims. The Coptic Church has long since internalized the idea that complaining about violence or oppression from Muslims only makes matters worse, and that the prudent course of action for Christians who want to survive is to keep quiet and say nothing that could possibly offend Muslims.

There were Catholics who agreed with him, though. Cardinal Jorge Maria Bergoglio, who in 2013 would succeed Pope Benedict XVI as Pope Francis, apparently was furious at words that he thought would harm Catholic-Muslim dialogue: "Pope Benedict's statements don't reflect my own opinions. These statements will serve to destroy in 20 seconds the careful construction of a relationship with Islam that Pope John Paul II built over the last twenty years."[7] Bergoglio did not point to any fruits of that "relationship with Islam" in protecting Christians from persecution by Muslims. Actually, he could not have done so, as the interfaith dialogue has borne no such fruits.

In fact the "relationship with Islam" that Bergoglio valued so highly did not prevent Muslims enraged at Benedict from terrorizing Christians across the world. In the West Bank and Gaza, Muslims opened fire at one church and firebombed four others.[8] Two Muslims in Mogadishu murdered an elderly Italian nun, Sister Leonella Sgorbati. A jihadi declared, "There is a very high possibility the people who killed her were angered by the Catholic Pope's recent comments against Islam."[9] Muslim leader Sheikh Mukhtar Robow acknowledged the "concrete possibility" that the murder was "a reprisal for the Pope's remarks on Islam."[10]

In Iraq, several Christians were murdered and

NOW WE CAN SEE THE FORCE OF YOUR ARGUMENT

One Muslim wrote on the door of the Chaldean Church of the Holy Spirit in Mosul, Iraq, "If the Pope does not apologise, we will bomb all churches, kill more Christians and steal their property and money."[12]

a number of churches firebombed; Muslims also threw a hand grenade at a priest's car.[11]

Muslims kidnapped Assyrian Christian priest Ameer Iskander and demanded a condemnation of the Pope's remarks from the Assyrian church and a $350,000 ransom. Iskander was eventually beheaded.[13]

Malaysia's Prime Minister Abdullah Ahmad Badawi placed the responsibility for the Muslim rage and violence solely upon the pope, who, he said, "must not take lightly the spread of outrage that has been created. The Vatican must now take full responsibility over the matter and carry out the necessary steps to rectify the mistake."[15]

What kind of steps Badawi had in mind was made clear when Pakistani President Pervez Musharraf called for the criminalization of "defamation of Islam" at the UN.[16]

A group of Muslim clerics in Gaza issued an invitation to the pope to convert to Islam—or else: "We want to use the words of the Prophet Muhammad and tell the pope: '*Aslim Taslam*'"—that is, embrace Islam and you will be safe.[18] The implication, of course, was that the one to whom this "invitation" is addressed would *not* be safe if he declined the invitation.

Benedict did not convert. But dismayed by the reaction to his speech, he apologized: "I am deeply sorry for the reactions in some countries to a few passages of my address at

TRUSTWORTHY, LOYAL, HELPFUL, FRIENDLY, COURTEOUS, KIND, OBEDIENT, CHEERFUL, THRIFTY, BRAVE, CLEAN, AND REVERENT

A jihad group calling itself the Islamic Salafist Boy Scout Battalions vowed that it would murder every Christian in Iraq if the Pope had not apologized to Muhammad within three days.[14]

the University of Regensburg, which were considered offensive to the sensibility of Muslims. These in fact were a quotation from a medieval text, which do not in any way express my personal thought.... I hope that this serves to appease hearts and to clarify the true meaning of my address, which in its totality was and is an invitation to frank and sincere dialogue, with great mutual respect."[19]

The Pope also added a footnote to the Vatican text of his speech: "In the Muslim world, this quotation has unfortunately been taken as an expression of my personal position, thus arousing understandable indignation. I hope that the reader of my text can see immediately that this sentence does not express my personal view of the Qur'an, for which I have the respect due to the holy book of a great religion. In quoting the text of the Emperor Manuel II, I intended solely to draw out the essential relationship between faith and reason. On this point I am in agreement with Manuel II, but without endorsing his polemic."[20]

> ## DON'T SAY MUSLIMS ARE INTOLERANT, OR THEY'LL KILL YOU
>
> • • •
>
> "Anyone who describes Islam as a religion as intolerant encourages violence."
> —Pakistani Foreign Ministry spokeswoman Tasnim Aslam, speaking on the Regensburg controversy, apparently without irony[17]

"Repeated negative references to Islam"

Pope Benedict would enrage Muslims again five years later, albeit without the same death toll. After a jihad terrorist murdered twenty-three Christians in a church in Alexandria in 2011, Benedict decried the "terrorism" that had "brutally affected worshippers" and the "strategy of violence" against Christians that "offends God and the whole of humanity." He called for the Christians of the Middle East to be protected.[21]

Ahmed al-Tayeb, the Grand Imam of al-Azhar, the most prestigious and influential institution in the Sunni Muslim world, was furious. He railed at Benedict for his "interference" and "unacceptable intervention in the affairs of Egypt," accusing the pontiff of "creating a negative political reaction in the East in general and in Egypt in particular." [22] He challenged the Pope: "I hope that His Holiness Benedict XVI will decide to send a message to the Islamic world. A message that might reestablish the points of trust, and dispel the origins of the misunderstandings." [23] Al-Azhar also broke off dialogue with the Vatican, denouncing Pope Benedict's "repeated negative references to Islam and his claims that Muslims persecute those living among them in the Middle East." [24]

But by September 2013, things had changed. That was when al-Azhar announced that Benedict's successor, Pope Francis, had sent a personal message to al-Tayeb. According to al-Azhar, Francis had declared his respect for Islam and his desire to achieve "mutual understanding between the world's Christians and Muslims in order to build peace and justice." [25] At the same time, al-Tayeb met with the Apostolic Nuncio to Egypt, Mgr. Jean-Paul Gobel, and told him in no uncertain terms that speaking about Islam in a negative manner was a "red line" that must not be crossed. [26] And so in May 2016, Francis welcomed al-Tayeb to the Vatican, embraced him, and was careful not to cross any "red line." [27]

So Pope Benedict had condemned a jihad attack, one that al-Azhar also condemned, and yet al-Azhar suspended dialogue because of the Pope's condemnation. [28] Then Pope Francis wrote to the Grand Imam of al-Azhar affirming his respect for Islam, and the Grand Imam warned him that criticizing Islam was a "red line" that he must not cross. That strongly suggested that the "dialogue" that Pope Francis reestablished would not be allowed to include any discussion of the Muslim persecution of Christians that was escalating worldwide—and that had led to the suspension of dialogue in the first place.

"If my good friend Dr Gasparri says a curse word against my mother, he can expect a punch"

In light of all this, it came as no surprise when, in January 2015, Pope Francis had nothing to say in defense of the *Charlie Hebdo* Muhammad cartoonists who had been murdered by Islamic jihadists. He even suggested that they deserved to be massacred. According to the *Independent*, "he said that freedom of speech and expression are fundamental human rights however he added that he believes there should be limits to offending and ridiculing the faiths and beliefs of others."[29]

The *Charlie Hebdo* cartoonists had apparently gone beyond those limits. Said the Pope, "If my good friend Dr Gasparri says a curse word against my mother, he can expect a punch," referring to the man who organized his trips. The Pope added, "It's normal. You cannot provoke. You cannot insult the faith of others. You cannot make fun of the faith of others."[30]

In February 2016, Jean-Clément Jeanbart, the Melkite Greek Catholic Archbishop of Aleppo, gave an interview with a French reporter in which he was highly critical of the mainstream media and even of his fellow bishops for ignoring the Muslim persecution of Middle Eastern Christians.

Archbishop Jeanbart was turning over a rock, exposing a scandal of catastrophic proportions within the Catholic Church.

"The European media," he charged, "have not ceased to suppress the daily news of those who are suffering in Syria and they have even justified what is happening in our country by using information without taking the trouble to verify it."[31] As for his brother bishops in France, "the conference of French bishops should have trusted us, it would have been better informed. Why are your bishops silent on a threat that is yours today as well? Because the bishops are like you, raised in political correctness. But Jesus was never politically correct, he was politically just!"[32]

The archbishop reminded them, "The responsibility of a bishop is to teach, to use his influence to transmit truth. Why are your bishops afraid of speaking? Of course they would be criticized, but that would give them a chance to defend themselves, and to defend this truth. You must remember that silence often means consent."[33]

Western governments, he said, were foolish to take in so many Muslim migrants without any possibility of vetting them for jihadist ties: "The egoism and the interests slavishly defended by your governments will in the end kill you as well. Open your eyes, didn't you see what happened recently in Paris?"[34]

No, they didn't see it—or at least they entirely failed recognize the significance of the *Charlie Hebdo* massacre. They didn't want to see it.

Archbishop Jeanbart was not the first to make these points. "Why, we ask the western world, why not raise one's voice over so much ferocity and injustice?" Cardinal Angelo Bagnasco, the head of the Italian Bishops Conference (CEI), had asked in September 2015.[35] The following month, Syriac Catholic Patriarch Ignatius Ephrem Joseph III Younan had appealed to the West "not to forget the Christians in the Middle East."[36] The month after that, Melkite Greek Catholic Patriarch Gregory III had said, "I do not understand why the world does not raise its voice against such acts of brutality."[37]

Actually, the Patriarch himself was a major part of the problem. After all, he had said—in January 2016, even after Muslims acting in the name of Islam had decimated his community and other Christian communities in the Middle East—"No one defends Islam like Arab Christians."[38] Defense of Islam and silence about the Muslim persecution of Christians were the favored strategies of many Catholic bishops. In February 2013, Robert McManus, the Roman Catholic Bishop of Worcester, Massachusetts, canceled my scheduled appearance at a Catholic Men's Conference on the grounds that my appearance would harm interfaith dialogue: "My decision to ask Mr. Spencer not to speak at the Men's Conference resulted from a concern voiced by members of the Islamic community in Massachusetts, a concern that I came to share. That concern was that Mr. Spencer's talk about extreme, militant Islamists and the atrocities that they have perpetrated globally might undercut the positive achievements that we Catholics have attained in our inter-religious dialogue with devout Muslims and possibly generate suspicion and even fear of people who practice piously the religion of Islam."[39]

I was later dropped from conferences by two other Catholic bishops, Jaime Soto of Sacramento and Kevin Farrell of Dallas, and was told when I was keynote speaker at a Lutheran conference in August 2015 that the U.S. Conference of Catholic Bishops, which sent a representative to that conference every year, had pulled out that year when it heard I was speaking. Apparently the interfaith dialogue that Catholic bishops in the United States were indefatigably committed to was predicated on not discussing the pressing issues that made the dialogue necessary in the first place.

Determined not to offend their Muslim interlocutors, Catholic leaders refrained from saying anything about Muslim persecution of Christians, and so ensured that their dialogue would be resoundingly fruitless, not saving a single Christian from persecution or preventing one church from being demolished.

"Robert Spencer's positions seem to be at odds with the magisterial teachings on what authentic Islam is . . . Robert seems to be a dissenter from the papal magisterium"

"I believe in one, holy, catholic and apostolic Church; I confess one baptism for the forgiveness of sins; and I look forward to the resurrection of the dead and the life of the world to come; and I believe that Islam is a religion of peace. Amen."

Apparently that is the creed of some in the Catholic Church—and they are determined to tar anyone who says otherwise as a dissenter and a heretic.

WHEN CATHOLICS BELIEVED IN SPEAKING THE TRUTH, REGARDLESS OF THE CONSEQUENCES

"Proclaim the truth and do not be silent through fear."
— St. Catherine of Siena, 1347–1380[42]

In August 2016 on Relevant Radio's Drew Mariani Show, I had a lively discussion with Monsignor Stuart Swetland, president of Donnelly College in Kansas City, Kansas, on the topic of whether or not Islam is a religion of violence.[40] Monsignor Swetland argued not only that Islam was a religion of peace, but that to believe otherwise was to place oneself in opposition to the teaching of the Catholic Church.

Later, in a written statement clarifying his remarks, Monsignor Swetland wrote, "Robert Spencer's positions seem to be at odds with the magisterial teachings on what authentic Islam is and what Catholics are called to do about it (accept immigrants, avoid hateful generalizations, show esteem and respect, etc.) At least in the area of morals, Robert seems to be a dissenter from the papal magisterium."[41]

Monsignor Swetland supported his claim that Catholics must believe that Islam was peaceful or be dissenters from Church teaching with quotations from Popes John Paul II, Benedict XVI, Francis, and documents of the Second Vatican Council. Swetland contended that statements of those popes to the effect that Islam is a religion of peace fall into the category of teachings to which Catholics must give "religious assent," as per the Second Vatican Council document *Lumen Gentium*, which states: "In matters of faith and morals, the bishops speak in the name of Christ and the faithful are to accept their teaching and adhere to it with a religious assent."

It seemed a bit odd for Monsignor Swetland to claim that the popes have authority to say definitively what Islam teaches. Isn't their magisterial authority supposed to be for teaching Catholicism? If Monsignor Swetland is correct, and Catholics must render "religious assent" to Pope Francis' claim that Islam is peaceful and rejects violence, then I am indeed, as he put it, "a dissenter from the papal magisterium." And so are millions of Catholics, including those from the Middle East who have borne the brunt of Muslim persecution of Christians and know what Islam teaches—such as a gentleman from Lebanon who phoned in to the Mariani Show during my discussion with Monsignor Swetland and vehemently agreed with what I was saying.

Of course Swetland's position is absurd. He never explained why Francis's remarks on Islam had to be given more weight by Catholics than those of, say, Pope Callixtus III, who in 1455 vowed to "exalt the true Faith, and to extirpate the diabolical sect of the reprobate and faithless Mahomet in the East."

What's more, if Swetland is correct, then the Catholic Church would be requiring that its faithful affirm the truth of what is an obvious and egregious falsehood. If it is Church teaching that all Catholics must believe that Islam is a religion of peace, then the Catholic hierarchy will have demonstrated that it does not have the authority or reliability in discerning and transmitting the truth that it claims to have; papal claims to speak in the name of Christ will be eviscerated and the Catholic Church as a whole exposed as a fraud.

Such were the risks that some churchmen were willing to take in order to preserve and protect their favorite new dogma, which they enforced with far

WHY WE NEED THE FREEDOM OF SPEECH

* * *

"Until every soul is freely permitted to investigate every book, and creed, and dogma for itself, the world cannot be free. Mankind will be enslaved until there is mental grandeur enough to allow each man to have his thought and say."

—Robert G. Ingersoll[43]

greater energy than they devoted to the propagation of the actual dogmas of their church. In 2016, with Francis as pope and so many bishops following his line, it was nearly universally unwelcome within the Church to speak the truth about Islam. The Catholic hierarchy was unwittingly falling into line with the OIC's agenda, and hoping that if it just made sure every Catholic stayed quiet, everything would be okay.

It was a far cry from the Church of saints and martyrs.

Chapter Ten

"NOT CONDUCIVE TO THE PUBLIC GOOD": FREE SPEECH DIES IN BRITAIN AND CANADA

Did you know?

- Britain banned me—while routinely admitting preachers of jihad to the country
- Some now condemn flying the English flag because of its supposed connection with "far-right nationalism"
- Canada is moving toward criminalizing "Islamophobia"

On June 25, 2013, the day before I had been planning to travel to Great Britain to lay a wreath at a memorial for Lee Rigby, the British soldier who was murdered on a street in London by an Islamic jihadi, I received a letter from the United Kingdom Home Office that read,

> You are reported to have stated the following:
>
> "…it [Islam] is a religion and is a belief system that mandates warfare against unbelievers for the purpose for establishing a societal model that is absolutely incompatible with Western society because media and general government unwillingness to face the sources of Islamic terrorism these things remain largely unknown."

The Home Secretary considers that should you be allowed to enter the UK you would continue to espouse such views. In doing so, you would be…behaving in a way that is not conducive to the public good.

You are therefore instructed not to travel to the UK as you will be refused admission on arrival.[1]

The Home Office garbled its quotation of me, but the import of the letter was clear: I was being barred from traveling to Britain because I had pointed out certain inconvenient facts: that Islam has a doctrine of warfare against unbelievers and that Sharia is incompatible with Western society. Ironically, just a week before I had been scheduled to arrive in Britain, the same Home Office admitted into the country Saudi sheikh Mohammed al-Arefe, who had said "Devotion to jihad for the sake of Allah, and the desire to shed blood, to smash skulls, and to sever limbs for the sake of Allah and in defense of His religion, is, undoubtedly, an honor for the believer. Allah said that if a man fights the infidels, the infidels will be unable to prepare to fight."[2]

So apparently you can believe that violent jihad is a tenet of Islam and still enter the United Kingdom—as long as you support that jihad. Al-Arefe was just one of numerous jihad supporters and preachers who were admitted into Britain both before and after I was banned. One particularly egregious example came on July 16, 2016, when Pakistani Muslim clerics Muhammad Naqib ur Rehman and Hassan Haseeb ur Rehman arrived in London for a speaking tour of mosques all over Britain. The day after they arrived, Justin Welby, the Archbishop of Canterbury, welcomed them to Lambeth Palace.

These clerics should not have been admitted into Britain, much less welcomed by the Archbishop of Canterbury, as they had led a campaign on behalf of Mumtaz Qadri, who murdered Pakistani politician Salmaan Taseer in 2011 over Taseer's opposition to Pakistan's blasphemy laws.

And they were not singular. In October 2016, the UK Home Office admitted Shaykh Hamza Sodagar into the country, despite the fact that he had said, "If there's homosexual men, the punishment is one of five things. One—the easiest one maybe—chop their head off, that's the easiest. Second—burn them to death. Third—throw 'em off a cliff. Fourth—tear down a wall on them so they die under that. Fifth—a combination of the above."[3]

Syed Muzaffar Shah Qadri's preaching of hatred and jihad violence was so hardline that he was banned from preaching in Pakistan, but in December 2016 the UK Home Office welcomed him into Britain.[4] That same month, the United Kingdom banned three bishops from areas of Iraq and Syria where Christians are persecuted from entering the country.[5]

"The Metropolitan police service is committed to working with our partners, including the mayor, to tackle all types of hate crime including offences committed online"

In November 2015, David Anderson QC, the UK's independent reviewer of terrorism legislation, recommended that Britain's Independent Press Standards Organisation (IPSO) be granted the authority to pursue complaints regarding criticism of Islam, rather than simply complaints of discrimination against a particular individual: "It's more difficult if there is a derogatory comment about Islam. And it seems to me that this is one thing that the press standards authority ought to think about."[7]

Britain was the cradle of the freedom of speech. The idea that any British official would propose making criticism of *any* belief system illegal was once unthinkable. But David Anderson wasn't alone.

It came to light in August 2016 that London's new Muslim mayor, Sadiq Khan, was allocating over two million dollars (£1,730,726) to an "online hate crime hub" enabling police to track and arrest "trolls" who "target...individuals and communities."[8] There could be no doubt, given the

THE OLD GOOD COP– BAD COP ROUTINE

In welcoming proponents of the violent enforcement of Sharia blasphemy law to the country while excluding critics like me, the British government was tacitly accepting Sharia blasphemy restrictions on speech: I was banned for being critical of Islam and Sharia, while Muhammad Naqib ur Rehman and Hassan Haseeb ur Rehman were admitted despite their repeated public praise of a man who had committed murder in favor of restrictions on speech. Once again, the forces of "tolerance" were enabling an absolutely intolerant belief system.[6]

nature of the British political establishment today, which "trolls" these new Thought Police would be going after, and which "communities" would be protected from "hate speech."

"The Metropolitan police service," said a police spokesman, was "committed to working with our partners, including the mayor, to tackle all types of hate crime including offences committed online." Given the fact that Mayor Khan had dismissed moderate Muslims as "Uncle Toms" in a 2009 interview (he later apologized under pressure) and has numerous ties to Islamic supremacists, the "types of hate crime" the police were cracking down on were unlikely to include the inflammatory statements coming from jihad preachers.[9]

The "partners" of the London police were likely to include Tell Mama UK, which says on its website, "we work with Central Government to raise the issues of anti-Muslim hatred at a policy level and our work helps to shape and inform policy makers, whilst ensuring that an insight is brought into this area of work through the systematic recording and reporting of anti-Muslim hate incidents and crimes."[10] Tell Mama UK had previously been caught classifying as "anti-Muslim hate incidents and crimes" speech on Facebook and Twitter that it disliked.[11] With the new initiative, it would have the help of the London police.

"The purpose of this programme," said the Metropolitan police, was "to strengthen the police and community response to this growing crime type." This "crime type" is "growing" only because Britain has discarded the principle of free speech and is increasingly committed to the idea that "hate speech" should be restricted by the government. An astonishingly broad range of speech is now subject to law enforcement action in the UK: Section 127 of the Britain's Communications Act of 2003 criminalized "using [a] public electronic communications network in order to cause annoyance, inconvenience or needless anxiety," as well as "sending, or causing to be sent, by means of a public electronic communications network, a message or other matter that was grossly offensive."[12] That's right. It's now illegal in Britain to annoy or even inconvenience anyone by what you say online.

The Communications Act of 2003 had already been used against the freedom of speech. A pastor in Northern Ireland, James McConnell, ran afoul of this law when he dared to criticize Islam. In a May 18, 2014 sermon that was streamed on the Internet, McConnell said: "The Muslim religion was created many hundreds of years after Christ. Muhammad, the Islam Prophet, was born around the year A.D. 570, but Muslims believe that Islam is the true religion. Now, people say there are good Muslims in Britain. That may be so, but I don't trust them. Islam's ideas about God, about humanity, about salvation are vastly different from the teaching of the holy scriptures. Islam is heathen. Islam is satanic. Islam is a doctrine spawned in hell."[13]

McConnell was duly arrested for "grossly offensive" material on a "public electronic communications network."[14]

In a June 2015 interview, McConnell said, "I have no regrets about what I said. I do not hate Muslims but I denounce Islam as a doctrine and I make no apologies for that. I will be pleading 'not guilty' when I stand in the dock in August."[15] Pointing out the absurdity of punishing him for speech as if he were a real criminal, he declared, "I am 78 years of age and in ill health but jail knows no fear for me. They can lock me up with sex offenders, hoodlums and paramilitaries and I will do my time."[16]

HATE SPEECH FOR THEE, BUT NOT FOR ME

• • •

The chief witness for the prosecution of McConnell was Dr. Raied Al-Wazzan of the Belfast Islamic Centre, who condemned the pastor's "terrible comments" and "general sweeping statements" as "offensive and disgusting." But Al-Wazzan himself had praised the Islamic State's conquest of his home city of Mosul in Iraq. "Since the Islamic State took over, it has become the most peaceful city in the world. Yes, there are other things going wrong there...they are murdering people, I agree, but you can go from east to west of the city without fear," he said on the BBC.

Al-Wazzan apologized after a public outcry, but he was not prosecuted for "hate speech."[24]

McConnell's solicitor, Joe Rice, noted that the case was "an absolute waste of scarce public funds" and vowed to make the trial a "defence of freedom of speech and freedom of religion."[17]

McConnell himself said that while he was being prosecuted, numerous Muslim clerics who had said far more genuinely hateful and incendiary things were not.[18]

He was absolutely right. Just days after McConnell's sermon first sparked a furor, videos surfaced of north London Muslim cleric Mizanur Rahman, who had previously been imprisoned for calling for jihad attacks across Europe. That was direct incitement to violence, but when he praised the kidnapping of two hundred schoolgirls in Nigeria by the jihad terror group Boko Haram, he was not prosecuted—nor when he said it was "not necessarily a bad thing" if they kill non-Muslims.[19] Then after the massacre of Muhammad cartoonists in the offices of the satirical magazine *Charlie Hebdo* in January 2015, Rahman praised the killers, saying that the victims were "insulting Islam" and that "they can't expect a different result."[20] Rahman even added, "Britain is the enemy of Islam."[21] Rahman was later arrested for working for the Islamic State—but never for "hate speech."

Likewise unprosecuted was Abu Waleed, another Muslim leader in Britain. In a video posted online on January 16, 2014, Abu Waleed approvingly quoted Muhammad saying, "Don't greet the Jews and the Christians before they greet you, and when you meet any of them on the road, force them to go on the narrower side of it." He noted that the caliph Umar, Muhammad's second successor, issued a charter stating that "infidels and Muslims were not allowed to wear the same clothes as one another. If a Muslim comes out on the day of *'Eid* and sees an infidel with nice clothes, the infidel has to take his clothes off and give them to the Muslim. When an infidel walks down the street, he has to wear a red belt around his neck, he has to have his forehead shaved, and he has to wear two shoes that are different from one another. He is not allowed to walk on the pavement. He has to walk in the middle of the road, and he has to ride on a mule."

Abu Waleed wanted these humiliating rules revived: "This is only for adults, not for the children. You can see how Islam would make the child become a Muslim. The child growing up in a state of heresy would turn to Islam. Why? Because the child would be walking along with his dad, and would say: 'Dad?' 'Yes.' 'Why have you got your forehead shaved?' 'I don't know, these Muslims make me do it.' 'Why can't you ride the animal like the Muslims, who ride like this? Why are you riding with both legs dangling on the side of the donkey?' 'Why is it that every time a Muslim comes and asks you for your clothes, you give them?' 'Why is it that every time he tells you to get down from the horse, you have to take it?'"[22]

Abu Waleed outlined more scenarios in which Muslims publicly humiliated Christians and the Christians decide to escape the humiliation by becoming Muslim.[23] He was not prosecuted.

There are numerous other examples. The gay rights group Outrage reported in October 2006 on a revealing conversation between Arshad Misbahi of the Manchester Central Mosque and John Casson, a local psychotherapist. The psychotherapist recounted, "I asked him if the execution of gay Muslims in Iran and Iraq was an acceptable punishment in Sharia law, or the result of culture, not religion. He told me that in a true Islamic state, such punishments were part of Islam: If the person had had a trial, at which four witnesses testified that they had seen the actual homosexual acts."[25]

Casson asked if this was the view of Muslims in Britain, and the answer was clear:

> I asked him what would be the British Muslim view? He repeated that in an Islamic state these punishments were justified. They might result in the deaths of thousands but if this deterred millions from having sex, and spreading disease, then it was worthwhile to protect the wider community. I checked again that this was not a matter of tradition, culture or local prejudice. "No," he said, "It is part of the central tenets of Islam: that sex outside marriage is forbidden; this is stated in the Koran and the prophet (peace and blessings be upon him) had stated that these punishments were due to such behaviours."[26]

East London imam Abdul Makin declared in 2008 that "non-Muslims are never innocent, they are guilty of denying Allah and his prophet. If you don't believe me, here is the legal authority, the top Muslim lawyer of Britain." That lawyer was the notorious Anjem Choudary, who after years of open support for jihad terror was finally found guilty of aiding the Islamic State in August 2016. Said Choudary, "You are innocent if you are a Muslim. Then you are innocent in the eyes of God. If you are not a Muslim, then you are guilty of not believing in God. As a Muslim, I must support my Muslim brothers and sisters. I must have hatred to everything that is not Muslim."[27]

In August 2009, the chief imam of the Grand Mosque in Mecca, Sheikh Abdul Rahman al-Sudais, spoke at the East London mosque in Whitechapel, despite having made anti-Semitic remarks and disparaged Christians and Hindus ("cross-worshippers" and "idol worshippers"). Peter Tatchell, the Green Party parliamentary candidate for Oxford East, pointed out, "Al-Sudais has stoked religious sectarianism and anti-Jewish racism. He has never expressed any regret." Tatchell called on the East London mosque to require al-Sudais to apologize as a condition for being allowed to speak, adding: "I don't understand why the Home Secretary is allowing al-Sudais into Britain, given that similar hate preachers have been banned. Is it because of the close business links between the British and Saudi establishments?"[28] That may indeed have been the case.

The Islamic Society at Queen Mary University came under fire in January 2011 for featuring as a speaker Abu Usamah, the imam at Green Lane Masjid in Birmingham. In 2007 Abu Usamah had been captured on hidden camera saying that Osama bin Laden was "better than a thousand Tony Blairs" and that non-Muslims were "liars." In 2009, he had declared, "Jihad is from our religion. We will not renounce our religion."[29]

Hidden cameras were unkind to many imams in Britain. Mohammed Abdul, the imam of Masjid al-Huda, a mosque in Bristol, was caught on camera in 2012 telling an undercover reporter to take his daughter abroad for genital mutilation, which was illegal in Britain: "In this country, it is not possible, we cannot do that. [For] any other Muslim who likes to practise the way of Prophet Muhammad, the best way is to go to other countries. Some families, they go to Africa or Arab countries. In this country you have to fight for your religion, your cultures, They don't like your Muslim cultures."[30]

In 2013 an undercover documentary team filmed another Muslim cleric in Britain, Ustadh Murtazah Khan, saying, "Take that homosexual man and throw him off the mountain." He complained that British authorities had given homosexuals "unprecedented rights, so that your child can be exposed and introduced to lesbians. Now they say 'if you discriminate against that, you're going to jail.' We'll discriminate, but we'll discriminate in a way where we don't get in trouble. The Muslim is a dentist, one of those people come, you want to take a big, big needle and stick it in his gums."[31] In December 2013, Britain allowed a speaking tour by a Saudi imam who called Shi'ites "apostates" and said that no churches should be allowed in Saudi Arabia.[32]

McConnell was acquitted after an eighteen-month investigation and a trial, but the Metropolitan police will not want to be seen as wasting their new "hate speech" money: others will not be as fortunate as McConnell.

Behind the push for "hate speech" laws is, of course, the increasingly authoritarian Left.

This is not the first time that a Sharia imperative and a leftist one have coincided during the relatively brief mayoral tenure of Sadiq Khan. The *London Evening Standard* reported on June 13 that "adverts which put Londoners under pressure over body image are to be banned from the Tube and bus network."[33] This was because "Sadiq Khan announced that Transport for London would no longer run ads which could cause body confidence issues, particularly among young people."[34]

Said Khan, "As the father of two teenage girls, I am extremely concerned about this kind of advertising which can demean people, particularly women, and make them ashamed of their bodies. Nobody should feel pressurised, while they travel on the Tube or bus, into unrealistic expectations surrounding their bodies and I want to send a clear message to the advertising industry about this."[35]

And so no more ads featuring women in bikinis on London buses. People often puzzle about how the hard Left and Islamic supremacists can make common cause, when they have such differing ideas of morality; Khan's ad ban showed how. The Left's concern with "body-shaming" and not putting people "under pressure over body image" meshed perfectly with the Sharia imperative to force women to cover themselves in order to remove occasions of temptation for men.

What next? Would London women be forced to cover everything except their face and hands (as per Muhammad's command) so as not to put others "under pressure over body image"? And if they were, would anyone who dared to complain about what was happening to their green and pleasant land be locked up for "hate speech" by London's new Thought Police?

Welcome to Sadiq Khan's London. Shut up and put on your hijab.

"The English flag used to have connotations with far-right nationalism"

Britain was avid to ban any expression that was deemed offensive to Muslims. As Europe geared up for the Euro 2016 soccer tournament, the BBC warned English soccer fans that they must not dress as Crusaders to attend the matches: to do so risked offending Muslims. This was because the Crusaders, the BBC explained one-sidedly, "were the perpetrators of violent attacks across Europe and the Middle East on Muslims, Jews and pagans." Even to fly the English flag was to cross over into the suspect camp because, the BBC helpfully explained, "the English flag used to have connotations with far-right nationalism."[36]

In September 2014, an English couple, Nick Barnfield and Sarah Cleaves, were riding on a bus with their fifteen-month-old autistic daughter Heidi. When Heidi began to cry, they started singing to her a song from the popular British children's show "Peppa Pig." A hijab-wearing Muslim woman approached them and then complained to the bus driver about the couple's "racism"; the driver asked Barnfield and Cleaves to get off the bus. Said Barnfield,

> It was humiliating. A lady came up to us and quite aggressively started telling us we were irresponsible parents and that we were being racist singing the song. She went up to the bus driver and told him we were being racist towards her and she wasn't happy. The driver came up to me and said we had to get off the bus or the police would have to come. He said: "just get off the bus—it's not worth the hassle." I was really shocked because we had done nothing wrong but he didn't listen to us.... I was more upset at the bus driver not taking in both sides—he just heard the word racism and kicked us off.[37]

The driver later denied having heard any charges of "racism," but the couple's story was more plausible, as charges of "racism" are extraordinarily powerful in Britain and all over the West today; the Left and their Islamic supremacist allies wield them like a cudgel to stigmatize and suppress all dissent.

At a Kentucky Fried Chicken outlet in Leicester, non-Muslim construction worker Graham Noakes was refused a hand-wipe, as they contain alcohol, which is forbidden in Islam: "They told me it might offend other customers. I explained that it wouldn't affect me. In fact—I told them I like alcohol, so it wouldn't bother me in the slightest. When they wouldn't give me one, I was disgusted. I will never be going to KFC again." Ironically, Noakes was in Leicester to help build a new Muslim community center.[38]

Beverley Akciecek of Beverley's Snack Shack in Manchester was told that Muslims who lived near her restaurant felt "physically sick" because of the "foul odor" of bacon frying. The Stockport Council of Greater Manchester told Akciecek that the smell was "unacceptable on the grounds of residential amenity," and that she would have to remove a fan that was apparently spreading the aroma into the area. Akciecek's husband is himself a Turkish Muslim, and Akciecek noted, "When we go to a cafe my husband wouldn't be offended by the smell of bacon. His friends are not offended by it, we have three visitors who come here for a sandwich, friends of my husband, and the smell doesn't offend them at all. My brother-in-law doesn't flinch if he comes and we've just taken out three trays of bacon."[39] Her husband's Muslim friends may not have been offended, but other Muslims were, and that was all that mattered.

And non-Muslim Britons are self-censoring even before Muslims complain. Birmingham vicar Canon Rob Morris declared preemptively that the name of the local Saracen's Head Pub was offensive to Muslims, and should be changed: "The name we have got does manage to be offensive to Muslims and that's not what Christians stand for. It's clearly disrespectful to another religious tradition in this city. We shall be looking for brilliant ideas for a name change that will signify something to all." Had he actually received any complaints from Muslims? Well, no.[40]

Dunni Odetoyinbo, pastor of the Immanuel International Christian Centre in north London, said that her church was known for its vibrant singing—until she was approached by an officer of the local governing authority, the Waltham Forest council, who asked her "to keep the noise down so as not to offend the Muslim community."[41] The congregation abandoned its building and moved to a new location.

"I'm getting locked up for sticking up for my own country"

While foreign Muslim clerics who preached jihad murder were welcomed, British authorities turned against their own citizens who dared to utter statements that were considered beyond the pale. In England in 2016, when a Facebook post from the Greater Manchester Police mentioned a sexual assault case involving a Muslim suspect, Stephen Bennett, a father of seven children, was incensed. He commented, "Don't come over to this country and treat it like your own. Britain first" and other remarks that Manchester Crown Court found to be "grossly offensive" to Muslims.[42] The *Manchester Evening News*, perhaps hoping to avoid prosecution itself, stated only that "one comment he made concerned Asian women, another was likely to be offensive to Muslims," without giving readers the opportunity to make up their own minds by reproducing his actual remarks.[43]

THE OLD GOOD COP– BAD COP ROUTINE

These non-Muslims demanding that other non-Muslims curtail their activities in order to avoid offending Muslims had imbibed Mohamed Atta's lesson: *just stay quiet and you'll be okay.* They were anxious to avoid giving offense to Muslims because they had been told repeatedly by the mainstream media that Muslims were a discriminated-against minority that deserved special consideration— and likely also because of the ever-present possibility of Muslim violence.

For this crime, Bennett was sentenced under Britain's Malicious Communications Act to 180 hours of unpaid labor. Justifying the sentencing, Recorder Andrew Long admonished the Bennett that he was "running the risk of stirring up racial hatred in the present climate."[44] (Long did not explain what race Islam was.) He also told Bennett that what he had done was "very serious," as it was "conduct capable of playing into the hands of the enemies of this country."[45] Long concluded in the tone of the politically correct schoolmarm he was: "Your remarks damaged the community in which you live, and it's the community that you must repay."[46]

When Bennett was arrested, he had cried out, "Is this about that Muslim thing on Facebook? I'm getting locked up for sticking up for my own country."[47]

His own country did not want his help.

"Several staff described their nervousness about identifying the ethnic origins of perpetrators for fear of being thought as racist"

The human cost of this politically correct silence was vividly and horrifically on display in the scandal involving Muslim rape gangs in Britain. In August 2014, the BBC reported that "at least 1,400 children were subjected to appalling sexual exploitation in Rotherham between 1997 and 2013, a report has found. Children as young as 11 were raped by multiple perpetrators, abducted, trafficked to other cities in England, beaten and intimidated, it said."[48]

The horrors of these abuse cases cannot be overstated. A report on this rampant abuse cited examples of "children who had been doused in petrol and threatened with being set alight, threatened with guns, made to witness brutally violent rapes and threatened they would be next if they told anyone."[49]

Yet months after the story broke in the summer of 2014, little been done to combat this scourge. On the contrary, it had grown explosively: hundreds of new cases had been discovered. One of the victims said that those who abused her were "untouchable."[50]

Sky News reported in January 2015 that in addition to the fourteen hundred cases revealed in August 2014, "hundreds more cases were known to authorities prior to its publication and that hundreds more are being reported."[51] The victim who spoke to Sky News said months after the news of the extent of this savage exploitation first broke, "It's still going on if not worse, because now they're having to hide it more. I'm still seeing my abusers driving young girls in their car."[52] She said of the police that "all they care about is getting a statement. Six months on we've had no arrests, we've had no charges, evidence is still being lost."[53]

These words were spoken a month after a team of government commissioners had taken over the Rotherham Council, after finding it in "complete denial" about the scandal.[54]

How could this have happened? What illness overtook British authorities, so that they were covering up horrific sex abuse cases and doing little or nothing to apprehend offenders? The answer lay in the fact that these were not simply criminal cases involving outlaw gangs. The rape gangs were overwhelmingly made up of Muslims. Nor was this simply a coincidence, or an inexplicable phenomenon sweeping through a community with no discernable relationship to the community's principles. The Qur'an tells Muslim men that along with as many as four wives, they may also enjoy the "captives of the right hand" (4:3, 4:24). These women are the "spoils of war" (33:50) and are to be used for sex, as men are to "guard their private parts except from their wives or those their right hands possess" (23:5–6).

A female Kuwaiti politician, Salwa al-Mutairi, explained several years ago that a Muslim cleric had told her, "With the law of sex slaves, there must be a Muslim nation at war with a Christian nation, or a nation which is not of the religion, not of the religion of Islam. And there must be prisoners of war." The cleric, she said, emphasized that "sex slaves are not forbidden by Islam."[55]

But surely the members of the British rape gangs didn't subscribe to this bizarre view, did they? They may well have. After all, many Muslims in the West consider the Western interventions in Iraq and Afghanistan to be neo-Crusades, the Christian West against the Islamic world. The nature of this new war between Islam and Christendom, however, has enabled many Muslims to settle behind what they consider to be enemy lines—while retaining their loyalty not to the Western state in which they live, but to the global umma. That would make non-Muslim British girls lawful to be captured as spoils of war and pressed into service as sex slaves.

Even if they didn't think this way, Muslim rape gang members in Britain who were reasonably devout and knowledgeable about their faith might have considered another Qur'an passage: "O Prophet, tell your wives and your daughters and the women of the believers to bring down over themselves of their outer garments. That is more suitable that they will be known and not be abused. And ever is Allah Forgiving and Merciful." (33:59) The implication is that if women do not cover themselves adequately with their outer garments, they *may* be abused—that such abuse would be justified. Western women, so often the subject of jihadist polemic and abuse for being dressed immodestly (thus supposedly demonstrating themselves to be "whores") would be prime candidates for this abuse.

If this revolting and barbaric behavior had been inspired and incited by any other belief system, British authorities would have moved swiftly to protect their girls and stamp it out. But since the attackers were overwhelmingly Muslim, British authorities feared to confront the problem in its full magnitude. It was the same dynamic that allowed U.S. Army major Nidal Malik Hasan to be promoted and left at large to plan a violent jihad attack, despite thoroughly alarming his coworkers with his talk of jihad: they were afraid of being called "racist."

The same cowardice explains Rotherham. Young non-Muslim girls by the hundreds were subjected to horrific abuse and forced into prostitution and sex slavery because, as a government report found "several staff described their nervousness about identifying the ethnic origins of perpetrators for fear of being thought as racist." Some of the officials, the BBC reported, "remembered clear direction from their managers not to do so."[56] Like Nidal Malik Hasan's superiors, they hoped that if they stayed quiet, they would be okay, and just like Hasan's superiors and the passengers on American Airlines flight 11, they weren't—and neither were a lot of other, entirely innocent people.

Still, the blame for their silence cannot be placed solely on the local authorities. They were quite correct in thinking that charges of "racism" in contemporary Britain could be the end of their professional careers, and possibly even result in criminal prosecution. "Racism" is de facto the worst of all crimes in modern-day Britain, as well as the United States, and even the threat of the charge has become one of the most effective tools in the arsenal of foes of the freedom of speech to chill discourse they don't like.

This is ironic, since the very idea that "racism" was a factor in the Rotherham sex abuse cases reflected the myopia of the British government and media elites; they consistently framed issues regarding jihad terror and Islamic supremacism as racial, despite the fact that Islam and its doctrines regarding jihad and the sexual enslavement of captive non-Muslim women are beliefs that can be and are held by people of all races. The rape gangs are explained not by the Pakistani origin of the perpetrators, but by their Muslim belief that infidel girls were nothing more than, in the immortal words of the Grand Mufti of Australia a few years ago, "uncovered meat."[57]

In any case, the fear of being stigmatized with the "racist" charge is unmistakably what hindered the proper prosecution of the rape gangs, and hinders it still. The perpetrators were untouchable. The prevailing culture—not just in Britain, but in the United States also, and all over the

West—consigns all concerns about the activity of Muslims, whether it be jihad terror or Sharia- and Qur'an-inspired sex trafficking, to "racism" and "Islamophobia." Officials stay quiet about such matters, hoping they will be okay, while the problems metastasize.

At least one British lawmaker wanted to codify this silence into law. On November 12, 2015, the day before the Paris jihad massacre in which Islamic jihadists murdered 130 people, Labour MP Keith Vaz said he would vote for the reimposition of blasphemy laws in Britain. "Religions are very special to people," he said, "and therefore I have no objection to [a blasphemy law]…but it must apply equally to everybody. It should apply to all religions. If we have laws, they should apply to everybody. If somebody brings it forward in parliament I'll vote for it.… Obviously it depends what's in the bill. But I have no objection to it being brought before parliament and having a debate about it."[58]

This initiative moved a bit closer to fruition in October 2016, when a report of the European Commission against Racism and Intolerance (ECRI) found an alarming increase in "hate speech" in Britain between 2009 and 2016. ECRI Chair Christian Ahlund declared, "It is no coincidence that racist violence is on the rise in the UK at the same time as we see worrying examples of intolerance and hate speech in the newspapers, online and even among politicians."[59]

STICKS AND STONES MAY BREAK MY BONES, BUT WORDS WILL NEVER HURT ME

Surprisingly, the British government responded to the ECRI call for censorship by defending the freedom of speech: "The Government is committed to a free and open press and does not interfere with what the press does and does not publish, as long as the press abides by the law."[62] How long it would maintain that resolve amidst the many pressures for censorship and blasphemy laws, however, was unclear.

The ECRI report stated that "in light of the fact that Muslims are increasingly under the spotlight as a result of recent ISIS-related terrorist acts around the world, fuelling prejudice against Muslims shows a reckless disregard, not only for the dignity of the great majority of Muslims in the United Kingdom, but also for their safety."[60]

According to this report, "where the media stress the Muslim background of perpetrators of terrorist acts, and devote significant coverage to it, the violent backlash against Muslims is likely to be greater than in cases where the perpetrators' motivation is downplayed or rejected in favour of alternative explanations."[61] Presumably, not mentioning that the jihad terrorist was Muslim in news reports about jihad attacks would lessen the risks to Muslims.

"And we have to tell them, you know what, if you're not going to allow us to do that, there will be consequences"

Blasphemy laws are already in force in Canada, under the guise of "hate speech" laws. Thus when on February 14, 2006—the seventeenth anniversary of the Rushdie fatwa—the *Western Standard* magazine reprinted the Danish Muhammad cartoons, the Islamic Supreme Council of Canada and the Edmonton Muslim Council complained that the *Standard* was inciting hatred against Muslims and filed a complaint against its publisher, Ezra Levant, with the Alberta Human Rights and Citizenship Commission. After Levant embarrassed both the Islamic groups and the Commission with an eloquent defense of the freedom of speech when answering questions before the Commission, the Islamic Supreme Council withdrew its complaint.[63]

Shortly thereafter, the Canadian Islamic Congress (CIC) charged that author Mark Steyn was "flagrantly Islamophobic" and had heaped "hatred and contempt" upon Muslims in Canada in his book *America Alone*; the

CIC filed complaints with three Canadian provincial Human Rights Commissions against *Macleans* magazine, which had published excerpts of *America Alone*.[64]

The problem with the CIC's complaint was that Steyn had not actually written the passages that the CIC found hateful; they were direct quotations from Muslim leaders. Nonetheless, Steyn did not want to win on a technicality; in fact, he wanted to lose: "We want to lose so we can take it to a real court and if necessary up to the Supreme Court of Canada and we can get the ancient liberties of free-born Canadian citizens that have been taken away from them by tribunals like this."[65]

One of the Muslims who had filed the complaints against *Macleans*, Khurrum Awan of the Canadian Arab Federation, knew what was at stake as much as Steyn did, saying, "And we have to tell them, you know what, if you're not going to allow us to do that, there will be consequences. You will be taken to the human rights commission, you will be taken to the press council, and you know what? If you manage to get rid of the human rights code provisions [regarding "hate speech"], we will then take you to the civil courts system. And you know what? Some judge out there might just think that perhaps it's time to have a tort of group defamation, and you might be liable for a few million dollars."[66]

WHY WE NEED THE FREEDOM OF SPEECH

• • •

"Those who make conversations impossible, make escalation inevitable."

—Stefan Molyneux[69]

In December 2016, Justin Trudeau's government advanced further down the road to criminalizing criticism of Islam. The Canadian Parliament passed a motion condemning "Islamophobia" and demanding that it be criminalized. The motion condemned "all forms of 'Islamophobia,'" without defining the term. Then Liberal MP Iqra Khalid, herself a Muslim, introduced another motion stating that "the government should recognize the need to quell the increasing public climate of hate and fear...condemn Islamophobia and all forms of systemic racism and religious discrimination."[67] Khalid called for "Islamophobia" to be prosecuted as a hate crime.

Then on the night of January 31, 2017, Montreal police arrested a man for "online hate speech targeting Muslims."[68] What exactly he had said was not released to the public.

No doubt the vast majority of Canadians knew by this time to stay quiet and hope they would be okay.

Chapter Eleven

THE NEW BROWNSHIRTS

Did you know?

- Leftist students now routinely intimidate and even physically menace pro-Israel students
- Conservative speakers face legions of hostile protesters
- UC–Berkley students used violent assaults and arson to shut down a Milo Yiannopoulos speech

On September 29, 2016, retired U.S. Army Lieutenant Colonel and former Congressman Allen West was scheduled to speak at Saint Louis University (SLU) on what he termed "the threat of radical Islam."[1] A group of leftist and Muslim student protesters, led by the SLU Rainbow Alliance and the Muslim Students' Association, packed the hall and then walked out, leaving West to speak to a nearly empty room.

That was the culmination of protests that had led SLU administrators to forbid the Young America's Foundation (YAF), the organization sponsoring West's speech, to use the words "radical Islam" on posters and fliers advertising it. West, not disposed to acquiesce to this censorship, had written before the event, "I along with the YAF activists will not back down from this challenge. And if this is just a case of ill-conceived political correctness, we'll rectify that. But, if this is a case of the influence of stealth jihad radical Islamic

SHUT UP, THEY EXPLAINED

YAF national spokeswoman Emily Jashinsky noted that what happened to West at SLU is common. "This is what happens when students attempt to bring one conservative speaker to a liberal campus. Threatened leftists do everything they can to erect obstacles."[4]

campus organizations such as the Muslim Student Association, an affiliate of the Muslim Brotherhood, then you will be exposed. And I recommend to the President of St. Louis University, you do not want it known that a radical Islamic organization is dictating speakers on your campus—that is not the type of PR you really want."[2]

But rather than affirming the importance of free discourse and the airing of dissenting views (never mind rejecting jihad and Islamic supremacism), SLU President Fred Pestello declared his "solidarity" with the protesters against the "provocateur" West.[3]

"Beyond academic discourse"

Campus leftists had been allied with Muslims for years in a campaign to shut down any speech critical of Islam. An ex-Muslim human rights activist, Nonie Darwish, was scheduled to speak at Princeton University on November 18, 2009, as she had spoken on numerous campuses in the past. Darwish is the founder of Former Muslims United and Arabs for Israel and an outspoken critic of jihad terror and its motivating ideology.

But Darwish's Princeton speech was canceled the day she was scheduled to appear. The university's Coordinator for Muslim Life, Sohaib Sultan, had called the director of the university's Center for Jewish Life to complain that Darwish's views went "beyond academic discourse."[5] Arab Society president Sami Yabroudi and former president Sarah Mousa issued a joint statement defaming Darwish: "Nonie Darwish is to Arabs and Muslims what Ku Klux Klan members, skinheads, and neo-Nazis are to other minorities, and we decided that the role of her talk in the logical, intellectual discourse espoused by Princeton University needed to be questioned."[6]

The two student groups sponsoring the event, Tigers for Israel (TFI) and the American Whig-Cliosophic Society (Whig-Clio), withdrew their sponsorship under pressure. Tigers for Israel, sounding more like Sheep for Israel, issued a statement that was a master-piece of cowardice and capitulation:

SHUT UP, THEY EXPLAINED

Increasingly unwilling (and doubtless unable) to engage its foes in rational discussion and debate, the Left is resorting more and more to the Alinskyite tactic of responding to conservatives only with ridicule and attempts to rule conservative views out of the realm of acceptable discourse. That coincides perfectly with the ongoing initiative of the Organization of Islamic Cooperation (OIC) to intimidate the West into criminalizing criticism of Islam.

> On Tuesday evening Tigers for Israel and Whig-Clio rescinded our cosponsorship of today's Nonie Darwish Lecture. Tigers for Israel accepted the opportunity for her to speak based on a misconception about what she actually believes. After her anti-Islam position was brought to my attention on Tuesday afternoon by the Center for Jewish Life director Rabbi Julie Roth and the Muslim Chaplain Imam Sohaib Sultan, I conducted extensive research and discussed the issue with TFI and Whig-Clio leadership, and we decided to rescind our cosponsorship after concluding that Tigers for Israel disagrees with and does not condone Ms. Darwish and her beliefs on Islam.... As President of TFI I take full responsibility for not vetting Ms. Darwish from the beginning, and I sincerely apologize for offending any person or group on campus, especially the Muslim community. Tigers for Israel deeply regrets the initial sponsorship and we do not in any way endorse her views.[7]

Whig-Clio's President Ben Weisman blamed Tigers for Israel, saying, "Our decision to co-host the event was based on our belief that by extending an offer to speak to Ms. Darwish, members of TFI deemed her views a legitimate element of the mainstream discourse and in part agreed with her incendiary opinions.... By rescinding their offer, TFI indicated their understanding that Darwish's views have no place in the campus community, essentially rendering irrelevant our attempt at opening them up for debate."[8]

Neither Tigers for Israel nor Whig-Clio—nor any of the protesting Muslims—took any public notice of the fact Darwish's "incendiary" "anti-Islam" beliefs had any basis besides irrational hatred or ignorant prejudice. In fact, her views are grounded in bitter personal experience and intimate knowledge of Islam from the inside. Darwish grew up a Muslim in Gaza, the daughter of Egyptian Colonel Mustafa Hafez, who was head of Egyptian intelligence in the Sinai and Gaza in the 1950s and was killed by the Israeli Defense Force; he is hailed as an Islamic martyr among Muslims in Egypt.[9] But even if her views had been less well grounded in reality, the idea that some intellectual positions are unacceptable to enunciate in a university setting is contrary to the idea of a university itself. And barring her from speaking on campus was grotesque in light of the jihad that was advancing globally under the aegis of a belief system that university officials (and indeed, the Western intelligentsia as a whole) is determined to label benign. The dogma that Islam is a religion of peace is simply not to be questioned on university campuses.

Occasionally the impetus to cancel speakers whose views are unwelcome comes not from Muslim groups, but from people anxious to curry favor with those groups. In May 2014, Darwish had been scheduled to speak at a pro-Israel event called iFest at the University of California, Irvine. But the Jewish group Hillel threatened to boycott and withdraw funding for iFest events if Darwish spoke. After Darwish's speech was duly canceled, Hillel issued a statement explaining that "Jewish campus organizations and their community partners, in partnership with the UCI administration, have worked hard to improve the campus climate for Israel and Jewish students. We will continue to take actions that serve the long-term best interests of the campus community."[10] The implication was clear: if Darwish spoke, the "campus climate for Israel and Jewish students" would be significantly impaired.

The whiff of a threat was unmistakable. And it was understandable that Jewish groups would feel intimidated, as groups such as Students for Justice in Palestine and the Muslim Students Association have been growing increasingly aggressive and even physically menacing toward those who dare to question support for the Palestinian jihad against Israel.

Leftist and Muslim solidarity with the Palestinians goes with across-the-the-board opposition to Israel, and opposition to Israel bleeds over into generalized anti-Jewish sentiment—in other words, anti-Semitism, which is now rife on American college campuses. In March 2016, transgender rights activist Janet Mock had been scheduled to speak at Brown University's Hillel Center—until leftist and Muslim students protested the fact that Mock was appearing at the university's Jewish student center. Under heavy pressure, Mock canceled the event. Mock's representative explained, "The focus of Janet's work was lost leading up to the proposed event, and her visit was received with controversy and resistance rather than open dialogue and discussion about the issues closest to Janet's work in movements for trans liberation, racial justice and intersectional feminism."[11] The leftist tropes of this statement did not mollify the mob calling for the event to be canceled. Thoudh Mock had not intended to speak about anything having to do with Jews, Israel, or Islamic jihad, the event was tainted by its association with Hillel so it had to be stopped.

"Propagating murder is not a responsible expression of free speech!"

In February 2010, the Israeli ambassador to the United States, Michael Oren, attempted to give a speech at the University of California at Irvine (UCI), on relations between the United States and Israel. He was ultimately unable to do so: after Muslim students heckled and interrupted him repeatedly, he left the stage.

Before Oren appeared, the UCI Muslim Student Union (MSU) chapter had issued a statement that read, in part,

> As people of conscience, we oppose Michael Oren's invitation to our campus. Propagating murder is not a responsible expression of free speech....
>
> We strongly condemn the university for cosponsoring, and therefore, inadvertently supporting the ambassador of a state that is condemned by more UN Human Rights Council resolutions than all other countries in the world combined....
>
> Oren took part in a culture that has no qualms with terrorizing the innocent, killing civilians, demolishing their homes, and illegally occupying their land. Oren is an outspoken supporter of the recent war on Gaza and stands in the way of international law by refusing to cooperate with the United Nation's Goldstone Report, a fact-finding mission endorsed by the UN Human Rights Council.[12]

The statement repeated Palestinian charges against Israel, claiming that the Jewish state had "massacred" fourteen hundred people in Gaza.[13] This was an extremely dubious charge, as was the assumption that the United Nations, in its incessant condemnations of Israel, was a neutral and impartial observer.

The most important aspect of the MSU statement, however, was not its claims about Israel and Gaza, but its assumption that the university was "inadvertently supporting" Oren's views just by cosponsoring the event. This was a complete rejection of the idea of the university as a place where all ideas can be discussed and accepted or rejected on their own merits. As far as the Muslim Student Union was concerned, giving someone a platform was tantamount to endorsing his views—so only those with acceptable opinions should be given a platform.

STICKS AND STONES MAY BREAK MY BONES, BUT WORDS WILL NEVER HURT ME

"This is beyond embarrassing.... This is no way for our undergraduate students to behave. We have an opportunity to hear from a policy-maker relevant to one of the most important issues facing this planet and you are preventing not only yourself from hearing him but hundreds of other people in this room and hundreds of other people in an overflow room. Shame on you! This is not an example of free speech."
—UC–Irvine professor Mark P. Petracca, castigating the hecklers who shut down Ambassador Michael Oren's speech on the UCI campus[14]

But applying that principle would mean turning universities into one-party states in which only one point of view is allowed. Surely on a university campus, if anywhere, the airing of opposing views should be viewed not as an intolerable affront but as an opportunity to grow intellectually and to learn to engage opposing viewpoints in a mature and effective manner.

In September 2011, seven Muslim students from UCI and three from the University of California, Riverside, were found guilty of disrupting Oren's speech and sentenced to informal probation and community service. But that hardly put a crimp in the anti-free speech campaign on campus. Shakeel Syed of the Islamic Shura Council of Southern California called the verdict "absolutely unbelievable... I believe the heart of America has died today."[15] Defenders of the students likened them to Martin Luther King Jr. and Rosa Parks.[16]

"A tremendous source of anti-Semitic expression and incitement of hatred for the Jewish state and Jews generally"

That was the academic Left in the second decade of the twenty-first century: unable to distinguish shouting down and physically menacing those with whom they disagreed from the peaceful civil disobedience of the Civil Rights Movement. No wonder Jewish students and supporters of Israel were increasingly menaced on American campuses. In a November 2015 rally organized by Students for Justice in Palestine (SJP) at Hunter College, a campus of the City University of New York (CUNY), protesters brandishing signs reading "Boycott Israel" and "Zionists out of CUNY" screamed at Jewish students: "Zionists go home!," "Zionists out of CUNY!," "Jews out of CUNY!," "Get out of America!," and "We should drag the Zionist down the street!"[18] In February 2016 at Brooklyn College, a group of hard-Left students burst into a Faculty Council meeting and began chanting "Zionists off campus!"[19]

These were just two of over a dozen incidents from around the same

STICKS AND STONES MAY BREAK MY BONES, BUT WORDS WILL NEVER HURT ME

· · · · · · · · · · · · · · · · · · ·

"History requires us to draw a line in the sand against this sort of organized thuggery."

—District Attorney Tony Rackauckas, decrying the "censorship by the few" that had driven Michael Oren from the UCI campus[17]

time in which Jewish stu-
dents were menaced on
CUNY campuses. The
underwhelming response
of CUNY officials was to
say that they were going to
establish a "working
group" and a "task force."[21]
Would their response have
been as limp if a group of

> ╾◆╾◆╾◆╾◆╾◆╾◆╾◆╾◆╾◆╾◆╾◆╾◆╾◆╾◆╾◆╾◆╾◆╾◆╾◆╾
>
> # NOW WE CAN SEE THE FORCE
> # OF YOUR ARGUMENT
>
> · · · · · · · · · · · · · · · · · · ·
>
> When a Jewish professor tried to get students to end their
> disruption of a Faculty Council meeting at Brooklyn College,
> they called him a "Zionist pig."[20]

Jewish and Christian students had been screaming, "Muslims out of CUNY"?

The Muslim students' behavior toward Oren and at Hunter College was
rapidly becoming the norm across U.S. campuses: it was becoming unsafe
to be pro-Israel at an American university. As colleges grow more authoritarian in their leftism, they are becoming increasingly inhospitable to
students who oppose the Left's pet causes. The pro-Palestinian "Israeli
Apartheid Week" has become an increasingly common feature of campus
life, with students and adult speakers denouncing Israel for its supposed
"ethnic cleansing" of Palestinians and "apartheid policies over the Palestinian people."[22] Israeli Apartheid Week often features a good deal of grievance
theater, with pro-Palestinian students constructing mock "apartheid walls"
and "Israeli checkpoints."

This is not an atmosphere conducive to open discussion and debate.
Tammi Rossman-Benjamin, cofounder and director of the Israel advocacy
AMCHA Initiative, explains that "Israeli Apartheid Week is a tremendous
source of anti-Semitic expression and incitement of hatred for the Jewish
state and Jews generally. Frequently during Israeli Apartheid Week and BDS
campaigns, Jewish students are singled out, harassed, intimidated and even
assaulted, regardless of their feelings on Israel. Jewish students report feeling afraid to display their Jewish Star necklaces, wear their Jewish sorority

or fraternity letters, or walk to Hillel for Shabbat dinner during these heightened weeks."[23]

Students for Justice in Palestine is one group that is particularly menacing to Jews on campus. In October 2014, journalist Daniel Mael described this group's agenda:

> Instead of promoting justice, SJP and/or its members spend almost all of their energy demonizing Israel, advocating for its eventual destruction, showing an unfortunate affinity for pro-terrorist figures, bullying and intimidating pro-Israel and Jewish students with vicious and sometimes anti-Semitic rhetoric, and even at times engaging in physical violence. While SJP may pay lip-service to peaceful aims, their rhetoric and actions make it hard to avoid the conclusion that a culture of hatred permeates nearly everything the group does—making the college experience increasingly uncomfortable, at times even dangerous, for Jewish or pro-Israel students. Perhaps equally disturbing is the limited response from university authorities that have an obligation to prevent such attacks and protect Jewish students.[24]

Amid all this, the U.S. Departments of Justice and Education urged educators to be vigilant and act decisively against bullying—of Muslims.[25] Bullying *by* Muslims didn't seem to concern them: as Jewish groups complained of on-campus harassment, Muslims and leftists continued their push to shut down speech, with the Muslim Students Association (MSA) chapter at San Diego State University (SDSU) demanding that administrators implement a "zero tolerance policy explicitly for Islamophobic speech and actions."[26]

According to the College Fix, an online journal chronicling campus leftism and authoritarianism, the SDSU MSA demanded not only restrictions on "Islamophobic speech," but "mandatory bystander training...more courses on Islam, and increase[d] funding for The Center for Intercultural Relations."[27] The MSA, fluently speaking the language of the politically correct Left, also demanded that "the SDSU administration address, alleviate, and eliminate systems of oppression that disproportionately target students of color, womyn, and all marginalized students on campus."[28]

"It was above all the students who drove forward the co-ordination process in the universities"

When Nonie Darwish spoke at the University of New Mexico in February 2012, according to one of the hosts of the event, the Students for Justice in Palestine were determined not to allow her to be heard:

> Halfway through the talk, Arab and Leftist anti-Israel students, mostly from the SJP group, stood up and began screaming and chanting in order to shut down the talk and make a disturbance that their wide network could use against us. They were surprised that people in the audience were angry and went to clear them out of the room. This was a first for UNM. Normally both sides have enough respect not to disrupt each other's events. Consequently UNM police didn't see the need to have officers at the event. However, there is a new wind blowing in the US, and the people who disrupted our talk showed us that what Nonie Darwish was saying is true.[29]

Syracuse University planned an international conference on "The Place of Religion in Film" for spring 2017 and one of the conference organizers, William L. Blizek, a professor of philosophy and religion at the University of Nebraska and founder of the *Journal of Religion & Film*, invited Israeli filmmaker Shimon Dotan to show his film *The Settlers* at the conference.

Shortly thereafter, Dotan received a letter from M. Gail Hamner of Syracuse University:

> Dear Professor Dotan,
>
> I know you have been in contact with my Omaha colleague, Bill Blizek, about screening *The Settlers* and serving as plenary speaker at a religion and film conference in Syracuse in March, 2017. I am the convener of that conference and I found Bill's description of your work, and the reviews I read of it exciting.
>
> I now am embarrassed to share that my SU colleagues, on hearing about my attempt to secure your presentation, have warned me that the BDS faction on campus will make matters very unpleasant for you and for me if you come.[30]

"The BDS faction on campus will make matters very unpleasant for you." Goebbels himself couldn't have said it more plainly. In his seminal history *The Coming of the Third Reich*, Richard J. Evans explains how, in the early days of National Socialist Germany, the universities became centers of Nazi indoctrination in which students collaborated with brownshirted storm-troopers to terrorize dissenters: "It was above all the students who drove forward the co-ordination process in the universities. They organized campaigns against unwanted professors in the local newspapers, staged mass disruptions of their lectures and led detachments of stormtroopers in house-searches and raids."[31]

Compare how the Nazi thugs behaved to what is now taking place on American university campuses:

1. "It was above all the students who drove forward the co-ordination process in the universities."

At Eastern Michigan University in April 2015, two showings of the film *American Sniper* were scheduled. But during the first, four Muslim students,

Ahmed Abbas, Layali Alsadah, Jenna Hamed, and Sabreen Dari, climbed onto the stage and began to denounce the film, which many Muslims complained was "Islamophobic" because it depicted Islamic jihad terrorists in a realistic manner. They were briefly arrested, but managed to get the second showing canceled.[32]

Student Body President Desmond Miller offered some airy and barely coherent double talk: "The conversation we had wanted to make sure student safety was at the forefront. We wanted to make sure whatever happens, students would be safe. The second part of it, which is actually just as important as the first part, was making sure we have a very serious dialogue about the movie and the propaganda associated with this movie."[33] Miller did not explain how a "serious dialogue" about a movie was possible if students were not allowed to see the movie in question.

2. "They organized campaigns against unwanted professors in the local newspapers.... "

Today, there are precious few professors saying anything that the new brownshirts disagree with. Instead, they turn their fire on speakers brought on campus from outside to express dissenting views. When David Horowitz spoke at the University of North Carolina at Chapel Hill in April 2015, Manzoor Cheema, "co-founder of Muslims for Social Justice," wrote a letter to the campus newspaper, the *Daily Tar Heel*, saying that it was "distressing" that Horowitz had spoken, and "especially distressing in the wake of Chapel Hill tragedy where three Muslim youth were murdered."[34]

Did Horowitz applaud or condone the murder of those students? Of course not. Were they even murdered because they were Muslim? No. The Chapel Hill Police had determined that a deranged man who was enraged over parking disputes, not Islam, perpetrated those killings.[35] The killer's wife, Karen Hicks, had added that her husband "often champions on his Facebook page for the rights of individuals.... He believes everyone is equal—doesn't matter what you look like or who you are or what you believe."[36] U.S. Attorney Ripley Rand had stated that the murders were "not part of a targeting campaign against Muslims in North Carolina," and that there was "no information this is part of an organized event against Muslims."[37]

But Cheema wasn't going to let facts get in the way of his defamation; he added: "Horowitz has supported work of such virulent Islamophobes as Robert Spencer, who was cited 162 times by the Norwegian mass-murderer Anders Breivik."[38]

Cheema didn't mention that in all his quotations of me, Breivik never quoted me calling for or justifying any vigilantism or violence; nor could he have, because I have never done so. Nor did Cheema mention that Breivik even criticized me for not doing so, saying of me and other critics of jihad terror, "If these authors are to [sic] scared to propagate a conservative revolution and armed resistance then other authors will have to."[39] Nor did Cheema note the well-documented fact that Breivik was set on his path to mass murder by certain experiences he had with Muslim immigrants in the early 1990s, years before I had published anything regarding the jihad threat.[40]

Cheema, however, didn't intend to discuss these matters rationally, and didn't want his readers to do so, either. He just wanted to sling enough mud at Horowitz (and me) that university invitations would not be extended again to those who deviated from the politically correct line. The same day, the *Daily Tar Heel* ran two other letters denouncing Horowitz, and (of course) none supporting him.

3. *". . . . staged mass disruptions of their lectures. . . . "*

Here again, it would be hard to find a professor that today's new Nazi thugs have any reason to want to silence, so they target campus speakers instead. In April 2012, I attempted to speak at Temple University, along with Nonie Darwish, Pamela Geller, and Sudanese activist Simon Deng, who had been kidnapped and enslaved by Muslims as a child.[41] I was the first speaker;

leftist students packed the hall, repeatedly heckled and interrupted me, and finally stood up en masse, held up photos of Anders Breivik, and stormed out, leaving only a handful in the audience. We learned later that many who had actually wanted to hear us speak were unable to get in because the leftist students had packed the hall.

"If U.C. Berkeley does not allow free speech and practices violence on innocent people with a different point of view—NO FEDERAL FUNDS?"

Those Left-fascists were out in force at the University of California at Berkeley (ironically, the home of the "Free Speech Movement" of the 1960s) on February 1, 2017, when Milo Yiannopoulos was scheduled to speak at the university. Chanting "shut him down," students and others started fires, smashed windows, and threw rocks at police, apparently oblivious to the irony of rioting violently against someone they accused of being "intolerant."[42]

Milo had previously had university appearances canceled at the University of California at Davis and elsewhere, but at his Berkeley appearance the Left crossed a line, declaring openly its contempt for the principles of free discourse and free expression, and making clear its determination to enforce its perspective by force.

This time, however, there was a new sheriff in town. President Donald Trump, in office for twelve days, tweeted, "If U.C. Berkeley does not allow free speech and practices violence on innocent people with a different point of view—NO FEDERAL FUNDS?"[43]

Defenders of the freedom of speech hoped those weren't empty words, as the situation on campuses nationwide for those who dissented from the leftist line was increasingly precarious. (And not just on campus. After the white nationalist Richard B. Spencer was punched in the face in Washington, D.C., on the inauguration day of Donald Trump as president of the United States, writer C. J. Werleman, author of the Islamic apologetic *Koran*

SHUT UP,
THEY
EXPLAINED

When Pamela Geller spoke at Brooklyn College in April 2015, Muslim students packed the hall and staged an unending series of disruptions: heckling, clapping, asking irrelevant and impertinent questions, and filing in and out of the hall repeatedly.[45] It was abundantly clear from the very beginning of her speech that the students had no intention of engaging her ideas; they were there to disrupt her speech, and that was all.

Curious, celebrated the violence on Twitter and recommended that more of those he hated be punched. He wrote to me, "I think a swift smack to the side of your head would make the world a much better place, too."[44] Twitter did not delete his account.)

"This opinion blog has been retracted because of personal safety concerns"

On campuses, this atmosphere of menace against conservative opinions increasingly curtailed the freedom of speech.

In the spring of 2015, a student at the University of California–Berkeley published an article in the *Californian*, Berkeley's campus newspaper, entitled "On Leaving Islam" and explaining why she no longer considered herself a Muslim. "If someone had told me six years ago that I would leave Islam and end up an atheist, I would never have believed him," she wrote. "But now, as a Muslim apostate and atheist, my journey couldn't have led me any further from what I once knew to be true."[46]

She wrote about Islamic beliefs with a frankness and honesty rarely seen on today's college campuses, to say nothing of the mainstream media: "I never accepted the male superiority and traditional gender roles that were part of my society. For most of my teen years, I felt torn apart by my contradictory beliefs. On one hand, I was a radical feminist who supported gay rights. But on the other hand, I was a practicing Muslim whose religion was clearly homophobic and placed men above women."[47]

The author defended some aspects of Islam but promised more detailed discussion of both its positive and negative aspects in future pieces: "Islam, after all, gave women the right to work and own property back in the seventh century—I also plan to ruthlessly point out areas that need reform (yes, Islam does allow men to have four wives and sex slaves)."[48]

A few days after this courageous article was posted, it was taken down. *Californian* editor-in-chief Kimberly Veklerov explained laconically, "This opinion blog has been retracted because of personal safety concerns."[49]

By 2015, it was no longer safe to criticize Islam on an American university campus. And so on some university campuses, non-Muslim students began to self-enforce Sharia blasphemy law.

"Even though freedom of speech and press is emphasized and is something all of us value as proud Americans, the University prides itself on diversity of people of different faith and backgrounds"

The April 5, 2016 issue of the *Gleaner*, the student paper of Rutgers University–Camden, published a cartoon of Muhammad, Buddha, and Jesus in a bar. Its content, however, cannot be known at this point, because at the behest of Muslims on campus the entire issue has been deep-sixed. This is an incident fraught with implications for the health of the freedom of speech today.

Two weeks after the cartoon was published, the April 19 issue of the *Gleaner* contained a letter from the Muslim Brotherhood campus group, the Muslim Students Association, saying that it found the image offensive and asking the *Gleaner* to remove the image from the April 5 issue and circulate a new edition of that issue without it. The MSA letter claimed that Christians and Jews on campus had told MSA members that they, too, found the image offensive.[50]

The MSA letter stated, "Even though freedom of speech and press is emphasized and is something all of us value as proud Americans, the University prides itself on diversity of people of different faith and backgrounds so we feel that it is necessary to respect those faiths and backgrounds by honoring their beliefs."[51]

The April 19, 2016, *Gleaner* contained a response to the MSA letter written by Christopher Church, the paper's editor in chief. Church apologized to the MSA and agreed to meet with it "so that we can rectify this issue and ensure that it doesn't happen again."[52] He also agreed to remove any copies of the offending April 5 issue from the *Gleaner* boxes around campus and destroy them.

Neither Church nor anyone at Rutgers appeared to be aware of, or to care about, the fact that the freedom of speech as a Constitutional right is not negated by anyone's taking offense. This incident could and should have been a chance for Rutgers and the *Gleaner* to explain why the freedom of speech must be protected as our fundamental bulwark against tyranny, and why that means that we must all learn to put up with material that offends us.

And once a group's feelings of offense are taken as decisive, that group has a license to take offense at other aspects of campus life. What if Muslim Student Association members declare themselves offended at men and women sharing classrooms at Rutgers, or pork being served in the Rutgers dining hall?

In light of the violent attacks on those who have depicted Muhammad, the *Gleaner* was bowing to the implicit threat of violence—which in the long run only encourages more violence. Around the same time the Rutgers Muhammad cartoon incident played out, the Rutgers Art Library featured an "artwork" depicting Jesus on a dartboard. It was ultimately removed, but not because it offended Christians.[53] No one cared if Christians were offended: Rutgers officials knew that offended Christians wouldn't murder them. Their solicitousness toward the MSA, by contrast, reveals that they knew offended Muslims might very well kill them. Rather than stand up for the freedom of speech and against this kind of bullying, they signaled their willingness to surrender and fall into line, accepting Sharia restrictions on speech.

The double standard was stark: Jesus crucified on a dartboard was art—and what's more, it was courageous—while a cartoon of Muhammad was beyond the bounds of acceptable expression. One Rutgers student chortled on Facebook that the dartboard "art" was "hilarious," and crowed that "we don't have to cater to the wills of the Church or any denomination of Christianity or religion."[54] A cartoon of Muhammad, on the other hand, was an outrage. No one was crowing about not having to cater to the will of the mosque.

This is the kind of respect being irrationally violent will win you. This respect won at the point of a sword does not bode well for the future of free expression in the West.

The brownshirts were back, and on American campuses. And administrators all too often appeared anxious to placate them, rather than determined to protect the freedom of speech and curb their influence.

> ## WHY WE NEED THE FREEDOM OF SPEECH
>
> "The best test of truth is the power of the thought to get itself accepted in the competition of the market."
>
> —Oliver Wendell Holmes[55]

Chapter Twelve

"THE UNIVERSITY PRIDES ITSELF ON DIVERSITY": ADMINISTRATORS VS. FREE SPEECH

Did you know?

- University administrators enable leftist students' campaigns to shut up speakers
- Administrators use the claim of "security risks" to keep critics of Islam off campus
- The propaganda term "Islamophobia" is taken seriously on campuses nationwide

Leftist and Muslim student groups have become notorious for their violent hostility to the freedom of speech. And university administrators are enabling their campaign to shout down, heckle, physically menace, and otherwise shut up speakers they do not want to be heard on college campuses.

This has been going on for quite some time. In 2007, campus Republicans at the University of Florida sponsored a showing of the film *Obsession: Radical Islam's War with the West*. To advertise it, they put up posters around campus reading, "Radical Islam Wants You Dead"—whereupon Patricia Telles-Irvin, the university's vice president for student affairs, sent a message to the entire student body, calling upon the Republican students to apologize and claiming that the posters "reinforced a negative stereotype…and contributed to a generalization that only furthers the misunderstanding of the religion of Islam."[1] Back in those days, such ham-handed efforts at politically biased censorship still received some pushback. Florida attorney general Bill McCollum rebuked the university for having "chilled free speech."[2]

"We will not tolerate an attack at our faith"

Voices speaking out for the freedom of speech and the consideration of unpopular ideas on American campuses were significantly more muted seven years later when, in April 2014, Brandeis University announced that it was awarding an honorary degree to human rights activist and ex-Muslim Ayaan Hirsi Ali. Widespread student protests quickly followed, including a Facebook page denouncing Hirsi Ali for "hate speech."[4] The Brandeis chapter of the Muslim Students Association charged that awarding Hirsi Ali an honorary degree was "a direct violation of Brandeis University's own moral code as well as the rights of all Brandeis students."[5] The MSA added ominously, "We will not tolerate an attack at our faith."[6] No fewer than eighty-six faculty members also demanded that the honorary degree should be rescinded.[7] The university soon reversed itself and dropped its plans to honor Hirsi Ali.

In a statement explaining its reversal, Brandeis

STICKS AND STONES MAY BREAK MY BONES, BUT WORDS WILL NEVER HURT ME

"...a great many Americans would disagree [with the University of Florida administrator who demanded that students apologize because they had 'reinforced a negative stereotype' of Islam] and argue that it is essential to the discussion and understanding of this war that the terrorists be properly and correctly labeled as radical Islamists who by their very actions clearly want us dead. Students and student organizations who hold this latter view should not be stifled in their free expression of it."

—Florida Attorney General Bill McCollum[3]

wrote, "She is a compelling public figure and advocate for women's rights, and we respect and appreciate her work to protect and defend the rights of women and girls throughout the world. That said, we cannot overlook certain of her past statements that are inconsistent with Brandeis University's core values. For all concerned, we regret that we were not aware of these statements earlier."[8]

Rashid Khalidi, a venomously anti-Israel professor at Columbia University who opposed Hirsi Ali's receiving an honorary degree from Brandeis, expressed astonishment that Brandeis professed not to have known about Hirsi Ali's remarks, commenting acidly, "You would think that someone at Brandeis would have learned to use Google."[9]

Anyone at Brandeis could have gone to Google and found Hirsi Ali observing that "violence is inherent in Islam," and asserting that Islam was "the new fascism" and "a destructive, nihilistic cult of death."[10] She had also stated in a 2007 interview that what the West needed to defeat was not "radical Islam," but

Islam, period. Once it's defeated, it can mutate into something peaceful. It's very difficult to even talk about peace now. They're not interested in peace.... I think that we are at war with Islam. And there's no middle ground in wars. Islam can be defeated in many ways. For starters, you stop the spread of the ideology itself; at present, there are native Westerners converting to Islam, and they're the most fanatical sometimes. There is infiltration of Islam in the schools and universities of the West. You stop that. You stop the symbol burning and the effigy burning, and you look them in the eye and flex your muscles and you say, "This is a warning. We won't accept this anymore." There comes a moment when you crush your enemy.[11]

When asked if she meant that Islam must be crushed militarily, Hirsi Ali responded, "In all forms, and if you *don't* do that, then you have to live with the consequence of being *crushed*."[12]

A key force in pressuring Brandeis to rescind the honorary degree was the Council on American-Islamic Relations (CAIR), which accused Hirsi Ali of being a "notorious Islamophobe."[13] CAIR's Ibrahim Hooper claimed that Hirsi Ali was "one of the worst of the worst of the Islam haters in America, not only in America but worldwide. I don't assign any ill will to Brandeis. I think they just kind of got fooled a little bit."[14]

Yes, but by whom?

Like Nonie Darwish's views on Islam, Hirsi Ali's criticisms of the religion of her birth were not born of racism or bigotry. They are reasoned and fact-based conclusions from her own bitter experiences growing up as a Muslim in Somalia, being subjected to genital mutilation and indoctrinated with hatred for Jews and other infidels. She immigrated to the Netherlands and left Islam, noting, "I left the world of faith, of genital cutting and forced marriage for the world of reason and emancipation. After making this voyage I know that one of these two worlds is simply better than the other. Not for its gaudy gadgetry, but for its fundamental values."[15] Hirsi Ali collaborated with Theo van Gogh's film *Submission* about the institutionalized mistreatment of women in Islam, and she was threatened in the note attached to van Gogh's body by his devout Muslim murderer.

Hirsi Ali's knowledge of Islam came from her lived experience, yet non-Muslim officials of a non-Muslim university felt compelled to dismiss her observations not on the basis of any knowledge of Islam—they didn't know whether or not violence was inherent in Islam, they just knew it was politically incorrect to say so—but because they were pressured by Islamic advocacy groups. Even those groups didn't demonstrate that what Hirsi Ali had said was false (because they couldn't); they just called her a hater.

Joseph Lumbard, the chairman of Brandeis's department of Islamic and Middle Eastern studies and a convert to Islam, also complained that the honorary degree to Hirsi Ali had frightened Muslim students: "This makes Muslim students feel very uneasy. They feel unwelcome here."[16] This was improbable in the extreme, and ironic in light of the fact that Muslim students are much more likely to brutalize Jewish students on American college campuses than the other way around, but it played well with the mainstream media's general desire to portray Muslims as victims of unfair suspicion, discrimination, and harassment.[17]

The *New York Times* asserted that rescinding the honor was simply a matter of Brandeis not wanting to appear to endorse Hirsi Ali's views: "Universities consider it important to make a distinction between inviting a speaker who may air unpopular or provocative views that the institution does not endorse, and awarding an honorary degree, which is more akin to affirming the body of a recipient's work."[18] But in rescinding the honorary degree to Hirsi Ali, Brandeis was affirming the views of her critics, that her work was indeed hateful and not worthy of being honored.

Brandeis didn't hesitate to award an honorary degree to playwright Tony Kushner, who has dubbed the creation of the State of Israel "a mistake" and blamed Israel for the "terrible peril in the world." Brandeis has also given an honorary degree to Archbishop Desmond Tutu, who has a long record of anti-Semitic remarks, according to journalist Lori Lowenthal Marcus: Tutu has "compared Israel to Hitler, attacked the 'Jewish lobby' as too 'powerful' and 'scary,' he has sanitized the gas chambers of the Holocaust which he said made for a 'neater death' than one under Apartheid, and he complained of the 'Jewish monopoly of the Holocaust.' He also insists that Jewish Holocaust victims should forgive the Nazis."[19]

Apparently, those were views that Brandeis was happy to endorse, "affirming the body of a recipient's work"—while Hirsi Ali's were beyond the pale of acceptable discourse.

STICKS AND STONES MAY BREAK MY BONES, BUT WORDS WILL NEVER HURT ME

"We need to make our universities temples not of dogmatic orthodoxy, but of truly critical thinking, where all ideas are welcome and where civil debate is encouraged."[20]
—Ayaan Hirsi Ali in the text of the address she had planned to deliver at Brandeis, published in the *Wall Street Journal*

At least in its statement rescinding its honorary degree to Hirsi Ali, Brandeis said, "In the spirit of free expression that has defined Brandeis University throughout its history, Ms. Hirsi Ali is welcome to join us on campus in the future to engage in a dialogue about these important issues."[21] The whole episode showed that the university's commitment to free expression was tenuous at best, but at least it had reiterated that Hirsi Ali was welcome on campus. On other campuses, that was not always true of speakers who enunciated unpopular and unwelcome truths about Islam.

"We had our event canceled due to 'security risks'"

In December 2009, Columbia University canceled a scheduled speech by Nonie Darwish. Daniel Hertz, a senior at the university, wrote on Facebook, "I am the CAMERA fellow for Columbia and the President of Campus Media Watch. We are the group that tried to bring Nonie Darwish to speak yesterday. It was very unfortunate that we had our event canceled due to 'security risks,' and I am still dealing with ways to respond to what happened."[22]

"Security risks" was becoming campus administrators' way of shutting down unwelcome politically incorrect speakers without bringing upon themselves charges of infringing upon the freedom of speech and banning unpopular ideas from campus. I encountered this tactic myself at Saint

Anselm College in Manchester, New Hampshire, when college officials invoked security risks to cover up their hostility to a point of view that veers too far from the acceptable leftist line.

In February 2013, a student group invited me to speak at Saint Anselm, and posters advertising the talk were being put up when Saint Anselm's then-president, Father Jonathan DeFelice, O.S.B., canceled my appearance, reportedly citing complaints he had received from Muslim students at the school.

If the story had ended there, Saint Anselm would have been no worse than dozens of other colleges and universities where officials have caved to pressure from Muslims who play the victimhood card to shut down those who air inconvenient truths about the nature and magnitude of the jihad threat. But it didn't.

The following year, after Father DeFelice had retired and been replaced as president of the college by Dr. Steven R. DiSalvo, Saint Anselm's philosophy department invited me to be the guest speaker at a symposium.

DiSalvo, following his predecessor's lead, nixed that appearance as well. Several Saint Anselm professors objected, complaining to DiSalvo that colleges were supposed to be centers of free inquiry and intellectual engagement, and that he was acting contrary to what institutions of higher learning were supposed to be all about by banning politically incorrect points of view.

Cornered, DiSalvo found an excuse: he was all for free inquiry and unpopular opinions (the unpopular opinion in my case being the rather obvious point that Islam is not really a religion of peace), but he just couldn't allow me to speak on campus because I had received death threats. He explained that, were I to be present on campus, Saint Anselm students would be endangered—what if a violent extremist were to burst onto campus while I was speaking?

The dubiousness of DiSavio's explanation was obvious. Numerous people who have received death threats speak on college campuses all over the country without incident. Since I personally first began receiving death threats, I have spoken at universities nationwide, including UCLA, Temple, Penn State, the University of North Carolina at Chapel Hill, the University of Virginia, Dartmouth, DePaul, SUNY in both Binghamton and Stony Brook, Brown, Cal Poly, and many, many others. In this instance, I met the Saint Anselm philosophy professors for an off-campus symposium, after which several of them told me that my positions were entirely reasonable and should have a place in campus discussion.

When people who have been threatened appear in public, they are generally accompanied by security personnel who are equipped and prepared to deal with any incident. Why Saint Anselm considered such security arrangements to be inadequate, DiSalvo didn't explain, suggesting the question: Why was Saint Anselm College so much less safe than all other campuses? Other colleges and universities nationwide can and do host speakers who have been threatened; they simply take measures to ensure everyone's safety. Saint Anselm apparently can't do that.

As implausible as it was, DiSalvo stuck with his security excuse. Often, as I speak around the country, I do TV appearances from a local studio; on one swing back up to New England in the summer of 2015, however, a Fox News producer told me that I couldn't do the segment from the Videolink at Saint Anselm's New Hampshire Institute of Politics (NHIOP), as she had been told that I was not welcome to use the Videolink there.

I found this curious and thought that while I was in the area I would go by Saint Anselm to ask why, certain that any misunderstanding could be cleared up. While there, I was told that I couldn't use the studio because of the death threats I had received. But while waiting to discuss this with Neil Levesque, the head of NHIOP, I was threatened and ultimately assaulted by a Saint Anselm security guard and told that I was henceforth barred from the Saint Anselm campus on pain of arrest for criminal trespass.

That is how a leftist "institution of higher learning" deals with dissenting points of view these days.

The dishonesty of Saint Anselm's position was obvious. The NHIOP is often the site of presidential debates during the New Hampshire primary season; Donald Trump spoke there in 2016 even after receiving death threats over his call for a border wall and a temporary moratorium on Muslim immigration. In regard to me, Saint Anselm officials claimed that they were utterly unable to stop those who make death threats from attacking their targets on campus; yet when it came to presidential candidates and other prominent figures who had been threatened, they had no difficulty providing adequate security.

I wrote to Levesque asking for a list of people who had used the NHIOP Videolink, expecting to find that a number of them had received death threats; he responded by having a member of the local Goffstown, New Hampshire police department call me to warn me that if I wrote to Levesque again, he would have me arrested for harassment (for the record: I wrote to Levesque only once, and my letter to him contained no abusive language, insults, threats, or anything of the kind).

Saint Anselm is not alone in its authoritarianism and use of thuggish security guards and local cops as enforcers: In October 2015 Adams State University in Colorado barred one of its former professors from campus, also on pain of arrest for trespassing, after he publicly questioned the university's pay scale and some of its other polices.[23] The following month, University of Missouri professor Melissa Click called for "muscle" to strong-arm a student photographer who had entered a meeting where he was unwelcome.[24]

Saint Anselm College, like so many other outposts of American academia, has swiftly descended from the days when ideas could be entertained and dismissed on their merits alone. In a world of microaggressions, trigger warnings, safe spaces, and mansplaining, American academia today subverts the free exchange of ideas by banning figures whose ideas they do not agree with. At this point I am barred not just from speaking at Saint Anselm College but even from setting foot on its campus. This is a new tactic in the academic Left's attempts to suppress ideas it disapproves of.

As colleges across America grow increasingly hostile to dissenting views, Saint Anselm, firmly clutching its "security risk" fig leaf, has placed itself squarely against the freedom of speech and free inquiry.

"If there is anyone who values free speech, it is a tenured professor!"

Professors all over the country now espouse the abridgement of the freedom of speech when it comes to criticism of Islam. In September 2012, as the Obama administration blamed the Benghazi jihad massacre on the obscure Muhammad video produced by Nakoula Basseley Nakoula (a.k.a Sam Bacile), Anthea Butler, a professor of religious studies at the University of Pennsylvania, joined Hillary Clinton in calling for the filmmaker's arrest.

"Words," Butler wrote, "have consequences" after receiving criticism for tweeting calls for Nakoula's arrest. She claimed she was doing so "not because I am against the First Amendment." Displaying a remarkable lack of self-awareness, she exclaimed, "If there is anyone who values free speech, it is a tenured professor!"[25]

Her call for the filmmaker's arrest, she said, "reflected my exasperation that as a religion professor, it is difficult to teach the facts when movies such as Bacile's *The Innocence of Muslims* are taken as both truth and propaganda, and used against innocent Americans." In the professor's mind, the moviemaker's free speech was only "free speech," in scare quotes: "The 'free speech' in Bacile's film is not about expressing a personal opinion about Islam. It denigrates the religion by depicting the faith's founder in several ludicrous and historically inaccurate scenes to incite and inflame viewers. Even the film's actors say they were duped."[26]

So denigrating a religion should land you in jail? If it results in other people behaving violently, yes: "Bacile's movie is not the first to denigrate a religious figure, nor will it be the last. *The Last Temptation of Christ* was protested vigorously. The difference is that Bacile indirectly and inadvertently inflamed people half a world away, resulting in the deaths of U.S. Embassy personnel."[27]

Of course no one was murdered over *The Last Temptation of Christ*. But the real difference between it and *The Innocence of Muslims* was that the people offended by the latter were not Christians but Muslims, who have a tradition of reacting to perceived insults with violent rage.

Butler concluded, "While the First Amendment right to free expression is important, it is also important to remember that other countries and cultures do not have to understand or respect our right."[28]

And apparently neither do University of Pennsylvania professors. Butler was saying that Muslims did not have to respect the freedom speech, but non-Muslims do have to respect Islamic blasphemy law. She did not explain, or even seem to notice, the inequity.

"Free speech areas"

In September 2016, the Young Americans for Freedom (YAF) chapter at Saddleback College in Mission Viejo, California, put up posters around campus for YAF's "9/11: Never Forget" project, marking the fifteenth anniversary of the largest-scale jihad terror attack on American soil. Margot Lovett, a professor of gender studies, proceeded to rip down the posters, telling the YAF members that they were allowed to put them up only in one of the college's "free speech areas."

No one seems to have reminded the professor that the entire United States is, or at least according the First Amendment ought to be, a "free speech area," but some students were well aware of what was at stake. The Saddleback YAF chapter's spokesman, Thomas Columbus, declared that Lovett had "blatantly infringed on our First Amendment rights by ripping down the posters."

While Lovett claimed that she was merely enforcing college policy, she may have had another agenda. In the immediate aftermath of the 9/11 attacks she had circulated among her Saddleback College colleagues a statement by the Black Radical Congress blaming the United States for "genocidal levels of death and destruction" worldwide and castigating the U.S. government for its "virtually uncritical" support of Israel. The statement proclaimed, "One clearly sees the callousness and evil intent with which U.S. imperialism treats the lives and property of others, especially non-white peoples around the globe." While the statement conceded that terrorism was not an "acceptable strategy" for dealing with this problem, it denounced "self-serving jingoism," warning against counterterror measures that would "strengthen the existing tendency toward a racist and classist police state."[29] Lovett called this hysterical bit of leftist agitprop the "most cogent analysis" of 9/11 and its aftermath that she had come across.[30]

And so while she may have indeed simply have been acting as a stickler for the rules when she tore down the YAF posters, it is likely that she would have been considerably less punctilious if the posters had been put up by, say, Black Lives Matter or Students for Justice in Palestine.

"A lot of people want to stereotype and say that Islam oppresses women"

For while they are more or less unanimously hostile spaces for conservative and particularly anti-jihad and pro-Israel views, university campuses are extremely hospitable environments for those who openly support jihad terror and Islamic supremacism. The Muslim Student Association, a group with links to the Muslim Brotherhood, held its first Islamic Awareness Week at Boston College, a Catholic institution, in March 2016. Among other activities, it invited non-Muslim women to don the hijab at a "Hijab Booth" and learn how, contrary to appearances, Muslim women are not really oppressed under Islamic law.

MSA president Ahad Arshad explained, "A lot of people want to stereotype and say that Islam oppresses women and makes them cover their hair, or something like that. But obviously there are women who do it in their own free will, and it's better if people can just see that." The "Hijab Booth," said Arshad, "eliminates that fear factor, like that 'Oh this is so foreign to me, I've never seen that before. If you see it on campus, you know girls wearing hijabs and talking openly about it and how they've made that choice on their own, independently, it definitely makes it less alien." Arshad said nothing about the many women who have been brutalized and even killed for not wearing the hijab.[31]

Unusually for an MSA leader, Arshad did admit that he had not faced "hate" at Boston College: "I have never really faced any stereotyping or ignorance or hatred, at least not to my face. I can't think of anyone who has done or said anything Islamophobic."[32]

"Cultivating academic freedom can be difficult and at times painful for any college community"

In February 2016, Joy Karega, a professor at Oberlin College, posted a series of paranoid and hateful Facebook messages blaming the Jews and Israel for the September 11 jihad terror attacks and the creation of the Islamic State. Amid the ensuing controversy, Karega found a defender in Oberlin College President Marvin Krislov, who sent a letter to the Oberlin College community:

> I am a practicing Jew, grandson of an Orthodox rabbi. Members of our family were murdered in the Holocaust. As someone who has studied history, I cannot comprehend how any person could or would question its existence, its horrors and the evil which

caused it. I feel the same way about anti-Semitic conspiracy theories. Regardless of the reason for spreading these materials, they cause pain for many people—members of our community and beyond.[33]

Nonetheless, he explained, he could not do anything about Karega, because of—of all things—the freedom of speech:

> Cultivating academic freedom can be difficult and at times painful for any college community. The principles of academic freedom and freedom of speech are not just principles to which we turn to face these challenges, but also the very practices that ensure we can develop meaningful responses to prejudice.
>
> This freedom enables Oberlin's faculty and students to think deeply about and to engage in frank, open discussion of ideas that some may find deeply offensive. Those discussions—in classrooms, residence halls, libraries, and across our campus and town—take place every day here. They are a vital part of the important work of liberal arts education at Oberlin and in our country.[34]

Administrators seldom spoke in such a high-minded manner about the freedom of expression when it came to conservative voices on campus. In any case, as the controversy over Karega's remarks continued, she was placed on paid leave in August 2016—in effect, given a vacation until the hullabaloo blew over.[35]

"Is Islamophobia accelerating global warming?"

It is remarkable that Karega's anti-Semitic rants caused any fuss at all. American universities are willing hosts to the most vitriolic, inaccurate, and bizarre speech without resistance or controversy—as long as it comes from the Left. Absurdities abound. In May 2016, posters appeared at the Massachusetts Institute of Technology (MIT) announcing a talk by Ghassan Hage, "Future Generation Professor in the School of Philosophy, Anthropology and Social Inquiry, University of Melbourne," presented by "the Ecology and Justice Forum In Global Studies And Languages" and sponsored by "Global Studies and Laguages [sic], Global Borders Research Collaboration, MIT Anthropology."[36] The topic: "Is Islamophobia Accelerating Global Warming?"[37]

The poster explained, "This talk examines the relation between Islamophobia as the dominant form of racism today and the ecological crisis. It looks at the three common ways in which the two phenomena are seen to be linked: as an entanglement of two crises, metaphorically related with one being a source of imagery for the other and both originating in colonial forms of capitalist accumulation. The talk proposes a fourth way of linking the two: an argument that they are both emanating from a similar mode of being, or enmeshment, in the world, what is referred to as 'generalised domestication.'"[38]

The man presenting this politically correct academic gobbledygook that united two leftist fantasies—Islamophobia and global warming—was an academic of impeccable pedigree:

> Ghassan Hage has held many visting [sic] positions across the world including in Harvard, University of Copenhagen, Ecoles des Hautes Etudes en Sciences Sociales and American University of Beirut. He works in the comparative anthropology of nationalism, multiculturalism, diaspora and racism and on the relation between anthropology, philosophy and social and political theory. His most well-known work is *White Nation: Fantasies of white supremacy in a multicultural society* (Routledge 2000). He

is also the author of *Alter-Politics: Critical Anthropology and the Radical Imaginary* (Melbourne University Press 2015). He is currently working on a book titled *Is Islamophobia Accelerating Global Warming?* and has most recently published a piece in *American Ethnologist*, titled: "Etat de Siege. A Dying Domesticating Colonialism?" (2016) that engages with the contemporary "refugee crisis" in Europe and beyond.[39]

Future generations will recognize that Ghassan Hage's work had all the academic rigor of that of any learned professor of alchemy; but in modern-day academia his perspective is not only mainstream, but dominant. American colleges are increasingly unwilling to host lectures on the threat of Islamic jihad, or the ways in which Islamic jihadis refer to Islamic texts and teachings in order to justify their actions and make recruits among peaceful Muslims. But a talk about how Islamophobia might be accelerating global warming? If only Ghassan Hage could find more time in his busy speaking schedule!

A pro-jihad, anti-American position was deeply ingrained in American academia. In September 2015, Alec Dent, a student at the University of North Carolina at Chapel Hill, revealed that "an English class offered at UNC Chapel Hill this fall called 'Literature of 9/11' explores the Sept. 11 terrorist attacks from the perspective of radical Islamists and those who view America as an imperialist nation."[40]

The course represented virtually everything wrong with American universities today. Its reading list consisted entirely of writings by leftists who viewed the War on Terror as a massive exercise in American racism and imperialism. Most of the other writings were by Muslims who...viewed the War on Terror as a massive exercise in American racism and imperialism.

In an article about the course, Dent identified the course's professor, Neel Ahuja, as "an associate professor of English, comparative literature, and geography at the University of North Carolina, Chapel Hill." UNC's website listed him more specifically as "associate professor of postcolonial studies in the Department of English and Comparative Literature at UNC." Postcolonial studies: that was as likely to present a positive or even fair view of the United States of America as the Department of Queer Theory is to present a course titled "The Wisdom of Pat Robertson." (After the controversy over Ahuja's course broke, the link to his page on the UNC website was sealed from the public; those trying to view it would see only "ACCESS DENIED. You are not authorized to access this page."[41])

Dent noted that "according to Ahuja's Blinkness rating page—similar to Rate My Professors but specific to Chapel Hill—he seems to be popular with his students, and received generally positive reviews. However, several students also warned not to disagree with Ahuja, especially in a graded assignment."[42]

Among the dismal and one-sided offerings in this propaganda session masquerading as a college class was Mohsin Hamid's *The Reluctant Fundamentalist*, an extended exercise in grievance-mongering, intending to show how U.S. policies were driving thoughtful people to become jihad terrorists. Despite the word "fundamentalist" in the title, there was little in the book about Islamic texts and teachings and the effects they could have upon a devout believer. No, jihad terrorism was all the fault of the big, bad United States.

UNC–Chapel Hill is a particularly ugly and virulent center of leftist indoctrination: the university employs the likes of Carl Ernst, who in 2008 won an award from the oppressive and brutal Islamic Republic of Iran for his work whitewashing Islamic jihad; the award was presented to Ernst in Tehran by Iran's genocidally anti-Semitic President Mahmoud Ahmadinejad.[43] UNC proudly employed a professor who had been presented an award by Ahmadinejad; would they employ a professor who had been given an award by President Donald Trump? To ask the question is to answer it.

WHY WE NEED THE FREEDOM OF SPEECH

• • •

"The moment you say that any idea system is sacred, whether it's a religious belief system or a secular ideology, the moment you declare a set of ideas to be immune from criticism, satire, derision, or contempt, freedom of thought becomes impossible."

—Salman Rushdie[44]

When the furor over this course broke nationwide, UNC tried to save face. Jim Gregory, UNC's director of media relations there, said, "Carolina offers academic courses to challenge students—not to advocate one viewpoint over another." Really? Then where was the counterpart course to this one, in which students could read accounts by 9/11 victims and the relatives of those who were killed? What courses did UNC offer about the Islamic doctrine of jihad, and the contemporary global jihad? What courses did UNC offer about Sharia and dhimmitude, in which students could read the works of the pioneering historian of dhimmitude, Bat Ye'or? What courses did UNC offer about the early origins of Islam, in which students could read the scholarship of Alphonse Mingana and Christoph Luxenberg?

The reality is that UNC, like most universities today, does nothing but advocate one viewpoint over another. And dissenting voices are not welcome.

Chapter Thirteen

"FACING THE NEW TOTALITARIANISM": FIGHTING BACK FOR THE FREEDOM OF SPEECH

There has been remarkably little pushback against the Islamic and leftist assault against the freedom of speech. For the most part, those in positions of power and influence seem not to realize the implications of what is happening, or else they don't care—when they aren't actively complicit in the steady muzzling of dissent.

There have been some small encouraging signs. In 2005, in the wake of the Muslim riots over the Danish Muhammad cartoons, a group of writers issued a manifesto called, "Together Facing the New Totalitarianism."[1] This genuinely anti-bigotry manifesto declared, "After having overcome fascism, Nazism, and Stalinism, the world now faces a new global totalitarian threat: Islamism.... We, writers, journalists, intellectuals, call for resistance to religious totalitarianism and for the promotion of freedom, equal opportunity and secular values for all. We refuse to renounce our critical spirit out of fear of being accused of 'Islamophobia,' a wretched concept that confuses criticism of Islam as a religion and stigmatization of those who believe in it. We defend the universality of the freedom of expression, so that a critical spirit can exist in every continent, towards each and every maltreatment and dogma."[2]

Words to live by. And to preserve free societies by.

A time of testing

But our society has not chosen to live by those words. Instead, we are living in the age of "the future must not belong to those who slander the prophet of Islam." Even when Barack Obama's presidency is just a distant memory, those words will stand as the pivotal moment when the United States sounded the retreat from the defense of the freedom of speech.

We could have acted so very differently—and we still can. The next time someone is menaced by Islamic jihadists for exercising free speech, he or she should not be forgotten like Molly Norris or demonized like Pamela Geller. Instead, that person's cause—the cause of the freedom of speech—should be taken up by all free people, not least the president of the United States.

Donald Trump's unexpected election to the presidency has undoubtedly thrown a bit of a wrench into the plans of the Organization of Islamic Cooperation and other organizations determined to extinguish Western nations' freedom of speech. His opponent in the 2016 election, Hillary Clinton, had been an active proponent of these efforts as Secretary of State, and even with her defeat, her recommendation that foes of jihad terror be silenced by means of "peer pressure and shaming" continues to be taken up by the Left on a daily basis.

However, the new president immediately broke with his predecessor by speaking of "radical Islamic terrorism" rather than the euphemistic and willfully ignorant "violent extremism" that was the focus of Barack Obama's counterterror efforts. This change in rhetoric could herald a willingness to restore study of the jihadis' motivating ideology to counterterror training, and even the beginning of a societal reaction against the tacit acceptance of Sharia blasphemy restrictions that continues to spread in the American public square.

But there is a great deal more that President Trump, and any president who values freedom, should do.

The president should explain that the freedom of expression is the foremost protection that free people have against tyranny. It is worth putting up with inconvenience and, yes, offense, as the price of not having one's own opinion violently suppressed.

The president will also need to go back to some basic principles that all people should know, but that many have forgotten. Chief among these is the proposition that human beings control their own reactions to things. If Muslims choose to riot and murder because of perceived insults to their religion, they are making that choice themselves, freely, out of an unlimited array of other choices.

The president could warn Western authorities that if they start altering or curtailing their statements and activities to avoid protest by Islamic supremacists, they are falling into the trap that has been laid for them, and internalizing the idea that they are responsible for the Muslim violence that may result from the articulation of unwelcome truths. In reality, that violence is in every case solely the responsibility of the perpetrator, not of anyone else.

An American president equipped with a courage and clarity of vision that are quite rare on the global stage today would also say that the very idea that any American would have to give up his or her career or live in hiding because of threats from Islamic jihadis over something spoken or written is unconscionable. The president would explain to the Islamic world that cartoons depicting Muhammad do not harm Muslims, and that the

WHY WE NEED THE FREEDOM OF SPEECH

. . .

"If there be time to expose through discussion the falsehood and fallacies, to avert the evil by the processes of education, the remedy to be applied is more speech, not enforced silence."

—Louis Brandeis[3]

willingness of some Muslims to commit murder over such depictions is the only thing that made people care to draw Muhammad in the first place.

Speaking calmly but with unmistakable force, the president would add that to threaten people with death because of cartoons is destructive to free speech and hence to free societies—and so it is something that the United States will do everything it can to resist. Added to that could be the announcement that anyone threatened for exercising the freedom of speech would be given full round-the-clock protection—and that if violent protests and riots over cartoons break out in areas where American troops are deployed, those troops will put down those riots and protect the innocent.

But if we do not change course, and the long retreat from the freedom of speech continues, then the United States and the West are in danger of descending into a totalitarianism more terrifying than all the totalitarian systems that have yet scarred the world. It is more terrifying for its potent combination of the new (the latest advances in technology, particularly weaponry and surveillance) with the old (the fourteen-hundred-year-old dogmas, incitements, and hatreds of Islam).

Our own leaders and the guardians of acceptable opinion in our own country have eagerly welcomed this totalitarianism—inviting its proponents to our shores, rebuking and stigmatizing its opponents, and complacently believing that once they have silenced their ideological foes once and for all, they will be able to maintain power in the new and brutal order that they have established.

They are in for a rude awakening. If the Left finally succeeds in ushering in the full implementation of Sharia blasphemy law, they will not be spared by the jihad to which they have surrendered the West. We must all hope—and work to assure—that that awakening never comes to them, that this new totalitarian order will never be imposed, that the jihad against the freedom of speech, aided and abetted by the authoritarian Left, will not triumph.

It is not too late; this sinister movement can still be stopped. But it is very, very late—past time for free people to rise to the test, to prove the love of freedom that is in their souls.

ACKNOWLEDGMENTS

As this is my sixteenth book, I have written a lot of Acknowledgments pages, and thanked a lot of people, and this time, I want to thank even more than usual. The real heroes of this book are all the individuals I have met as I travel around the country and the world speaking, who stand up and enunciate unpopular and unwelcome truths despite the contempt, hostility, and even personal and professional risk that doing so involves. I am heartened by them even as the assaults on the freedom of speech continue. Because I have had the privilege to meet them, I know that the forces of darkness and authoritarian oppression will never fully succeed, and the human spirit will never be completely bound and silenced.

Narrowing the circle just a bit, I owe a debt of gratitude to all those among my friends and colleagues who have been, as I have, the objects of the hatred, smears, defamation, lies, and character assassination that leftists and Islamic supremacists employ against those they hate, and have stood unbowed and kept fighting. Pamela Geller, the epitome of the happy warrior, has for years inspired me with her courage, grit, and grace under fire. Steve Emerson and Frank Gaffney, with both of whom I have had the privilege to work, likewise have given me worthy models to emulate: warriors who keep advancing despite the risks, the unjust attacks they routinely receive, and the white-hot rage of the foes of freedom.

Meanwhile, I am eternally grateful to my Jihad Watch colleagues: the acute, perceptive and indefatigable Christine Williams, who has given me a great deal of important information about the fight for the freedom of speech in Canada and elsewhere, and Hugh Fitzgerald, whose wit, erudition, and eloquence are unparalleled. Without their work on Jihad Watch, I couldn't have written this book or much of anything else, or had many of the worthwhile insights that may be contained in it.

Then we come to the actual book as it stands, for which I once again owe an immense debt of gratitude to the remarkable Elizabeth Kantor, my longtime friend and editor at Regnery Publishing. Hers is the keen eye and steady hand that kept this book from running aground; as determined as I was to dash it into the rocks, she kept it afloat. She is, indeed, a veritable Admiral Dewey of editors.

This is my tenth Regnery book. I am extremely proud of this long association, and grateful to Regnery's Marji Ross and Harry Crocker, as well as to my witty and patient publicist, Caitlyn Reuss, for all their support over the years, and for their refusal to succumb to the peer pressure and shaming that the enlightened Left have subjected them to because of their association with me.

No Acknowledgments page would be complete without a nod to Jeffrey Rubin, who brought me to Regnery, gave me the idea for my bestselling *The*

Politically Incorrect Guide to Islam (and the Crusades), and helped me in so many other ways. Cheers, Jeff. I hope we will be able to meet again on my next Acknowledgments page.

NOTES

Chapter One: "Just Stay Quiet and You'll Be Okay"

1. Michael Ellison, "'We Have Planes. Stay Quiet'—Then Silence," *Guardian*, October 17, 2001.
2. "Fear Pervades Danish Art Community," *DR Nyheder*, September 18, 2005.
3. Paul Belien, "Jihad against Danish Newspaper," *Brussels Journal*, October 22, 2005.
4. "Imam Demands Apology for Mohammed Cartoons," *Jyllands-Posten*, October 9, 2005.
5. "Muslim Anger at Danish Cartoons," BBC, October 20, 2005.
6. Jan M. Olsen, "Cartoons of Muhammad Anger Muslims Worldwide," Associated Press, December 11, 2005.
7. "Imam Demands Apology."
8. Clive Hibbert, "Onward Christian Soldiers," *Guardian*, December 9, 2003.
9. "Cartoons Have Muslims Threatening Newspaper," *Jyllands-Posten*, October 12, 2005.
10. "PM Ditches Muslims for Freedom of Speech," *Copenhagen Post*, October 25, 2005.

11.   "PM Ditches Muslims."

12.   Kate Connolly, "Muslims March over Cartoons of the Prophet," *Telegraph*, November 4, 2005.

13.   Olsen, "Cartoons of Muhammad."

14.   "Prophet Cartoons Prompt Egypt to Cut off Danish Dialogue," *Copenhagen Post*, November 3, 2005.

15.   Kate Connolly, "Muslims March over Cartoons of the Prophet," *Telegraph*, November 4, 2005.

16.   "New Death Threats against Mohammed Cartoonists," *Copenhagen Post*, December 2, 2005.

17.   Hjörtur J. Guðmundsson, "Bounty Offered for Murdering Cartoonists," *Brussels Journal*, December 4, 2005.

18.   "Protest Strike against Blasphemous Cartoons in Kashmir," *World Bulletin*, February 6, 2006.

19.   "Protest against Cartoon Cripples Life in Kashmir," *Pak Tribune*, February 6, 2006.

20.   Adel Abdel Halim, "Al-Azhar Takes Anti-Prophet Danish Cartoons to UN," Islam Online, December 11, 2005.

21.   Olsen, "Cartoons of Muhammad."

22.   "'Muhammad cartoon' proved fake," World Net Daily, February 8, 2006.

23.   "Gaza EU Offices Raided by Gunmen," BBC News, January 30, 2006.

24.   "Gazans Burn Danish Flags, Demand Cartoon Apology," Reuters, January 31, 2006.

25.   "EU Press Reprints Explosive Cartoons," IslamOnline, February 1, 2006.

26.   Alan Cowell, "European Papers Join Danish Fray," *New York Times*, February 8, 2006; "Protests Over Muhammad Cartoon Grow," Associated Press, January 30, 2006.

27.   "Group Stokes Cartoon Protest," Reuters, February 1, 2006; "Fatwa Issued against Danish Troops," Agence France Press, February 1, 2006.

28.   "Q&A: The Muhammad Cartoons Row," BBC News, February 7, 2006; "Kashmir Shutdown over Quran Desecration, Prophet Caricature," India-Asia News Service, December 8, 2005; "Cartoons of Mohammed Cause Death Threat," *DR Nyheder*, December 3, 2005; "Muslim World League Calls for UN Interventions against Disdaining Religions," Kuwait News Agency, January 28, 2006.

29.   "Cartoon Body Count," http://www.cartoonbodycount.com/.

30.   "Clinton Warns of Rising Anti-Islamic Feeling," *Agence France Presse*, January 30, 2006.

31.   Jonathan Duffy, "The Right to Be Downright Offensive," BBC News, December 21, 2004.

32. "'Offensive Cartoons Like 9/11 of Islamic World,'" *The Journal of Turkish Weekly*, February 14, 2006.

33. Ibid.

34. Ibid.

35. Doudou Diène, "Racism, Racial Discrimination, Xenophobia and Related Forms of Intolerance: Follow-Up To and Implementation of the Durban Declaration and Programme of Action," United Nations Human Rights Council, August 21, 2007.

36. Rukmini Callimachi, "Defame Islam, Get Sued?," Associated Press, March 14, 2008.

37. Ibid.

38. Ekmeleddin Ihsanoglu, "Speech of Secretary General at the Thirty-Fifth Session of the Council of Foreign Ministers of the Organisation of the Islamic Conference," June 18, 2008.

39. "UN resolution against Islamophobia, Judeophobia and Christianophobia," Reuters, November 24, 2010.

40. Daniel Greenfield, "The Cartoonphobia War Rages On," FrontPageMagazine.com, July 22, 2011.

41. Abigail R. Esman, "Could You Be A Criminal? US Supports UN Anti-Free Speech Measure," Forbes, December 30, 2011.

42. Patrick Goodenough, "New Name, Same Old Focus for Islamic Bloc," CNSNews.com, June 30, 2011.

43. "Journalist Sigolene Vinson says she was spared by gunmen because of her gender," News.com.au, January 10, 2015.

44. Meabh Ritchie, "'I'd rather die standing than live on my knees': Charlie Hebdo, told in quotes," Telegraph, January 8, 2015.

45. "Journalist Sigolene Vinson says she was spared by gunmen because of her gender," News.com.au, January 10, 2015.

46. Ibn Ishaq, *The Life of Muhammad: A Translation of Ibn Ishaq's Sirat Rasul Allah*, A. Guillaume, trans. (Oxford University Press, 1955), 365.

47. Ibid., 367.

48. Ibid.

49. Ibid.

50. Ibid., 675.

51. Ibid.

52. Ibid.

53. Ibid.

54. Ibid.

55. Ibid., 676.

56. Ibid.

57. Ibid.

58. Ibid.

59. Abu Dawud, *Sunan Abu Dawud, English Translation with Explanatory Notes*, Ahmad Hasan, trans. Kitab Bhavan, 1990, book 38, number 4348.

60. Abu Dawud, *Sunan Abu Dawud, English Translation with Explanatory Notes*, Ahmad Hasan, trans., Kitab Bhavan, 1990, book 38, number 4349.

61. Ahmed ibn Naqib al-Misri, *Reliance of the Traveller ('Umdat al-Salik): A Classic Manual of Islamic Sacred Law*, translated by Nuh Ha Mim Keller. Amana Publications, 1999. O11.10.

62. Shaykh 'Abd al-Rahmaan al-Barraak, "It is essential to respond to those who defame the Prophet (peace and blessings of Allaah be upon him)," Islam Question and Answer, http://islamqa.info/en/14305.

63. Peter Berkowitz, "The Left's Crusade Against Free Speech," RealClearPolitics, May 10, 2015.

64. "Quotes about Freedom of Speech," Goodreads, http://www.goodreads.com/quotes/tag/freedom-of-speech.

Chapter Two: "Tailored in an Appropriate Way": Can Free Speech Really Be Restricted in the United States?

1.   *W. Blackstone's Commentaries on the Laws of England*, T. Cooley 2nd revised edition, 1872, 151-52.

2.   "An Act in Addition to the Act, Entitled 'An Act for the Punishment of Certain Crimes Against the United States.'" United States Congress, July 14, 1798, The Avalon Project, http://avalon.law.yale.edu/18th_century/sedact.asp.

3.   James Madison, *The Debates in the Several State Conventions: On the Adoption of the Federal Constitution, as Recommended by the General Convention at Philadelphia, in 1787, Volume 4* (J. B. Lippincott Company, 1901), 539.

4.   Terri Diane Halperin, *The Alien and Sedition Acts of 1798: Testing the Constitution* (JHU Press, 2016); Phillip I. Blumberg, *Repressive Jurisprudence in the Early American Republic: The First Amendment and the Legacy of English Law* (Cambridge University Press, 2010), 107.

5.   Douglas Alan Cohn, *The President's First Year: None Were Prepared, Some Never Learned—Why the Only School for Presidents Is the Presidency* (Rowman & Littlefield, 2016), 27.

6.   *The Defence of Young and Minns, Printers to the State, Before the Committee of the House of Representatives [in Answer to the Accusation of Having Published a Libellous Article on T. Jefferson's Character. in the "New England*

Palladium"], with an Appendix, Containing the Debate, Etc. (Young and Minns, 1805), 20.

7. John Davison Lawson, *American State Trials: A Collection of the Important and Interesting Criminal Trials which Have Taken Place in the United States, from the Beginning of Our Government to the Present Day: with Notes and Annotations, Volume 10* (Thomas Law Book Company, 1918), 837.

8. David Barton, *The Jefferson Lies: Exposing the Myths You've Always Believed About Thomas Jefferson*, Thomas Nelson Inc, 2012, 17.

9. Phillip I. Blumberg, *Repressive Jurisprudence in the Early American Republic: The First Amendment and the Legacy of English Law*, (Cambridge University Press, 2010), 107.

10. Geoffrey R. Stone, *Perilous Times: Free Speech in Wartime from the Sedition Act of 1798 to the War on Terrorism* (W. W. Norton & Company, 2004), 64.

11. "An Act in Addition to the Act, Entitled 'An Act for the Punishment of Certain Crimes Against the United States.'" United States Congress, July 14, 1798, the Avalon Project, http://avalon.law.yale.edu/18th_century/sedact.asp.

12. "Text of the Supreme Court's Opinion in Libel Case against the New York Times," *New York Times*, March 10, 1964.

13. "Primary Documents—U.S. Espionage Act, 7 May 1918," FirstWorldWar.com, http://www.firstworldwar.com/source/espionageact1918.htm.

14. *Schenck v. United States*, March 3, 1919, Legal Information Institute, Cornell University, https://www.law.cornell.edu/supremecourt/text/249/47.

15. Ibid.

16. *Frohwerk v. US*, March 10, 1919, FindLaw, http://caselaw.findlaw.com/us-supreme-court/249/204.html.

17. Ibid.

18. *Debs v. US*, March 10, 1919, FindLaw, http://caselaw.findlaw.com/us-supreme-court/249/211.html.

19. Ibid.

20. *Abrams v. United States*, November 10, 1919, Legal Information Institute, Cornell University, https://www.law.cornell.edu/supremecourt/text/250/616.

21. Ibid.

22. Ibid.

23. Ibid.

24. Ibid.

25. Michael Daly, "Nidal Hasan's Murders Termed 'Workplace Violence,'" Daily Beast, August 6, 2013, http://www.thedailybeast.com/articles/2013/08/06/nidal-hasan-s-murders-termed-workplace-violence-by-u-s.html.

26. Kevin Johnson, "Justice Dept. Reverses Course on Redacting Transcript of Orlando Gunman," *USA Today*, June 20, 2016, http://www.usatoday.com/story/news/nation/2016/06/20/fbi-release-orlando-911-transcripts/86130520/.

27. See "What Do They Have in Common?," Youtube, March 4, 2007, https://www.youtube.com/watch?v=Rd8cRvZZv44.

28. Neil H. Cogan, *The Complete Bill of Rights: The Drafts, Debates, Sources, and Origins*, (Oxford University Press, 2015), 275.

29. Ibid.

30. "Getting A NYC Handgun Permit," New York City Guns, http://newyorkcity-guns.com/getting-a-nyc-handgun-permit/.

31. Ibid.

32. Ibid.

33. Jake Malooley, "5 steps to getting a gun in Chicago," TimeOut Chicago, May 2, 2011.

34. Hillary Clinton, "Remarks on the mass shooting at community college in Oregon," HillaryClinton.com, January 31, 2016.

35. Jeremy Diamond, "Trump says Clinton wants to abolish the 2nd Amendment," CNN, May 7, 2016.

36. Jeremy Diamond, "Trump says Clinton wants to abolish the 2nd Amendment," CNN, May 7, 2016.

37. Hillary Clinton, "Remarks on the mass shooting at community college in Oregon," HillaryClinton.com, January 31, 2016.

38. H.Res.569—Condemning violence, bigotry, and hateful rhetoric towards Muslims in the United States.114th Congress (2015-2016), Congress.gov, https://www.congress.gov/bill/114th-congress/house-resolution/569/text.

39. "Wife of Bataclan Shooter 'Proud' and 'Happy,'" The Local, December 28, 2015.

40. "Christmas Celebrations Banned in Somalia, Tajikistan and Brunei," *Guardian*, December 23, 2015.

41. Ibid.

42. Kate Ng, "Malaysia: World's First Sharia-Compliant Airline Revealed," *Independent*, December 23, 2015.

43. Barbara Pinto, "Muslim Cab Drivers Refuse to Transport Alcohol, and Dogs," ABC News, January 26, 2007, http://abcnews.go.com/International/story?id=2827800.

44. Daniel Greenfield, "Muslim Imam Claims Women Who Don't Wear Hijabs Are 'Asking to Be Raped,' Arrested for Trying to Rape Woman," FrontPageMag, March 7, 2013, http://www.frontpagemag.com/point/180393/muslim-imam-claims-women-who-dont-wear-hijabs-are-daniel-greenfield.

45. Rick Noack, "Leaked Document Says 2,000 Men Allegedly Assaulted 1,200 German Women on New Year's Eve," *Washington Post*, July 11, 2016, https://www.washingtonpost.com/news/worldviews/wp/2016/07/10/leaked-document-says-2000-men-allegedly-assaulted-1200-german-women-on-new-years-eve/?utm_term=.01625db1c204.

46. Lubna Thomas Benjamin, "'Justice' in Pakistan: Asia Bibi," Gatestone Institute, August 3, 2016, https://www.gatestoneinstitute.org/8603/pakistan-asia-bibi.

47. Lizzie Dearden, "Teenaged Christian Boy Arrested for Sharing 'Blasphemous' Facebook Post in Pakistan," *Independent*, September 21, 2016, http://www.independent.co.uk/news/world/asia/teenage-boy-christian-arrested-sharing-blasphemous-facebook-post-in-pakistan-nabeel-chohan-kaaba-a7321156.html.

48. "Quotes about Freedom of Speech," Goodreads, http://www.goodreads.com/quotes/tag/freedom-of-speech.

Chapter Three: "Now Obviously This Is a Country That Is Based on Free Speech, but. . . . ": The U.S. Government vs. Free Speech

1. Jonathan Turley, "Just Say No To Blasphemy: U.S. Supports Egypt in Limiting Anti-Religious Speech," *USA Today*, October 19, 2009.

2. Ibid.

3. Eugene Volokh, "Is the Obama Administration Supporting Calls to Outlaw Supposed Hate Speech?," Huffington Post, October 1, 2009.

4. Eugene Volokh, "Is the Obama Administration Supporting Calls to Outlaw Supposed Hate Speech?," Huffington Post, October 1, 2009.

5. Trent Franks, "High Ranking DOJ Official Refuses to Affirm 1st Amendment Rights," YouTube, July 26, 2012.

6. Ibid.

7. Hillary Rodham Clinton, "Statement on the Attack in Benghazi," U.S. Department of State, September 11, 2012.

8. "The Secretary's Call with Egyptian PM Kandil," September 12, 2012 (email released by U.S. Department of State to Benghazi Select Committee), http://benghazi.house.gov/sites/republicans.benghazi.house.gov/files/documents/Tab%2079.pdf.

9. Hillary Rodham Clinton, "Remarks at the Opening Plenary of the U.S.-Morocco Strategic Dialogue," U.S. Department of State, September 13, 2012.

10. Hillary Rodham Clinton, "Remarks at the Transfer of Remains Ceremony to Honor Those Lost in Attacks in Benghazi, Libya," U.S. Department of State, September 14, 2012.

11. This classic defense of the freedom of speech, often attributed to Voltaire, is actually a summary of Voltaire's position by Evelyn Beatrice Hall (writing under the pen name S. G. Tallentyre) in her 1903 *The Life of Voltaire.*

12. David Rutz, "Hannity Plays Montage of Obama Administration Members Falsely Blaming Video for Benghazi Attack," Washington Free Beacon, October 23, 2015.

13. Ibid.

14. "Judicial Watch: Benghazi Documents Point to White House on Misleading Talking Points, Judicial Watch, April 29, 2014.

15. Rutz, "Hannity Plays Montage."

16. "Judicial Watch: Benghazi Documents Point to White House."

17. Ibid.

18. "Father of Navy SEAL Killed at Libyan Embassy Reveals the Shocking Details of His Meeting with Obama, Biden, and Clinton in Interview with Glenn Beck," GlennBeck.com, October 25, 2012.

19. Pamela K. Browne and Catherine Herridge, "Diary Entry from Benghazi Victim's Dad: 'I Gave Hillary a Hug,' She Blamed Filmmaker," Fox News, October 23, 2015.

20. Robert Jonathan, "Benghazi Committee: Hillary Clinton Is Lying, Says Benghazi Mom Pat Smith [Video]," Inquisitr, October 22, 2015.

21. "Remarks by the President to the UN General Assembly," Whitehouse.gov, September 25, 2012.

22. Ahmed ibn Naqib al-Misri, *Reliance of the Traveller ('Umdat as-Salik): A Classic Manual of Islamic Sacred Law*, trans. Nuh Ha Mim Keller (Amana Publications, 1999), r2.2.

23. "Man behind Anti-Islam Film Arrested, Authorities Say," Associated Press, September 27, 2012.

24. Hollie McKay, "Blamed for Benghazi: Filmmaker jailed after attack now lives in poverty, fear" Fox News, September 12, 2016.

25. Audrey Hudson, "Filmmaker Blamed for Benghazi Attack set for Jail Release," Newsmax, September 22, 2013.

26. McKay, "Blamed for Benghazi."

27. Ibid.

28. Byron Tau, "Feds Suggest Anti-Muslim Speech Can Be Punished," Politico, May 31, 2013.

29. Ibid.

30. Ibid.

31. Ibid.

32. Ibid.

33. Ibid.

34. "Justice For Our Children," iPetitions.com, June 18, 2016. This petition has been edited from its original form in order to correct factual errors.

35. Betsy Z. Russell, "False Story on Social Media Charges Syrian Refugees Raped Idaho Girl," *Spokesman-Review*, June 20, 2016.

36. Ibid.

37. Amanda Marcotte, "No, Syrian Refugees Didn't Rape a Child in Idaho: Right-Wing Urban Legend Shows How Ugly Anti-Refugee Movement Has Become," Salon, June 22, 2016.

38. Anna Merlan, "Right-Wing News Sites Are Circulating a Fake Story About Syrian Refugees Raping a Child in Idaho," Jezebel, June 22, 2016.

39. Michelle Goldberg, "If You Want to Live Here, You Need to Live by the Rules Here," Slate, July 31, 2016.

40. Pamela Geller, "Pamela Geller: Shocking New Details Emerge in Idaho Muslim Migrant Rape Case," Breitbart, August 7, 2016.

41. Ibid.

42. Leo Hohmann, "Cops, Media Hide Idaho Girl's Sex Assault by Muslim Migrants," World Net Daily, June 20, 2016.

43. Eugene Volokh, "Chief Idaho Federal Prosecutor Warns: 'The Spread of False Information or Inflammatory or Threatening Statements…May Violate Federal Law,'" *Washington Post*, June 26, 2016.

44. Ibid.

45. Ibid.

46. Ibid.

47. Eugene Volokh, "Idaho Federal Prosecutor Issues Follow-Up Statement about Twin Falls Child Sexual Assault controversy," Washington Post, June 28, 2016.

48. Ibid.

49. James Barrett, "Loretta Lynch Vows to Prosecute Those Who Use 'Anti-Muslim' Speech That 'Edges Toward Violence,'" Daily Wire, December 4, 2015.

50. Ibid.

51. Ibid.

52. John Stanton, "Loretta Lynch: 'Actions Predicated On Violent Talk' Toward Muslims Will Be Prosecuted," BuzzFeed, December 3, 2015.

53. Ibid.

54. Kaitlyn Schallhorn, "Former Congressman Unleashes on Attorney General in Rant Against Islam: 'Go Ahead and Prosecute Me. I Dare You,'" The Blaze, December 5, 2015.

55. Neil Munro, "Pataki Demands That AG Lynch Arrest Him For Urging War against Islam," Breitbart, December 4, 2015.

56.　Oliver Darcy, "Clinton Makes Questionable Claim: Islamic State 'Showing Videos of Donald Trump' to Recruit Fighters," The Blaze, December 19, 2015.

57.　"Quotes about Freedom of Speech," Goodreads, http://www.goodreads.com/quotes/tag/freedom-of-speech.

58.　"Quotes about Freedom of Speech," Goodreads, http://www.goodreads.com/quotes/tag/freedom-of-speech.

Chapter Four: The "Hate Speech" Scam

1.　Cal Poly College Republicans, "Robert Spencer on Radical Islam (Cal Poly, SLO)," YouTube, May 13, 2014.

2.　Mark Steyn, "Stay Quiet and You'll Be Okay," Steyn Online, May 9, 2015.

3.　Lauren Carroll, "CNN's Chris Cuomo: First Amendment doesn't cover hate speech," Politifact, May 7, 2015.

4.　Ibid.

5.　Lyle Denniston, "Constitution Check: Are There No Limits on Second Amendment Rights?," National Constitution Center, January 9, 2014.

6.　Carroll, "CNN's Chris Cuomo."

7.　Ibid.

8.　Eugene Volokh, "No, there's no 'hate speech' exception to the First Amendment," Washington Post, May 7, 2015.

9.　Ibid.

10.　Carroll, "CNN's Chris Cuomo."

11.　"Twitter, Facebook, YouTube and Microsoft agree to help EU fight hate speech," Associated Press, May 31, 2016.

12.　Ibid.

13.　Ibid.

14.　Ibid.

15.　Ibid.

16.　http://obaidkarki.blogspot.com/; https://alakhtal.com.

17.　Obaid Karki, "Robert Spencer mustn't featured but lynched from his scrotum along with Zionists scumbags, Pamela Geller, Pat Condell, Daniel Pipes, Debbie Schlussel and JIHADWATCH Jackass duo Baron Bodissey & Geert Wilders for inspiring Anders Behring Breivik to innocent students in 2011," Suicide Bombers Magazine, May 29, 2016.

18.　https://twitter.com/stsheetrock/status/736678919277973505.

19.　https://twitter.com/rules.

20.　https://twitter.com/stsheetrock/status/465788312771231744.

21.　https://twitter.com/stsheetrock/status/380431800545603584.

22. William Hicks, "10 Times Facebook Censored Conservatives," Heat Street, May 26, 2016.

23. Ian Tuttle, "Conservatives Are Going to Have to Build a Better Internet," *National Review*, June 18, 2016.

24. Joshua Philipp, "Hackers Say Twitter Isn't Telling the Whole Story About Anti-Terror Fight," Epoch Times, March 4, 2016.

25. Nina Rosenwald, "CENSORED: Facebook deletes a Gatestone author's page!," Gatestone Institute, June 2, 2016.

26. Ibid.

27. Ibid.

28. Ibid.

29. Ibid.

30. Christian Datoc, "Reddit Bans Users, Deletes Comments That Say Orlando Terrorist Was Muslim," Daily Caller, June 12, 2016.

31. Pamela Geller, "Facebook removes 'Stop Islamization of America' (SIOA) page in wake of gay jihad slaughter in Orlando," PamelaGeller.com, June 12, 2016.

32. Ibid. Pamela Geller, "Facebook BANS Pamela Geller from posting in wake of Orlando Nightclub Jihad Massacre," PamelaGeller.com, June 12, 2016.

33. Allum Bokhari, "Pamela Geller And 'Stop Islamization Of America' Reinstated on Facebook Following Breitbart Story," Breitbart, June 14, 2016.

34. Chris Tomlinson, "Facebook Bans Gay Magazine Critical Of Islam," Breitbart, June 17, 2016.

35. Ibid.

36. Tuttle, "Conservatives Are Going to Have to Build."

37. Hicks, "10 Times Facebook."

38. Internal Jihad Watch site data, February–March 2017.

39. "CENSORED: YouTube Uses Anti-ISIS Policy to Pull CounterJihad Video. Watch It Here," Counter Jihad, July 6, 2016.

40. Ibid.

41. "Facebook Blocks Michael Savage for Posting News on Islamic Crime," World Net Daily, August 1, 2016.

42. Ibid.

43. Ibid.

44. Joe Newby, "Facebook: Page Opposing Sharia Law Violates Community Standards, Gets Unpublished," Conservative Firing Line, September 6, 2016.

45. Charlie Warzel, "Twitter Permanently Suspends Conservative Writer Milo Yiannopoulos," BuzzFeed News, July 19, 2016.

46. Milo Yiannopoulos, "Here's Everything I Wanted To Say About Islam Yesterday, but Couldn't," Breitbart News, June 16, 2016.

47.   Federal Government Authorizes Facebook, Twitter, and YouTube to Censor 'Anti-Islam' Speech; Lawsuit Filed," American Freedom Law Center, July 13, 2016.

48.   Ibid.

49.   Ibid.

50.   Eric Lieberman, "Obama Admin Wants To Surrender US Control Over Internet To Global Bureaucracy," Daily Caller, September 24, 2016.

51.   Ibid.

52.   Ibid.

53.   Laura Sydell, "Republicans Say Obama Administration Is Giving Away the Internet," WBHM, September 26, 2016.

54.   John Hayward, "John Bolton: Hostile Foreign Governments Will Use Obama's Internet Surrender to Their Advantage," Breitbart News, September 29, 2016.

55.   "Quotes about Freedom of Speech," Goodreads, http://www.goodreads.com/quotes/tag/freedom-of-speech.

Chapter Five: "Peer Pressure and Shaming" to Rein in Free Speech

1.   Barack Obama, "Remarks by the President on a New Beginning," WhiteHouse.gov, June 4, 2009.

2.   Hillary Rodham Clinton, "Remarks at the Organization of the Islamic Conference (OIC) High-Level Meeting on Combating Religious Intolerance," U.S. Department of State, July 15, 2011.

3.   Hillary Rodham Clinton, "Remarks at the Organization of the Islamic Conference (OIC) High-Level Meeting on Combating Religious Intolerance," U.S. Department of State, July 15, 2011.

4.   Ibid.

5.   Ibid.

6.   Ibid.

7.   Ibid.

8.   Ibid.

9.   Paula Newton, "Artist Defiantly Draws Prophet Mohammed," CNN, October 16, 2007.

10.   Jana Winter, "Iranian Artist Fights to Have Muhammad Art Displayed in Dutch Museums," FoxNews, May 3, 2008.

11.   David Petraeus, "David Petraeus: Anti-Muslim Bigotry Aids Islamist Terrorists," Washington Post, May 13, 2016.

12.   Ibid.

13.   Ibid.

14. Ibid.

15. Meena Hartenstein and Michael Sheridan, "Obama Tells Rev. Terry Jones to Call Off 'International Burn-a-Koran Day,'" *New York Daily News*, September 9, 2010.

16. Ibid.

17. Ibid.

18. Ibid.

19. Ibid.

20. Frank James, "Preacher Terry Jones Got Call from Defense Secretary Gates," National Public Radio, September 9, 2010.

21. Hartenstein and Sheridan, "Obama Tells Rev. Terry Jones."

22. Ibid.

23. Ibid.

24. "Petraeus Condemns Quran Burning as Protests Rage On," CNN, April 4, 2011.

25. "Afghan Quran-burn protests enter 3rd day," CBS News, April 3, 2011.

26. Nick Schifrin, Agha Aleem, Lee Ferran, and Matt Gutman, "U.N. Staffers Killed in Afghanistan Over Terry Jones Koran Burning, Police Say," ABC News, April 1, 2011.

27. Tom A. Peter, "Why Terry Jones Quran burning spurred two days of deadly Afghan protests," Christian Science Monitor, April 2, 2011.

28. Enayat Najafizada and Rod Nordland, "Afghans Avenge Florida Koran Burning, Killing 12," New York Times, April 1, 2011.

29. Mark Potok, "Enraged by Florida Pastor, Afghan Crowds Kill Foreigners," Southern Poverty Law Center, April 1, 2011.

30. Aliyah Shahid, "Pastor Terry Jones on deadly Afghanistan protests at United Nations compound: Don't blame me!," New York Daily News, April 2, 2011.

31. "Libya Attack: General Martin Dempsey Calls Pastor Terry Jones Over Film," Reuters, September 12, 2012.

32. Hartenstein and Sheridan, "Obama Tells Rev. Terry Jones.".

33. Benjamin Weiser, "M.T.A. Violated Rights of Group, Judge Says," *New York Times*, July 20, 2012.

34. Itamar Marcus and Nan Jacques Zilberdik, "Hamas: Killing Jews Is Worship of Allah," Palestinian Media Watch, November 27, 2012.

35. Emma G. Fitzsimmons, "M.T.A. Must Run Bus Ad From Pro-Israel Group, Judge Says," New York Times, April 21, 2015.

36. Ibid.

37. Emily Saul and Danielle Furfaro, "MTA's Ban on Anti-Muslim Subway Ads Is Legal, Court Rules," *New York Post*, March 3, 2016.

38.   Jonathan Stempel, "New York's MTA Must Run 'Muslim' Movie Posters in Subways: Judge," Reuters, October 7, 2015.

39.   Pamela Geller, "Sharia Judge Colleen McMahon Rules Muslims Get Special Privileges," Breitbart, October 15, 2015.

40.   Pamela Geller, "Geller: NYC & Boston Run Nazi and Anti-Semitic Ads, Ban AFDI Pro-Israel Ads," Breitbart, November 25, 2015.

41.   Paul Miller, "Lamar Outdoor Advertising Under Fire for Anti-Israel Billboard," The Observer, February 19, 2016.

42.   Ibid.

43.   Paul Miller, "Lamar Outdoor Advertising Under Fire for Anti-Israel Billboard," The Observer, February 19, 2016.

44.   Adelle Nazarian, "EXCLUSIVE: Pam Geller Places Anti-Jihadi Ads on San Francisco Buses," Breitbart, September 9, 2016.

45.   "Quotes about Freedom of Speech," Goodreads, http://www.goodreads.com/quotes/tag/freedom-of-speech.

Chapter Six: "Is That Being Racist?": Americans Learn Self-Censorship

1.   Tom Gjelten, Daniel Zwerdling, and Steve Inskeep, "Officials Begin Putting Shooting Pieces Together," National Public Radio, November 6, 2009.

2.   "Final Report of the William H. Webster Commission on the Federal Bureau of Investigation, Counterterrorism Intelligence, and the Events at Fort Hood, Texas, on November 5, 2009," 46, https://s3.amazonaws.com/s3.documentcloud.org/documents/779134/fort-hood-report.pdf.

3.   "Final Report of the William H. Webster Commission," 54.

4.   Ibid., 65.

5.   Molly Hennessy-Fiske, "Ft. Hood Shooter Received Glowing Evaluations before Attack," *Los Angeles Times*, August 24, 2013.

6.   Ibid.

7.   Paul von Zielbauer, "5 Men Are Convicted in Plot on Fort Dix," *New York Times*, December 22, 2008.

8.   Jana Winter, "Clerk Rings Up N.J. Jihad Jerks," *New York Post*, May 13, 2007.

9.   The article can be read in its entirety here: "Robert Spencer in The Hill: Lindsay Lohan may have made her worst life choice yet," Jihad Watch, January 18, 2017.

10.   Robert Spencer, "Sharia at The Hill: Robert Spencer Article Pulled after Pressure from Leftists and Islamic Supremacists," Jihad Watch, January 18, 2017.

11. Cindy Boren, "Curt Schilling Compares Muslim Extremists to Nazis in Deleted Tweet," *Washington Post*, August 25, 2015; Ted Berg, "Curt Schilling Compares Muslims to Nazis in Baffling Deleted Tweet," *USA Today*, August 25, 2015.

12. Claire McNear, "Curt Schilling Tweets, Deletes Awful Meme about Muslims and Nazis," SB Nation, August 25, 2015.

13. Max Fisher, "Curt Schilling's Tweet Comparing Muslims to Nazis Is Even Worse Than It Sounds," Vox, August 26, 2015.

14. Ibid.

15. Dick Uliano, "Muslims Hold Interfaith Rally on National Mall," WTOP, July 23, 2016.

16. "Around 50 People Take Part in 'Not in Our Name' Demonstration," RTE News, July 26, 2015.

17. Robert Spencer, "Hamas-Linked CAIR Rally against the Islamic State Draws around Ten People," Jihad Watch, October 4, 2014.

18. Gal Tziperman Lotan, "Young Muslims Try to Show Others Islam Urges Peace," *Boston Globe*, August 19, 2013.

19. Wendy Gillis, "Progressive Muslims Group Launched in Toronto to Reclaim 'Hijacked' Faith," *Toronto Star*, June 17, 2013.

20. John Hinderaker, "Muslims To March Against Terror," Powerline, April 18, 2005.

21. Ibid.

22. "Local Group Leads March against Terror," *Washington Times*, May 14, 2005.

23. Ted Thornhill and Steph Cockroft, "Growing Anger across Muslim World over Charlie Hebdo Magazine as Hundreds of Thousands March in Chechnya and Iranians Chant 'Death to France' (but Pakistanis Mistakenly Burn the Wrong Flag)," *Daily Mail*, January 19, 2015.

24. "Anti-Charlie Hebdo Protests Continue in Pakistan," Press Trust of India, January 19, 2015.

25. Andrew Carswell and Ian Walker, "Sydney's Muslim Community Rallies in Lakemba in Response to Terror Attacks That Rocked Paris," *Daily Telegraph*, January 24, 2015.

26. "About 1,000 Attend 'I Am Not Charlie' Rally In Kyrgyzstan," Radio Free Europe/Radio Liberty, January 20, 2015.

27. Richard Sandomir, "Curt Schilling, ESPN Analyst, Is Fired Over Offensive Social Media Post," New York Times, April 20, 2016.

28. Gabriel Arana, "Charlie Hebdo 'Wandered into The Realm Of Hate Speech,' Says Doonesbury Cartoonist Garry Trudeau," Huffington Post, April 10, 2015.

29. "Garry Trudeau on Charlie Hebdo, Doonesbury and the Future of Satire," NBC News, April 25, 2015.
30. Ibid.
31. Ibid.
32. Ibid.
33. Robert Spencer, "Doonesbury's Trudeau: 'I Certainly Wouldn't Draw Pictures of the Prophet,'" Jihad Watch, April 26, 2015.
34. Salman Rushdie, *In Good Faith* (Penguin, 1990), 19.
35. English PEN, https://www.englishpen.org/.
36. PEN America, https://pen.org/about.
37. Jennifer Schuessler, "Six PEN Members Decline Gala after Award for Charlie Hebdo," *New York Times*, April 26, 2015.
38. Ibid.
39. Alison Flood and Alan Yuhas, "Salman Rushdie Slams Critics of PEN's Charlie Hebdo Tribute," *Guardian*, April 27, 2015.
40. Ibid.
41. Ibid.
42. Schuessler, "Six PEN Members Decline Gala."
43. Flood and Yuhas, "Salman Rushdie Slams Critics."
44. Ibid.
45. Ibid.
46. Ibid.
47. Glenn Greenwald, "204 PEN Writers (Thus Far) Have Objected to the Charlie Hebdo Award—Not Just 6," The Intercept, April 30, 2015.
48. Ibid.
49. Alan Yuhas, "Two dozen writers join Charlie Hebdo PEN award protest," Guardian, April 29, 2015.
50. Ibid.
51. Robert Spencer, "Joyce Carol Oates: 'Is there nothing celebratory & joyous' about ISIS?," Jihad Watch, November 24, 2015.
52. Elsa Keslassy, "Gunmen Kill 12 at French Satirical Magazine Charlie Hebdo," *Variety*, January 7, 2015.
53. Abigail R. Esman, "Attacking Free Speech Is a Core Element of Terrorism," *Algemeiner*, May 3, 2015.
54. Sharon Otterman, "Film at 9/11 Museum Sets Off Clash over Reference to Islam," *New York Times*, April 23, 2014.
55. Ibid.
56. "Translation of Sept. 11 Hijacker Mohamed Atta's Suicide Note: Part One," ABC News, September 28, 2001.

57. Otterman, "Film at 9/11 Museum."
58. "Apostates Refused Service at Wegmans Bakery—Fear of Invoking Offense Led to Discrimination, says Ex-Muslims of North America," Ex-Muslims of North America, June 20, 2016.
59. Todd Clausen, "Clausen: Wegmans Says Ex-Muslims Group Can Buy Cake," *Democrat & Chronicle*, June 23, 2016.
60. Hannah McDonald, "Advertisement Removed After Resident Expresses Offense," WPTZ.com, August 23, 2014.
61. Ray Bogan, "Quran Burned at Anti-Islam Rally in Gillette," KCWY13, August 29, 2016.
62. Patricia Cohen, "Yale Press Bans Images of Muhammad in New Book," *New York Times*, August 12, 2009.
63. Ibid.
64. Christopher Hitchens, "Yale Surrenders," Slate, August 17, 2009.
65. "Quotes about Freedom of Speech," Goodreads, ttp://www.goodreads.com/quotes/tag/freedom-of-speech.

Chapter Seven: "Irresponsibly Provocative": The Erosion of Free Speech from Rushdie to Geller

1. Daniel Pipes, *The Rushdie Affair: The Novel, the Ayatollah, and the West* (Transaction, 1990), revised edition 2003, 27.
2. Eliot Weinberger, "The Month of Rushdies," *Boston Review*, March 15, 1989.
3. Ibid.
4. Ibid.
5. Andrew Anthony, "How One Book Ignited a Culture War," *Observer*, January 10, 2009.
6. Pipes, *The Rushdie Affair*, 28.
7. Ibid.
8. Sarah Womack, "Rushdie Does Not Need Police Guard Say Asian Peers," *Telegraph*, October 30, 2000.
9. Pipes, *The Rushdie Affair*, 29-30.
10. Baqir Moin, *Khomeini: Life of the Ayatollah,* Thomas Dunne Books, 1999, 284.
11. Andrew Anthony, "How One Book Ignited a Culture War," *Observer*, January 10, 2009.
12. Rushdie's Conversion to Islam is Not Acceptable, 2 Muslims Say," *Deseret News*, May 5, 1991.
13. "I Was Deranged When I Embraced Islam: Rushdie," *DNA India*, April 6, 2008.
14. Anthony, "How One Book Ignited."

15.   Ibid.

16.   Daniel Pipes, *The Rushdie Affair*, 157–58.

17.   Ibid., 163.

18.   Ibid., 156.

19.   Ibid., 157.

20.   Ibid., 160.

21.   Eliot Weinberger, "The Month of Rushdies," *Boston Review*, March 15, 1989; Robert D. McFadden, "Naguib Mahfouz, 94, Nobel Laureate in Literature, Dies," *New York Times*, September 1, 2006.

22.   Daniel Pipes, *The Rushdie Affair*, 161.

23.   Ibid., 161.

24.   Ibid., 159.

25.   Craig R. Whitney, "Cat Stevens Gives Support to Call for Death of Rushdie," *New York Times*, May 22, 1989.

26.   Ibid.

27.   Emilio Pérez Miguel, "Why Was Cat Steven's 'Peace Train' Removed from US Copies Of 10,000 Maniacs' 'In My Tribe'?," MusicKO.com, January 23, 2011.

28.   Craig R. Whitney, "Cat Stevens Gives Support to Call for Death of Rushdie," *New York Times*, May 22, 1989.

29.   Duncan Campbell, "Reid Cites Life of Brian over Rushdie Award," *Guardian*, June 20, 2007.

30.   Mark D. Fefer, "On the Advice of the FBI, Cartoonist Molly Norris Disappears from View," *Seattle Weekly*, September 14, 2010.

31.   Dave Itzkoff, "'South Park' Episode Altered after Muslim Group's Warning," *New York Times*, April 22, 2010.

32.   "Leader of Revolution Muslim Pleads Guilty to Using Internet to Solicit Murder and Encourage Violent Extremism," U.S. Attorney's Office, February 9, 2012.

33.   Itzkoff, "'South Park' Episode Altered."

34.   Ibid.

35.   Ibid.

36.   Jimmy Orr, "Creators of 'Everybody Draw Muhammad Day' Drop Gag after Everybody Gets Angry," *Los Angeles Times*, April 26, 2010.

37.   Ibid.

38.   Ibid.

39.   Ibid.

40.   Fefer, "On the Advice of the FBI."

41.   Ibid.

42. Michael Coren, "The 'Draw Mohammad' Contest Was Not an Attempt to Start a Conversation but a Single Act of Bravado," *National Post*, May 7, 2015.

43. "'Radicalization' Hearings Reignite US Muslim Debate," Agence France Presse, March 10, 2011.

44. Andrew Kaczynski and Molly Ward, "Peter King: Pam Geller Event Put 'People's Lives at Risk for No Good Reason,'" BuzzFeed, May 7, 2015.

45. Evan McMurry, "Pamela Geller Battles CNN Host over Garland Shooting: Why Is Media 'Targeting' Us?," Mediaite, May 4, 2015.

46. Jenn Selby, "Donald Trump Lambasts 'Disgusting' Pam Geller for Baiting Muslims with 'Draw the Prophet' Contest in Texas," *Independent*, May 5, 2015.

47. "Salman Rushdie Says the World Learned the 'Wrong Lessons' from His Iran Fatwa ordeal," Agence France-Presse, July 22, 2015.

48. "Salman Rushdie says the world learned the 'wrong lessons' from his Iran fatwa ordeal," Agence France-Presse, July 22, 2015.

49. Evan Perez, Pamela Brown, and Jim Sciutto, "Texas Attacker Had Private Conversations with Known Terrorists," CNN, May 7, 2015.

50. Mia De Graaf, "Iranian Mullah Revives Death Fatwa against Salman Rushdie over Satanic Verses 25 Years after It Was Issued," *Daily Mail*, February 16, 2014.

51. Mia De Graaf, "Iranian mullah revives death fatwa against Salman Rushdie over Satanic Verses 25 years after it was issued," Daily Mail, February 16, 2014.

52. Dina Vakil, "'Don't Allow Religious Hooligans to Dictate Terms,'" *Times of India*, January 16, 2008.

Chapter Eight: "Can't We Talk about This?": The Death of Free Speech in Europe

1. "Disney's Piglet Banned in Middle East!," QatarLiving.com, January 28, 2007.

2. "Pigs' Faces Blackened Out in Papers in Malaysia," AFP, January 21, 2014.

3. "Swiss Muslims File Suit Over 'Racist' Fallaci Book," *IslamOnline*, June 20, 2002.

4. Ibid.

5. Ibid.

6. "Italian Judge Bans Crucifix from School," Associated Press, October 27, 2003.

7. "Paper: Italian Church Attack Plotted," Associated Press, June 23, 2002.

8. "Muslim Activist Sues Pope, Cardinal," Associated Press, February 29, 2004.

9. "Fallaci to Go on Trial for Defaming Islam," AGI, May 24, 2005.

10. "Italian Author to Face Charges of Defaming Islam," Reuters, May 25, 2005.

11.   Tunku Varadarajan, "Prophet of Decline," *Wall Street Journal*, June 23, 2005.

12.   Ibid.

13.   "Fallaci, Processo Aggiornato a Dicembre," *L'Eco di Bergamo*, June 25, 2006.

14.   Liz McGregor and John Hooper, "Oriana Fallaci," *Guardian*, September 15, 2006.

15.   Chris Allen, *Islamophobia* (Ashgate, 2013), 175.

16.   Bruno Cousin and Tommaso Vitale, "Italian Intellectuals and the Promotion of Islamophobia After 9/11," in *Global Islamophobia: Muslims and Moral Panic in the West*, George Morgan and Scott Poynting, eds. (Ashgate, 2013), chapter 3.

17.   "Rome Nixes Naming Street after Journalist Fallaci, Citing Past Statements on Islam," *Haaretz*, September 17, 2014.

18.   Andrew Osborn, "'I Shot Fortuyn for Dutch Muslims,' Says Accused," *Guardian,* March 28, 2003.

19.   Toby Sterling, "Dutch Filmmaker Theo Van Gogh Murdered," Associated Press, November 2, 2004.

20.   "Slaughter and 'Submission,'" CBS News, August 20, 2006.

21.   "Ayaan Hirsi Ali: My Life under a Fatwa," *Independent*, November 26, 2007.

22.   Sterling, "Dutch Filmmaker."

23.   Philippe Naughton, "Van Gogh Killer Jailed for Life," Times Online, July 26, 2005.

24.   "Ayaan Hirsi Ali."

25.   "Prison Gives Van Gogh's Killer Ultra-Orthodox Islam Books," NIS News, May 14, 2007.

26.   "Dutch Filmmaker Killed, Muslims Condemn," IslamOnline.net, November 2, 2004.

27.   Lucia Kubosova, "Brussels Defends Pope's Freedom of Expression," *EU Observer*, September 18, 2006.

28.   Soeren Kern, "'A Black Day for Austria,'" Gatestone Institute, December 26, 2011.

29.   Muhammed Ibn Ismaiel Al-Bukhari, *Sahih al-Bukhari: The Translation of the Meanings*, translated by Muhammad M. Khan, Darussalam, 1997, vol. 5, book 63, no. 3896; cf. Bukhari, vol. 7, book 67, no. 5158.

30.   Muhammed Ibn Ismaiel Al-Bukhari, *Sahih al-Bukhari: The Translation of the Meanings*, trans. Muhammad M. Khan (Darussalam, 1997), vol. 5, book 63, no. 3894.

31.   Soeren Kern, "'A Black Day for Austria,'" Gatestone Institute, December 26, 2011.

32.   Ibid.

33.   Ibid.

34.   Ibid.

35.   "Next Stop: The European Court of Human Rights," Gates of Vienna, December 11, 2013.

36.   Kern, "'A Black Day for Austria.'"

37.   "Islam Film Dutch MP to Be Charged," BBC, January 21, 2009.

38.   Ibid.

39.   Ibid.

40.   "Mixed Reactions to Wilders Court Decision," DutchNews.nl, January 21, 2009.

41.   Hillel Fendel, "Geert Wilders to INN: 'Traditional European Freedom at Stake,'" Israel National News, September 2, 2010.

42.   Patrick Goodenough, "Anti-Islam Dutch Lawmaker Says He's Being Denied a Fair Trial; Court Rejects Most of His Witness List," CNS News, February 4, 2010; Robert Spencer, "Dutch Court Railroading Wilders: Disallows All but Three of His Witnesses," Jihad Watch, February 3, 2010.

43.   "Geert Wilders Cleared of Hate Charges by Dutch Court," BBC, June 23, 2011.

44.   Ibid.

45.   Toby Sterling and Anthony Deutsch, "Dutch Far Right Leader Geert Wilders on Trial for Discrimination," Reuters, March 18, 2016.

46.   Sofia Lotto Persio, "Anti-Islam Politician Geert Wilders Found Guilty of Inciting Discrimination in Hate Speech Trial," International Business Times, December 9, 2016.

47.   "WATCH—Geert Wilders's Opening Statement to Court During 'Hate Speech' Trial: 'I Will Never Give It Up,'" Breitbart, March 22, 2016.

48.   Soeren Kern, "Free Speech Found Guilty by Europe," Gatestone Institute, April 23, 2012.

49.   Lars Hedegaard, "Response to Charges of Hate Speech," Gatestone Institute, April 16, 2012.

50.   Soeren Kern, "Free Speech Found Guilty."

51.   Ibid.

52.   "Bardot Fined Over Racial Hatred," BBC News, June 3, 2008.

53.   Aurelien Breeden, "French Court Acquits Marine Le Pen of Hate Speech," New York Times, December 15, 2015.

54.   Giulio Meotti, "Western Publishers Submit to Islam," Gatestone Institute, September 11, 2016.

55.   Kern, "Free Speech Found Guilty."

56.   Ibid; Soeren Kern, "Free Speech Found Guilty by Europe," Gatestone Institute, April 23, 2012.

57.   Ibid.

58.   Ibid.

59.   Giulio Meotti, "Western Publishers Submit to Islam," Gatestsone Institute, September 11, 2016.

60.   Ibid.

61.   Alice Philipson, "Italians Outraged After Headmaster Scraps Christmas Carol Concert following Paris Attacks," *Telegraph*, November 29, 2015.

62.   Virginia Hale, "Christians Told to 'Pray In Silence…Don't Disturb the Migrants,'" Breitbart, June 6, 2016.

63.   "Quotes about Freedom of Speech," Goodreads, http://www.goodreads.com/quotes/tag/freedom-of-speech.

Chapter Nine: Catholics against Free Speech

1.   Benedict XVI, "Faith, reason and the university: memories and reflections," Papal Address at University of Regensburg, September 12, 2006.

2.   Ibid.

3.   "In Quotes: Muslim Reaction to Pope," BBC, September 16, 2006.

4.   Ibid.

5.   Lucia Kubosova, "Brussels Defends Pope's Freedom of Expression," *EU Observer*, September 18, 2006.

6.   "Christian Leader Joins Muslims in Denouncing Pope's Remarks," Associated Press, September 16, 2006.

7.   Alasdair Baverstock, "Pope Francis' Run-In with Benedict XVI over the Prophet Mohammed," *Telegraph*, March 15, 2013.

8.   "Report: Rome Tightens Pope's Security after Fury Over Islam Remarks," *Haaretz*, September 15, 2006.

9.   "Nun's Death May Be Linked to Pope: Somali Islamist," Reuters, September 17, 2006.

10. "Nun Shot Dead as Pope Fails to Calm Militant Muslims," Times Online, September 18, 2006.

11. "Violence against Christians grows in Iraq," Ekklesia, September 29, 2006.

12. Ibid.

13. "Iraq Priest 'Killed over Pope Speech,'" Al-Jazeera, October 12, 2006.

14. "Christian Killed in Iraq in Response to Pope's Speech: Islamic Website," Asia News, September 16, 2006.

15. "Pope Sorry for Offending Muslims," BBC, September 17, 2006.

16. "Pakistan Calls for Ban on 'Defamation of Islam' in Veiled Attack on Pope," Agence France-Presse, September 19, 2006.

17. "Pakistan's Parliament Condemns Pope Benedict XVI," Associated Press, September 15, 2006.

18. Khaled Abu Toameh, "Gazans Warn Pope to Accept Islam," *Jerusalem Post*, September 18, 2006.

19. "Text of Pope's Statement," BBC, September 17, 2006.

20. "Meeting with the Representatives of Science, Lecture of the Holy Father, Aula Magna of the University of Regensburg," Vatican.va, September 12, 2006, footnote 3.

21. Sandro Magister, "Bloody Christmas Between the Nile and the Indus," Chiesa, January 7, 2011; Andrea Gagliarducci, "Pope Francis Wants More Dialogue with Islam. Is Egypt the Key?," Catholic News Agency, February 25, 2016.

22. Magister, "Bloody Christmas."

23. Ibid.

24. "Sunni Islam's Al-Azhar Freezes Talks with the Vatican," Deutsche Presse Agentur, January 20, 2011.

25. "Francis Calls for Mutual Understanding between Christians and Muslims in Letter to Al-Azhar," Vatican Insider, September 18, 2013.

26. Ibid.

27. Nicole Winfield, "Pope Embraces Al-Azhar Imam in Sign of Renewed Relations," Associated Press, May 23, 2016.

28. "Interior Ministry: Suicide Bomber behind Egypt Church Blast," CNN, January 1, 2011.

29. Lamiat Sabin, "Charlie Hebdo: Pope Francis Says If You Swear at My Mother—or Islam—'Expect a Punch,'" *Independent*, January 15, 2015.

30. Ibid.

31. "The Last Christians in Aleppo," Gallia Watch, February 5, 2016.

32. Ibid.

33. Ibid.

34. Ibid.

35. "West Silent on 'Cull' of Christians—Italian Bishops' Head," ANSA, September 30, 2015.

36. "Synod: The West Must 'Not Forget the Christians in the Middle East,' says Patriarch Younan," Asia News, October 8, 2015.

37. Joop Koopman, "Bodies of Christian Family Discovered in a Syrian Well," Aid to the Church in Need, November 6, 2015.

38. Deborah Danan, "Greek Catholic Patriarch: No One Defends Islam Like Arab Christians," Breitbart, January 21, 2016.

39. "Catholic Men's Conference Opens Ticket Sales," Catholic Free Press, February 8, 2013.

40.   "Robert Spencer & Msgr. Stuart Swetland debate: Is Islam violent?," YouTube, August 11, 2016.

41.   Robert Spencer, "Is There Room in the Catholic Church for those who don't believe Islam is a religion of peace?," Jihad Watch, August 13, 2016.

42.   "Quotes About Freedom of Speech," Goodreads, http://www.goodreads.com/quotes/tag/freedom-of-speech.

43.   "Quotes about Freedom of Speech," Goodreads, http://www.goodreads.com/quotes/tag/freedom-of-speech.

Chapter Ten: "Not Conducive to the Public Good": Free Speech Dies in Britian and Canada

1.   Robert Spencer, "Britain Capitulates to Jihad," Jihad Watch, June 26, 2013.

2.   Oren Kessler, "'Saudi Clerics Use Social Media to Spread Hate,'" Jerusalem Post, May 10, 2012.

3.   Raheem Kassam, "'Behead, Burn, and Crush Gays' Islamic Preacher to Deliver 10 Days of Lectures in London," Breitbart, October 4, 2016.

4.   Jamie Doward, "Muslim cleric banned in Pakistan is preaching in UK mosques," Observer, December 17, 2016.

5.   Caroline Wheeler, "Britain BANS heroic bishops: Persecuted Christian leaders from war zones refused entry," Express, December 4, 2016.

6.   Tom Porter, "Pakistani 'Hate Preacher' Who Glorifies Islamist Murder Welcomed by Archbishop of Canterbury," International Business Times, July 21, 2016.

7.   Ben Flanagan, "UK Press Watchdog Urged to Act against Media slurs on Muslims," Al Arabiya, November 13, 2015.

8.   Liam Deacon, "London Mayor to Set Up Police 'Online Hate Crime Hub' in 'Partnership' with Social Media Firms," Breitbart, August 16, 2016.

9.   James Tapsfield, "Sadiq Khan Issues Grovelling Apology After Video Shows Him Using 'Uncle Toms' Slur against Moderate Muslims," Mailonline, May 4, 2016; Raheem Kassam, "London Is about to Elect a Muslim Mayor Who Has Defended Islamists, 9/11 Terrorists, and Who Is Endorsed by Anti-Semites," Breitbart, May 3, 2016; Porter, "Pakistani 'Hate Preacher.'"

10.   "About Us," Tell Mama, http://tellmamauk.org/about-us/.

11.   Andrew Gilligan, "The Truth about the 'Wave of Attacks on Muslims' after Woolwich Murder," Telegraph, June 1, 2013.

12.   "Communications Act 2003," legislation.gov.uk, http://www.legislation.gov.uk/ukpga/2003/21/section/127.

13. Billy Hallowell, "'Islam Is a Doctrine Spawned in Hell': Embattled Pastor Warns of 'Uprising' if He's Jailed over Anti-Muslim Sermon," The Blaze, January 4, 2016.

14. "Pastor James McConnell's Islamic Remarks Investigated by Police," BBC, May 21, 2014.

15. Suzanne Breen, "'Satanic Islam' Sermon Belfast Pastor James McConnell Says He Faces Six Months in Jail," *Belfast Telegraph*, June 19, 2015.

16. Ibid.

17. Ibid.

18. Ibid.

19. David Churchill, "London Hate Preacher's 'Disgusting' Sermon Praising Boko Haram's Kidnap of Schoolgirls," London Evening Standard, May 29, 2014.

20. Keiligh Baker, "British Hate Preacher Backs Paris Massacres and Tells His Followers 'Britain Is the Enemy of Islam,'" MailOnline, January 10, 2015.

21. Ibid.

22. "British Islamist Abu Waleed: Muslims Should Humiliate Christians in Order to Make Them Convert to Islam," Middle East Media Research Institute, January 16, 2014.

23. Ibid.

24. Suzanne Breen, "Muslim who praised IS drove case against 'Satanic Islam' sermon Belfast pastor McConnell," Belfast Telegraph, July 10, 2015.

25. Robert Spencer, "It's OK to Kill Gays—British imam," Jihad Watch, October 27, 2006.

26. Ibid.

27. "Report: Non-Muslims Deserve to Be Punished," FoxNews, April 1, 2008.

28. Robert Spencer, "Saudi Imam Who Called Jews 'Scum, Rats, Pigs, Monkeys' Speaks in London—Geert Wilders Still barred," Jihad Watch, August 5, 2009.

29. Robyn Rosen, "London University to Host Imam Who Called Jews 'Enemy,'" *Jewish Chronicle*, January 18, 2011.

30. Ian Garland, "'Cheat Genital Mutilation Ban by Going Abroad': British Muslim Leader Caught on Camera Advocating Female Circumcision" *Daily Mail*, April 29, 2012.

31. Omar Kuddus, "Throw Gays off a Mountain Imams to Speak at London Conference," GayStarNews, October 3, 2013.

32. Robert Spencer, "UK Allows Speaking Tour by Saudi Imam Who Calls Shi'ites 'Apostates' and Says No Churches Should Be Allowed in Saudi Arabia," Jihad Watch, December 17, 2013.

33. Pippa Crerar, "Sadiq Khan: There Will Be No More 'Body Shaming' Adverts on the Tube," *London Evening Standard*, June 13, 2016.

34. Ibid.

35. Ibid.

36. Donna Rachel Edmunds, "BBC Warns Football Fans Dressing as Crusaders 'Offensive' to Muslims," Breitbart, June 4, 2016.

37. Jennifer Smith, "Couple Singing Peppa Pig Tune to Toddler 'Forced off Bus after Complaints They Were Being Racist' Because It Goes against Muslim Pork Ban," *Daily Mail*, September 26, 2014.

38. Yasmin Duffin, "Leicester KFC Customer Shocked as He is Refused Hand-Wipe Because of Branch's Halal Policy," *Leicester Mercury*, September 28, 2014.

39. "Cafe Owner Ordered to Remove Extractor Fan Because Neighbour Claimed 'Smell of Frying Bacon Offends Muslims,'" *Daily Mail*, October 21, 2010.

40. "UK: Christian Cleric Calls for Renaming of Pub That May Offend Muslims," *Guardian*, August 3, 2004.

41. Worshippers Quit Church After Council Noise Ban 'Takes Away Their Ability to Praise God," *Daily Mail*, October 8, 2009.

42. Chris Osuh, "Online Troll Caught Out after Posting 'Grossly Offensive' Anti-Muslim Comments on Police Facebook Page," *Manchester Evening News*, August 5, 2016.

43. Ibid.

44. Ibid.

45. Ibid.

46. Ibid.

47. Ibid.

48. "Rotherham Child Abuse Scandal: 1,400 Children Exploited, Report Finds," BBC, August 26, 2014.

49. Ibid.

50. Jason Farrell, "Video: Rotherham: Hundreds of New Cases," Sky News, January 29, 2015.

51. Ibid.

52. Ibid.

53. Ibid.

54. "Government in Rotherham Council Takeover after Abuse Inquiry," BBC, February 4, 2015.

55. Raymond Ibrahim, "Video: Kuwaiti Activist: 'I Hope that Kuwait Will Enact a Law for....ex Slaves,'" Translating Jihad, June 22, 2011.

56. "Rotherham Child Abuse Scandal."

57. Mark Tran, "Australian Muslim Leader Compares Uncovered Women to Exposed Meat," *Guardian*, October 26, 2006.

58. "'Bring back blasphemy laws, apply them equally to all faiths'—Labour MP," RT, November 16, 2015.

59. Katie Mansfield, "FREE SPEECH CRACKDOWN: EU orders British press NOT to reveal when terrorists are Muslims," *Express*, October 5, 2016.

60. Ibid.

61. Ibid.

62. Ibid.

63. Syed Soharwardy, "Why I'm Withdrawing My Human Rights Complaint against Ezra Levant," *Toronto Globe and Mail*, February 15, 2008.

64. "Neocon Book Offends Canada Muslims," IslamOnline, January 1, 2008.

65. "Maclean's Writer Dares B.C. Human Rights Tribunal to Rule against Him," Canadian Press, June 6, 2008.

66. Brian Hutchinson, "Steyn watches as tribunal winds up," National Post, June 7, 2008.

67. David Krayden, "Canada Inching Toward 'Islamophobia' Law," Daily Caller, January 26, 2017.

68. "Montreal Police Arrest Kirkland Man Accused of Online Hate Speech Targeting Muslims," CBC News, February 1, 2017.

69. "Quotes about Freedom of Speech," Goodreads, http://www.goodreads.com/quotes/tag/freedom-of-speech.

Chapter Eleven: The New Brownshirts

1. William Nardi, "Students Walk Out of Veteran's Speech to Protest His Use of Term 'Radical Islam,'" The College Fix, September 30, 2016.

2. Ibid.

3. Ibid.

4. Ibid.

5. Adam Kissel, "More Unsavory Disinvitations: This Time, Nonie Darwish at Princeton and Columbia," FIRE, December 10, 2009.

6. Pamela Geller, "Free Speech Silenced at Columbia and Princeton," American Thinker, November 24, 2009.

7. Ibid.

8. Kissel, "More Unsavory Disinvitations."

9. Nicole Hungerford, "UC Irvine Hillel Forces Cancellation of Pro-Israel Speaker," FrontPage Magazine, May 5, 2014.

10. Ibid.

11. Aiden Pink, "Black Trans Rights Activist Cancels Speech at Brown Hillel after Anti-Israel Protests," *The Tower*, March 16, 2016.

12.   "Oren heckled at US College," *Jerusalem Post*, February 9, 2010.

13.   Ibid.

14.   Ibid.

15.   Lauren Williams, Nicole Santa Cruz, and Mike Anton, "Muslim Students Found Guilty of Disrupting Speech," *Los Angeles Times*, September 24, 2011.

16.   Ibid.

17.   Ibid.

18.   Shlomo Greenwald, "Critics Slam CUNY Response to Campus Anti-Semitism," *Jewish Press*, March 16, 2016.

19.   Ibid.

20.   Ibid.

21.   Ibid.

22.   Matt Lebovic, "'Apartheid Week' Really Does Threaten Israel, Some Experts Warn," Times of Israel, March 18, 2016.

23.   Ibid.

24.   Daniel Mael, "On Many Campuses, Hate is Spelled SJP, *The Tower*, October 2014.

25.   Michael Melia, "Educators Update Anti-Bullying Messages to Protect Muslims," Associated Press, March 5, 2016.

26.   Alec Dent, "Muslim Student Association Demands All 'Islamophobic Speech' Be Punished," College Fix, December 28, 2015.

27.   Ibid.

28.   Ibid.

29.   "UNM Students Assaulting Nonie Darwish Talk," YouTube, February 24, 2012.

30.   Conor Friedersdorf, "How Political Correctness Chills Speech on Campus," *The Atlantic*, September 1, 2016.

31.   Richard J. Evans, *The Coming of the Third Reich* (Penguin Books, 2005).

32.   Chad Dees, "Protesters Disrupt 'Sniper' Screening, Arrested at Eastern Michigan," Campus Reform, April 15, 2015.

33.   Chad Dees, "Protesters disrupt 'Sniper' screening, arrested at Eastern Michigan," Campus Reform, April 15, 2015.

34.   Manzoor Cheema, "Letter: Speech was harmful in wake of murders," Daily Tar Heel, April 15, 2015.

35.   "Families: Hate Sparked Chapel Hill Shooting, Not Parking Issue," WNCN, February 11, 2015.

36.   "'He Hates Us': Muslim Father of NC Victims Says Daughter Had Run-Ins with Alleged Killer," FoxNews.com, February 11, 2015.

37.   Ibid.

38.   Cheema, "Letter."

39. Andrew Berwick (Anders Behring Breivik), *2083: A European Declaration of Independence*, 743.

40. Breivik, *2083*, 1348.

41. "Robert Spencer and 'Islamic Apartheid' at Temple University," YouTube, April 24, 2012.

42. "Trump Threatens UC Berkeley Funds over Breitbart Protests," AFP, February 1, 2017.

43. "Trump Threatens UC Berkeley Funds."

44. https://twitter.com/cjwerleman/status/823278985073131520

45. "Pamela Geller Speaks at Brooklyn College, Speech, Q&A," YouTube, April 23, 2015.

46. Austin Peterson, "Student's Anti-Islam Article Retracted Due to 'Safety' Risk," Libertarian Republic, June 8, 2015.

47. Ibid.

48. Ibid.

49. Ibid.

50. Robert Spencer, "Rutgers' Student Paper Complies with MSA's Demand, Destroys All Copies of Issue Containing Muhammad Cartoon," Jihad Watch, April 27, 2016.

51. Ibid.

52. Ibid.

53. Todd Starnes, "What the Hell? Artist Crucifies Jesus on Dartboard," FoxNews.com, April 25, 2016.

54. Ibid.

55. "Quotes about Freedom of Speech," Goodreads, http://www.goodreads.com/quotes/tag/freedom-of-speech.

Chapter Twelve: "The University Prides Itself on Diversity": Administrators vs. Free Speech

1. Scott Jaschik, "Quick Takes: Gender Gap in Tenure at MIT, 'Obsession' and Free Speech, Obama's National Service Plan, Academics for Ron Paul, RIT in Dubai, $200M for U.S.-Canadian Telescope Project, University's Crime Report Upheld, Grawemeyer for Education," Inside Higher Ed, December 6, 2007.

2. Ibid.

3. Ibid.

4. Lori Lowenthal Marcus, "Brandeis Caves to Pressure, Withdraws Honor to Ayaan Hirsi Ali," Jewish Press, April 9, 2014.

5. Ibid.

6. Ibid.

7. Ibid

8. Ibid.

9. Richard Pérez-Peña and Tanzina Vega, "Brandeis Cancels Plan to Give Honor-
    ary Degree to Ayaan Hirsi Ali, a Critic of Islam," *New York Times*, April 8,
    2014.

10. Ibid.

11. Rogier van Bakel, "'The Trouble Is the West': Ayaan Hirsi Ali on Islam, Immi-
    gration, Civil Liberties, and the Fate of the West," Reason, November 2007.

12. Ibid.

13. Pérez-Peña and Vega, "Brandeis Cancels Plan.

14. Ibid.

15. Lori Lowenthal Marcus, "Brandeis Caves to Pressure, Withdraws Honor to
    Ayaan Hirsi Ali," Jewish Press, April 9, 2014.

16. Benjamin Wallace-Wells, "What Was Brandeis Thinking When It Invited
    Ayaan Hirsi Ali to Speak?," *New York*, April 15, 2014.

17. See, for example, Jamie Glazov, "Hostile Environment for Jewish Students at
    U.C. Berkeley," July 22, 2012, and Camilla Turner "Police Called to UCL over
    'Violent' Anti-Israel Protest Which Left Jewish Students Barricaded in Room,"
    Telegraph, October 28, 2016.

18. Pérez-Peña and Vega, "Brandeis Cancels Plan."

19. Marcus, "Brandeis Caves to Pressure."

20. Ayaan Hirsi Ali, "Here's What I Would Have Said at Brandeis," *Wall Street
    Journal*, April 10, 2014.

21. Marcus, "Brandeis Caves to Pressure."

22. Adam Kissel, "More Unsavory Disinvitations: This Time, Nonie Darwish at
    Princeton and Columbia," FIRE, December 10, 2009.

23. Adam Prendergast, "Adams State Bans from Campus Ex-Prof Who Criticized
    Pay Scale," Westword, October 19, 2015.

24. Edgar Sandoval and Leonard Greene, "University of Missouri Football Play-
    ers Return to Practice After President Resigns; School Issues Alert Warning
    Students of Threats," *New York Daily News*, November 11, 2015.

25. Anthea Butler, "Opposing View: Why Sam Bacile Deserves Arrest," *USA
    Today*, September 12, 2012.

26. Ibid.

27. Ibid.

28. Ibid.

29. Matt Coker, "Lovett or Leave It," *OC Weekly*, September 27, 2001.

30. Ibid.

31. Susan Berry, "Women Try on Hijabs at Catholic Boston College Islamic Aware-
     ness Week Event," Breitbart, March 18, 2016.
32. Ibid.
33. "Oberlin College President Appears to Defend Controversial Professor in Let-
     ter," FoxNews.com, March 3, 2016.
34. Ibid.
35. "Oberlin Suspends Professor Who Blamed Israel for 9/11," FoxNews.com,
     August 8, 2016.
36. "Is ISLAMOPHOBIA Accelerating Global Warming?," MIT Global Studies
     and Languages, May 9, 2016.
37. Ibid.
38. Ibid.
39. Ibid.
40. Alec Dent, "UNC's 'Literature of 9/11' Course Sympathizes with Terrorists,
     Paints U.S. as Imperialistic," College Fix, August 28, 2015.
41. http://englishcomplit.unc.edu/people/ahujan.
42. Dent, "UNC's 'Literature of 9/11' course."
43. Yonat Shimron, "Iranians Honor UNC scholar: Ahmadinejad Will Present
     the Award," Raleigh News & Observer, December 25, 2008.
44. "Quotes about Freedom of Speech," Goodreads, http://www.goodreads.com/
     quotes/tag/freedom-of-speech.

Chapter Thirteen: "Facing the New Totalitarianism": Fighting Back for the Freedom of Speech

1.   "Full Text: Writers' Statement on Cartoons," BBC, March 1, 2006.
2.   Ibid.
3.   "Quotes about Freedom of Speech," Goodreads, http://www.goodreads.com/
     quotes/tag/freedom-of-speech.

INDEX